FASHIONING THE NINETEENTH CENTURY

Habits of Being

Fashioning the

CRISTINA GIORCELLI AND

PAULA RABINOWITZ *editors*

HABITS OF BEING 3

NINETEENTH CENTURY

UNIVERSITY OF MINNESOTA PRESS

MINNEAPOLIS · LONDON

The publication of this book was supported by an Imagine Fund grant for the Arts, Design, and Humanities, an annual award from the University of Minnesota Provost's Office.

Published by the University of Minnesota Press
111 Third Avenue South, Suite 290
Minneapolis, MN 55401-2520
http://www.upress.umn.edu

Library of Congress Cataloging-in-Publication Data
    Fashioning the Nineteenth Century : Habits of Being 3 / Cristina Giorcelli and Paula Rabinowitz, editors.
    (Habits of Being ; 3) Includes bibliographical references.
    ISBN 978-0-8166-8746-6 (hc) — ISBN 978-0-8166-8747-3 (pb)
    1. Clothing and dress in literature. 2. Fashion in literature. 3. Literature and society—History—19th century. 4. Clothing and dress—Social aspects. 5. Fashion—Social aspects.
    I. Giorcelli, Cristina, editor of compilation. II. Rabinowitz, Paula, editor of compilation.
    PN56.C684F45 2014
    809'.933564—dc23

                                                          2013040906

Printed in the United States of America on acid-free paper

The University of Minnesota is an equal-opportunity educator and employer.

21 20 19 18 17 16 15 14   10 9 8 7 6 5 4 3 2 1

Contents

Preface and Acknowledgments

This four-volume English-language series extracts over forty of the best essays included in the ongoing editions *Abito e Identità: Ricerche di storia letteraria e culturale*, edited by Cristina Giorcelli and published since 1995 by Edizioni Associate (volumes 1–3) and Ila Palma Press (volumes 4–12) of Rome, Italy, augmenting these Italian-published essays with a few newly commissioned ones and with examples of work by contemporary artists who explore the interface between text and textile. The result of almost two decades of research by international teams of scholars from Algeria, France, Hungary, Italy, and the United States, the series focuses on the multiple forms and meanings attached to various articles of clothing in literature, film, performance, art, and other cultural arenas as well as on the social, economic, and semiotic connotations of clothing. Bringing together the work of literary and film critics, art and fashion historians, semioticians, sociologists, historians, and ethnographers, as well as psychoanalysts, artists, and fashion designers, these volumes offer an English-speaking audience a rare glimpse of the important work being published in Italy, that most modish of nations.

Moving among thematic, chronological, and aesthetic concerns, this series tracks clothing (and especially accessories) around four cardinal points—top, bottom, inside, outside—to allude to the complex implications of power, meaning, and sensibility associated with, for example, the head (of state as much as of body) or the foot, interiority or exposure. Each book addresses a complex of ideas encased within a set of terms that at times appears contradictory. The first volume, *Accessorizing the Body,* reconsiders the cliché that clothes represent a "second skin" by showing how the body itself became an accessory within various political and artistic movements of the twentieth century. Volume 2, *Exchanging Clothes,* focuses on the transnational circulation and exchange of apparel and its appropriations across time and space to consider how depictions of clothing in classic texts (for instance, Homer's epics) might migrate into understandings of how items of clothing actually mutate within the secondary economy of used-clothing stores. This volume, *Fashioning the Nineteenth Century,* is more traditional, organized as it is by period (the nineteenth century) and place (Europe and the United States) to explore a crucial era within the consolidation and spread of Western culture, when dress signified class and other distinctions through excess and detail, even as mass production turned clothing into an available commodity. The fourth and final volume in the series will interrogate connections between ornamentation and the quotidian, considering how aspects of apparel decorate everyday lives as the extravagant becomes mundane and the ordinary excessive.

Each book addresses social and economic processes involving dress as well as psychic and ontological aspects of identity. For instance, "circulation" references global exchange of commodities or a pair of shoes walking the streets; "movement" stresses the fluidity of meaning—political, sexual, historical—attached to articles of clothing when worn in various contexts; "detail" focuses on accessorizing the body and the role of clothing in the construction of social formations; "intimacies" exposes how what appears outside is a complex of social meanings extending deep inside to the interior of the body and its psychic formations; and "value" addresses economic disparities coded within dress as well as examines how replication and individuation differentiate affect. Obviously these are fluid categories that leak one into another, because any attention to clothing and its representation necessitates some awareness of what is seen and what is remembered for and by whom for what purpose activating which desires.

As an ongoing research project, the subjects covered range from boarding-school attire to Futurist vestments, from lesbian pulp to Henry James, from used-clothing stores to analysts' couches, from Spanish Fascist promotion of appropriate female dress to Hungarian Jewish tailors embroidering the yellow star. The mix of essays provides a compelling argument for the inherent interdisciplinarity of fashion studies. Looking at how dress is represented in a work of fiction necessarily opens into a discussion of class, of social procedures, of psychic dimensions, of the very texture of language itself; after all, text and textile share the same Latin root *texere*, to weave. Considering materials— literally the stuff out of which stuff is made—requires a discourse that brushes economics up against aesthetics. That so many scholars (experts in the history of Italian education, in the history of East European socialism, in the ethnography of Algerian wedding practices, to name a few) can unite through attention to items of clothing speaks to the transhistorical and cross-cultural ubiquity of clothing. It is a basic human need. Yet the vast differences and arcane meanings attached to any particular fashion trend or item of dress vary and change across classes, genders, time, and space. These vital embellishments appear utterly unnecessary. Such is the contradiction we all face daily.

Fashion studies extend from the ethnographic approach of Joanne Eicher to the art historical readings of Anne Hollander, from literary critic Marjorie Garber's inventive readings of transvestism to Germano Celant's exhibition of Giorgio Armani's couture at the Guggenheim Museum in 2000, which has inspired many others since then. This fluidity has attracted many distinguished scholars to our project. Most considered clothing for the first time in their careers. Yet, once analyzed, the subject captivated them so deeply that they willingly extended their research to create original meditations on the materials covering bodies both real and imagined. By no means exhaustive, the essays offer a range of styles—from rigorously archival to deeply textual—on objects and the affects they induce in their wearers and in those who observe them, describe them, desire them, and perhaps also shop for them.

As literary critics, much of our focus is on the ways in which literature relies on and participates in the construction of bodily presence through narrative or lyrical obsession with dress and habit. Because dress is at once tactile and visual—and often aural as well, as the crinkly sound of a crinoline or the swish of satin attests—the art of creating literary effects of touch and sight (and sound), especially when they are so intimately associated with character, offers tour de force examples of a writer's skill in conveying affect through description. More obviously, film, photography, and visual culture in general present opportunities to foreground clothing, tracking its changing sensations over time. Film, especially from Hollywood's Golden Era, worked hand in glove with the fashion industry, displaying the latest styles or costuming actresses in period clothing again and again to convey a world of opulence and ease seemingly accessible to all. Dress codes, whether in the form of school uniforms or corporate and government protocols, enforce, by contrast, a sense of clothing as a restrictive binding controlling one's ability to express individuality. Clothing both opens up and clamps down the body and its myriad identities. Even the same article of clothing can be at once freeing and restrictive—an empty sign full of meaning.

The essays in these collections are concerned with how subjectivity and identity, intimately tied to processes of incorporation, projection, and desire, are evoked by an item of dress. Thus, before scholars engage the subject, each volume commences with an essay by a woman psychoanalyst. Given the complexity of the problematic of clothes, it seemed essential to open each book with a reflection that ponders over their meaning in relation to identity from the point of view of her school—Freudian, Lacanian, Jungian. In every case, her evocative, even innovative, elaboration on the sparse shreds that the various masters have incidentally jotted down in their works calls for new ways of thinking about the habits of being. For instance, Freud noted Dora's *schmuckasten* but could never fathom what she meant when she asserted her right to own, and show off, such a fashionable item—sometimes a cigar is just a cigar, but a purse is never just a purse. In every volume we have also included a conversation with or a statement by a noted fashion designer; these views by masters of fashion design, with hands-on expertise and attention to detail, augment the psychoanalytic and philosophical considerations of the analysts. Then we open the arena to scholars. In addition, each book includes an example of women artists who appropriate traditional Western assumptions that weaving and sewing are aspects of women's work to create stunning visual links between text and textile. Like careful shoppers, we have been very selective in our choices. They remind us that all clothing is at once conceptual (someone designed each piece) *and* material (someone made it). Made for use yet extravagant, quotidian yet unique—what else is culture?

Attention to the mechanisms by which clothing and its representation affect psychic and social structures underlies most of the essays included, no matter how diverse their approaches. Representations of clothing, like the items themselves, can take on a fetishistic quality. Identity is perhaps little more than a matter of habit, of what is put on every day, to construct one's being. A habit of being. Clothed in the world and in the imagination.

This book is the result of the deep commitments of our many contributors; we are grateful for their collaboration, enthusiasms, and insights. We would like to thank our research assistants, Sara Cohen and Laura Brennan, for formatting and securing permissions for parts of this volume. Terese Austin of the Clements Library of the University of Michigan and Margaret Borg, assistant curator at the James Ford Bell Library of the University of Minnesota, helped with locating images for chapter 3. Support for the entire project has come from the Dipartimento di Studi Euro-Americani of the Università degli Studi di Roma Tre, and the Department of English, the Samuel Russell Chair in the Humanities of the College of Liberal Arts, and the Imagine Fund of the University of Minnesota. Our editor at the University of Minnesota Press—Douglas Armato, who has been devoted to this effort from the beginning—and his assistant, Danielle Kasprzak, as well as Nancy Sauro and Laura Westlund, helped guide us and trusted us to follow them throughout the process of turning an Italian series into an American one. Our reviewers, Caroline Evans, Cynthia Kuhn, and an anonymous reader, gave us cogent and encouraging suggestions; these have helped make this a stronger work.

The essays by Carmela Covato and Bianca Iacarrino Idelson first appeared in Italian in *Abito e Identità: Ricerche di storia letteraria e culturale,* vol. 1 (1995). Cristina Giorcelli's essay on "Charlie" was first published in Italian in *Abito e Identità* 2 (1997). Marta Savini's essay first appeared in Italian in *Abito e Identità* 3 (1999). Dagni Bredesen's essay originally appeared in English in *Abito e Identità* 4 (2001). Anna Scacchi's essay was published in Italian in *Abito e Identità* 5 (2004). Anna Masotti's essay originally appeared in Italian in *Abito e Identità* 6 (2006). The essays by Bruno Monfort and Agnès Derail-Imbert were published in English in *Abito e Identità* 7 (2007). Giuseppe Nori originally published his essay in Italian and Clair Hughes's essay first appeared in English in *Abito e Identità* 8 (2008). Carroll Smith-Rosenberg first published her essay in English in *Abito e Identità* 9 (2009).

Clothing, Dress, Fashion: An Arcade

The woman shall not wear that which pertaineth unto a man,
neither shall a man put on a woman's garment:
for all that do so are abominable unto the LORD thy God.

DEUTERONOMY 22:5

You must needs have dresses embroidered with gold;
you like to do your perfumed hair in countless different ways;
you must have sparkling rings upon your fingers.
You adorn your necks with pearls brought from the East,
pearls so big that your ears can scarcely bear the weight of them.

OVID, *The Art of Beauty*

Know, first, who you are, and then adorn yourself accordingly.

EPICTETUS

A complete description of people's costumes is apt to be tedious, but as in stories
the first thing that is said about the characters is invariably *what they wore*, I shall
once in a way attempt such description.

LADY MURASAKI, *The Tale of Genji*

Apparel may well be a part of majesty.

THOMAS ELYOT, *The Governor*

But seest thou not, I say, what a deformed thief this fashion is?

WILLIAM SHAKESPEARE, *Much Ado about Nothing*

Clothing is the sign that separates men from animals.

JEAN-ANTOINE CONDORCET, *Sketch for an Historical Picture of the Progress of the Human Mind*

Those who make their dress a principal part of themselves will, in general, become of no more value than their dress.

WILLIAM HAZLITT, "On the Clerical Character"

Man was an animal compounded of two dresses, the natural and celestial suit, which were the body and the soul: that the soul was the outward, and the body the inward clothing. . . . By all which it is manifest that the outward dress must needs be the soul.

JONATHAN SWIFT, "A Tale of a Tub"

The first spiritual want of a barbarous man is Decoration.

THOMAS CARLYLE, *Sartor Resartus*

What shall we call our "self"? Where does it begin? Where does it end? It overflows into everything that belongs to us—and then it flows back again. I know a large part of myself is in the clothes I choose to wear. I've a great respect for *things!* . . . these things are all expressive.

HENRY JAMES, *Portrait of a Lady*

It was dressed entirely in black, and of the very finest cloth;
it had patent leather boots, and a hat that could be folded together,
so that it was bare crown and brim; not to speak
of what we already know it had—seals, gold neck-chain, and diamond rings;
yes, the shadow was well-dressed, and it was just that which made it quite a man.

HANS CHRISTIAN ANDERSEN, "The Shadow"

Fashion is what one wears oneself. What is unfashionable is what other people wear.

OSCAR WILDE, "An Ideal Husband"

Fashion includes a peculiar attraction of limitation, the attraction of a simultaneous beginning and end, the charm of novelty coupled to that of transitoriness.

GEORG SIMMEL, "The Philosophy of Fashion"

The clothes are the background, the frame, if you like: they don't make success, but they are part of it.

EDITH WHARTON, *The House of Mirth*

The human animal shows in its clothing as conspicuously as in many other ways, the peculiar power of extraphysical expression.

CHARLOTTE PERKINS GILMAN, *The Dress of Women*

A blue coat is guided away, guided and
guided away, that is the particular color that is used
for that length and not any width not even more
than a shadow.

GERTRUDE STEIN, "A Blue Coat"

The clothes . . . seem to exist, not so much in the author's mind, as in the emotional penumbra of the characters themselves.

WILLA CATHER, "The Novel Démeublé"

What a strange power there is in clothing!

I. B. SINGER, "Yentl the Yeshiva Boy"

There is much to support the view that it is clothes that wear us and not we them.

VIRGINIA WOOLF, *Orlando*

The eternal is in any case far more the ruffle on a dress than some idea.

WALTER BENJAMIN, *The Arcades Project*

Let there be fashion, down with art.

MAX ERNST, *Let There Be Fashion, Down with Art*

Fashion is art's permanent confession that it is not what it claims to be.

THEODOR ADORNO, *Aesthetic Theory*

"Nuncle, you're looking wonderful this evening. Black suits you perfectly. But what are you looking at? Are you courting death?"

GIUSEPPE TOMASI DI LAMPEDUSA, *The Leopard*

If there's one thing I know, it's how to wear the proper clothing.

GRACE KELLY to **JIMMY STEWART** in *Rear Window*

The male subject, like the female subject, has no visual status apart from dress and/or adornment.

KAJA SILVERMAN, "Fragments of a Discourse on Fashion"

Dress is a sculpture in movement.

VIVIANE AUBRY, *Costumes II*

As a playful and gratuitous representation and a factitious sign, fashionable dress has broken all ties with the past; it draws the essence of its prestige from the ephemeral, scintillating, fascinating present.

GILLES LIPOVETSKY, *The Empire of Fashion*

A contemporary metropolis is that social site where individuals present and represent themselves first of all through the form and style of appearances.

ROBERTO GRANDI, "Fashion and the Ambiguous Representation of the Other"

A person without clothes is a person without language.

WEST AFRICAN PROVERB

The real opposition is not between soul and body, but between life and garment.

MARIO PERNIOLA, *The Sex Appeal of the Inorganic*

I enter the garment. It is as if I were going into the water. I enter the dress as I enter the water, which envelops me and, without effacing me, hides me transparently.

HÉLÈNE CIXOUS, "Sonia Rykiel in Translation"

Clothes like lovers, or, better, instead of lovers.

SEAN BLAZER, *Merchants of Fashion*

To write on clothing implies trying to consider garments no longer . . . as secondary elements, as accessories, but as primary, founding elements that determine individual behaviors as well as social structures.

FRÉDÉRIC MONNEYRON, *The Essential Frivolity: On Clothing and Fashion*

Fashion is the foundation of dress. Style is imparted to it by the wearer, and the accessories are its expression.

CARRIE A. HALL, *From Hoopskirts to Nudity*

Marie Antoinette sold her soul, and eventually the crown of her husband's realm, to her milliner, Rose Bertin.

COLIN MCDOWELL, *Hats, Status, and Glamour*

For clothing, its style is its essence.

ANNE HOLLANDER, *Seeing through Clothes*

Among primates, only humans regularly use adornment.

VALERIE STEELE, "Appearance and Identity"

Adornment *is* the woman, she exists veiled; only thus can she represent lack, be what is wanted.

STEPHEN HEATH, "Joan Riviere and the Masquerade"

Dress is the way in which individuals learn to live in their bodies and feel at home in them.

JOANNE ENTWISTLE, *The Fashioned Body*

Perfume . . . is our own shadow. It is a luxurious mirage, our transparency, a majestic choreography, a kind of inner palace, an architecture of exquisite crystal.

SERGE LUTENS, "My Perfumes"

Clothes are inevitable. They are nothing less than the furniture of the mind made visible.

JAMES LAVER, *Style in Costume*

I think my clothes allow someone to be truly an individual.

VIVIENNE WESTWOOD, in "A Conversation
with Vivienne Westwood" by Tara Sutton

I never thought people would want to wear clothes with monkeys and bananas
on them. It gave me great insight into people, into how willing people are to put
themselves out there. Fashion is an incredible tool for understanding people,
for understanding the world.

MIUCCIA PRADA, *Schiaparelli and Prada: Impossible Conversations*

If we think to distance ourselves from current fashion by finding another
fashion from which to fashion ourselves, chances are it will be the one that
current fashion predicted we'd pick.

MARK STRAND, "A Poet's Alphabet"

FASHIONING A CENTURY

Cristina Giorcelli

He who esteems trifles for themselves, is a trifler, but he who esteems them for the conclusions to be drawn from them, or the advantage to which they can be put, is a philosopher.
EDWARD BULWER-LYTTON, *Pelham*

Reflect on the whole history of women: ... they "put on something" even when they take off everything.
FRIEDRICH W. NIETZSCHE, *The Gay Science*

Accessorizing the Body, the first volume of this series, featured essays primarily referring to twentieth-century fashion accessories for women and men. Scholars from Hungary, the United States, and Italy examined them across various disciplines. *Exchanging Clothes*, the second volume, included essays that dealt mainly with both female and male accessories and clothes worn in ancient Greece and Rome up to contemporary United States, England, Algeria, and Italy—thus, with apparel that was donned from the ninth century BC to the twentieth century AD, from Homer to Sid Vicious. Again such accessories and clothes were analyzed through several disciplinary perspectives. This third volume, *Fashioning the Nineteenth Century*, presents essays concerning garments and accessories worn mostly by women in Italy, England, and the United States chiefly in nineteenth-century fiction, and specifically in canonical, more philosophical, "high" literature, proving that no matter how sophisticated the authors (male as well as female), they could not bypass such "marginal" items even when they were meant to talk of and denote characters who were not frivolous or irrational or false (although, one must remember, the state of being dressed may convey a shade of artifice, of inauthenticity). And this, not only because characters, in the majority of cases, must be dressed, but because of the intrinsic expressive potential of apparel: it covers and yet also uncovers, it hides and yet also reveals the body, our corporeal self. As Cynthia Kuhn and Cindy Carlson have argued, "the *written* clothed body" may function as "a narrative element with multiple dimensions."[1] In effect, clothes possess a performativity of their own, that is, they can be "mirror or lamp," either of the perceptive capacities or of the social (in terms of class or of money) identity of a character.[2]

Although not always easy to decode or univocal in their possible decodings, literary dresses are often revelatory. As symbolic systems, if they "articulate the soul," they are also "shifting, capable of infinite deferral."[3] A reader must be on guard for the slightest variations of tone and of perspective. Why, otherwise, would masters of the mind and of the pen, such as Nathaniel Hawthorne and Henry James or Gabriele D'Annunzio and Elizabeth Gaskell, be so punctiliously precise in the description of a veil and a spat, or of a pleat and a cap? As a manifestation of life, fashion and clothes signify both one's difference from others and one's consideration of oneself, while revealing yet another, important facet of their times. Paul Poiret, the great innovator of fashion at the beginning of the twentieth century, changed not only the style of women's clothes, but also that of a whole period. Tellingly, he titled his book *En habillant l'èpoque* (Dressing the Belle Epoque). Thus, beyond his author's ironic intention, Thomas Carlyle's Diogenes Teufelsdröckh may well be right when he wishes to use clothes as a key to read the world! Frédéric Monneyron, for instance, pushes this concept even further when he asserts that fashion may prefigure the future state of a society.[4]

Clothes indicate one's power over real as well as over fictitious people.[5] Clair Hughes has maintained that dresses are "a visible aspect of history, a material index of social, moral, and historical change which helps us understand and imagine historical difference." In her opinion, they are "crucial to the construction of an imagined world as well as an integral part of the way a novel is constructed as an artwork, part of the novelist's modernist concern with the life of the mind."[6] And this not only as of the last century.

Less exotic and less temporarily dislocated—at least for a Western audience—more traditional in content and more compact in time than the previous two volumes, this present one offers samples for the investigation of garments, accessories, and fashion at a period of significant social changes: when apparel was entering the field of consumerism; when the city was emerging as the anonymous, public arena where gendered bodies were displayed; when the flaneur, the female shopper, and the prostitute became iconic figures of modernity; when department stores were created as sites for the purchase and performance of elite goods; and when, after the French Revolution—as Friedrich Nietzsche maintained—individuals were eager to free themselves from any form of authority, the sartorial one included.[7] The fact that, in the nineteenth century, Paris and London were imperial cities helps explain their centrality in the fashion process: they were places of inevitable reference whenever garments were discussed, both within Europe and in their numerous colonies.

As far as women's fashions were concerned, the century saw radical changes taking place: while the discovery of synthetic dyes made possible more colorful fabrics, the patenting of the sewing machine (1853) accelerated the process of making dresses and, consequently, the possibility of their frequent innovations in style and of their more numerous acquisitions due to their lower costs. From the point of view of shapes and devices, the novelties were profound: from the neoclassical or empire style, with its high-waisted, loose-fitting rectangular dresses that allowed for breasts to be prominently visible, to the reintroduction of the corset, with its tight, stifling lacing, the crinoline, and multiple layers of petticoats (creating the bell-shaped figure); from the bustle to the mutton sleeve to the hourglass-shaped figure; from the bonnet to the large hat adorned with feathers, stuffed animals, veils, and ribbons; from the unattractive bloomers to the divided skirt, culottes, and knickerbockers when women saw in bicycling new possibilities for movement and sport. This more masculine attire was the harbinger of the different roles women were ready to take upon themselves in society.

Each of these changes implied a new way in which the female body was displayed and thus perceived. Clothes—at the frontier between the self and the not-self (they "link [the] body to the social world, but also more clearly separate the two"),[8] between the inside and the outside, or even as the outer layer of the inside—have always answered the function of expressing an identity through representation (the self to others), self-perception (the self to oneself), and designation (the recognition of oneself by others). During the nineteenth century, the relationship between clothes and desire reached a high level of signification for the amused entertainment of the most vivacious minds. Even if, especially in the first half of the century, feminine fashion was not as varied as it is today (when not only many looks are in vogue at the same time, but hybridization multiplies these looks ad infinitum), some artists understood how intriguing the signification of those often ostentatious clothes really was. These artists soon discovered that clothes and fashion are rich in aesthetic, social, economic, and moral meanings. (In the next century, alert people would find that clothes also help the construction of sex, gender, race, and ethnicity.) Although during that period, the dialectic was still between what is ephemeral and what is eternal, between the artificial and the natural, between the transitory and the permanent, clothes started acquiring an ideological and political value as well: European fashion set the pattern for distinction—therefore, according to the time's parameters, for self-serving cultural superiority.

In the nineteenth century, however, the most revolutionary changes occurred, as Anne Hollander has demonstrated, in male clothing: the tailored dark coat, dark close-fitting pants, vest, a clean shirt, and tie.[9] This austere apparel was befitting the bourgeoisie's declared belief in hard work, saving, seriousness, and moral rigor; such a severe suit, the expression of a philosophy of life, became the costume for middle-class men—unchanged for over a century. So much darkness and sternness inevitably brought with it a compelling desire for a spark of color, for a mark of originality, for what was often seen as a sign of "mannered effeminacy."[10] Suffice to think, for instance, of the dandy-ism of Lord George "Beau" Brummel, Honoré de Balzac, Charles Baudelaire, or Oscar Wilde, who quipped that one should either *be* a work of art or *wear* a work of art. With them, we may recall, the futile was metamorphosed into the sublime, and the pleasure and the quest were, in Baudelaire's words, to be amazing without being amazed. As Elizabeth Wilson has maintained, "The dandies invented Cool."[11] But dandies did not change the basic male attire, just insisted on the perfection of cut, line, and materials to make it even simpler: Ellen Moers observes that this "arrogant simplicity was an affirmation of the aristocratic principle"; it stood "on an isolated pedestal of self."[12] With so much uniformity to men's haberdashery, it was left mostly to accessories, to items on the body's periphery, such as ties, snuff boxes, pocket watches, walking sticks, gloves, hats, spats, and cufflinks, to signal some sort of individuality and provocatively destabilize bourgeois respectability.

At the end of the nineteenth century two sociologists, Thorstein Veblen and Georg Simmel, took clothes and fashion as their object of investigation and expressed ideas that are of interest to this day. For Veblen, who saw fashion as nonsensical, trivial, even wasteful, women's dresses were tools meant to disclose their wearers' bourgeois status and, at a time when women from the bourgeoisie up were not supposed to be other than wives and mothers, to reveal the wealth of the men who supported them (fathers, husbands, brothers).[13] Dresses were thus meant above all for the social world, that is, for those who would judge and be judged on the basis of their garments. (Now, a century later, dresses must above all signify for their wearer, for the way in which one feels in them.)[14] For his part, Simmel tried to assess who establishes fashion and why.[15] Following comments found in Adam Smith (*The Theory of Moral Sentiments*, 1759), Immanuel Kant (*Anthropology from a Pragmatic Point of View*, 1798), and Herbert Spencer (*The Principles of Sociology*, 1882), he reached the conclusion that two social tendencies are essential for the rise of fashion: the socializing impulse and the differentiating impulse. He deemed that, thanks to these two forces, fashion trickles down from the higher classes that invent it to the lower ones that copy it, until the former, to differentiate themselves from the latter, create a new one. (More recently, not only has this theory been contested by another sociologist, René König, but the contrary movement, the "bubble up," that is, the inspiration that comes to designers from what is worn in the streets, is also taken into consideration.)[16] Simmel understood that fashion is a perpetual compromise between individualism and conformity. If too individualistic, one risks trespassing the borders of fashion; if one conforms too slavishly, one's style is no longer an appealing badge of distinction.

In the United States, beginning in the 1880s, in several of her writings (which culminated in 1915 with the pamphlet entitled "The Dress of Women" serialized in her journal the *Forerunner*), the American sociologist, feminist, and novelist Charlotte Perkins Gilman forcefully battled for dresses that, against the prevailing flamboyant fashion, she wanted functional and comfortable. Aware that "cloth is a social tissue," as she wrote in the first installment of her series, and that "you only are when clothed,"[17] she understood that dresses are an integral part of the way women are and, specifically, that they bespeak their wearers' relationship with the world: they, in fact, extol women's personalities.[18] Anticipating observations made years later (with the less moralistic third wave of feminism of the 1990s), Gilman proclaimed that "the human animal shows in its clothing as conspicuously as in many other ways, the peculiar power of extra-physical expression."[19] Rather than condemning women's interest in fashion, she saw it as another way through which they revealed themselves—even to themselves.

At a time when the rational dress movement was sponsoring clothes that were practical but not becoming, Gilman advocated dresses that would not hamper but leave freedom of movement to the body and would not turn their wearers into sexual objects on display to catch a husband (and thus financial support). In her opinion, however, clothes also had to be beautiful and to beautify. With an eye on the shoe fashion of today, with its exasperatingly vertiginous heels, I select Gilman's comment on the shoes worn at her time: she wrote that they hazarded "grave mechanical injury."[20] But she also added that such dangers and harms occurred because fashion designers, being mostly men, knew "what taste to please."[21] Is it true today as well? Certainly the most prominent shoe designers are still men, but do women risk breaking their ankles (or necks) only to please men? Or do they do it because (besides competing with and showing off to other women) they wish to improve their silhouette or raise their height, or simply prove something about themselves to themselves? On this subject one must recall that Oscar Wilde held a high opinion of feminine clogs because, while avoiding the risk of soiling dresses with mud and dust, they would not make the body bend forward and compel women to make short steps, thus depriving them of the grace that comes from freedom of movement.[22]

At the end of the century, symbolist, decadent, and art nouveau writers evoked the sensuous, voluptuous, and even erotic power of clothes. In some of these writers the descriptions of garments went so far as to assume fetishist characteristics: fabrics seemed to take on a life of their own, clothes became cult objects, and bodies were meant to lose substance and corporeality in favor of a cold, merciless, morbid, indifferent, perverse femininity: that of the femme fatale. Significantly, in the new century, an English psychologist, John C. Flügel, underlined the sexual dimension of clothes and their role as sexual differentiators: in his opinion a man is more conservative in his dress as he gives up exhibitionism and narcissism for social power, whereas women are more whimsical and gaudy in their clothes to compensate for their social subordination.[23] As far as these points of view are concerned, Flügel's work is now dated not only because men are as interested in physical appearance as women are, but also because of the fragmentary messages sent by dresses about our current fluid (male and female) identities. Yet, as far as the psychological meaning of clothes is concerned, his book has still valuable insights to offer.

This succinct overview shows how comprehensive and far-reaching the debate over clothes and fashion already was more than a century ago, prefiguring the more recent (since the 1980s) emergence of cultural and fashion studies that have finally acknowledged the importance of these items of material culture to appropriately and legitimately help define a time, a place, and an individuality. In fiction as well as in painting, with their shapes and colors, garments do not simply cover a character, but they tell us *more* about him or her. And if to understand, for instance, the many variations of white in color and textures that there may be in a dress one should read Théophile Gautier's poem "Symphonie en blanc majeur" (1849) or Emile Zola's *Au bonheur des dames* (1883), to understand the many variations of black in shades, hues, and textures one should examine Giovanni Boldini's portraits of women swathed in evening gowns of such a color.[24] Each of those hues, each of those textures (taffeta, lace, brocade, silk, satin), besides manifesting the artist's extraordinary control over his palette, hints at the woman's multifaceted personality. Readers and onlookers are thus implicitly asked to retrieve the significations of such deliberate and virtuoso details by letting them play in their eyes and, imaginatively, in their ears (in the case of textiles, not by chance the vocabulary used to described them is often that of music). Having learned how to read such a zero degree of color, one is tempted to imagine the many unwritten but implicitly not unimaginable different hues that Hawthorne's "Minister's Black Veil" must have assumed as the Reverend Hooper was talking, whispering, breathing, bending, in light or in darkness. As the title indicates, the veil, that "simple piece of crape," no less than its wearer, is the story's protagonist.[25]

Close attention to the garments and accessories described by a writer is an act of respect toward the dedication to his or her craft that manifests itself *also* through and thanks to them. In the United States, Henry James and Edith Wharton show how quickly they became aware of fashion as a reality and how subtly they incorporated its evolutions into their work. Can we ever forget, from this specific perspective, the telling encounter in the evening between Longmore, the Comte de Mauves, and the latter's dandy friend in the Parisian Boulevard toward the end of "Madame de Mauves" (1874) or Lily Bart's trying to make a living by trimming hats in *The House of Mirth* (1905)? For both writers, moreover, clothes were signs immediately gauged by the upper class to which they belonged and that they were eminently addressing. And how can we bypass the information that James gives at the beginning of the narratives about both Daisy Miller and Isabel Archer when, naively spontaneous, they appear to the sophisticated and scrutinizing male gaze in the garden of the Vevey Hotel and in the park of Gardencour, respectively, "hatless"? Surely "dress functions as hieroglyph: its material presence drapes the body, revealing and concealing intricate patterns easily read by the members of the tribe and clearly setting limits on those included and excluded from its web of meaning."[26]

We are then not only many centuries away, but also at the opposite end from Plato's allegory of the cave in which appearance, the image, is the inverse of reality.[27] Today— in the so-called civilization of images—the image, stigmatized by Plato, but also by Blaise Pascal and Immanuel Kant, among others, is rehabilitated as a link between the intelligible and the sensible by philosophers and sociologists such as Gaston Bachelard, Mircea Eliade, Gilbert Durand. Indeed clothed (and unclothed) appearances are social constructions with which we must daily come to terms. More important, as fashion is, in principle, constantly in movement, constantly modern, constantly up-to-date, fashion is one of the areas of human life in which there is an impelling urge to move forward, to try new adventures, to release new energies, even to return anew to the past. In such depressing times of recession, this push forward should not be underestimated.

NOTES

1. Cynthia Kuhn and Cindy Carlson, "Introduction," in *Styling Texts: Dress and Fashion in Literature,* ed. Cynthia Kuhn and Cindy Carlson (Youngstown, N.Y.: Cambria Press, 2007), 1.

2. Paola Colaiacomo and Vittoria C. Caratozzolo, *Cartamodello: Antologia di scrittori e scritture sulla moda* (Rome: Luca Sossella, 2000), 8 (my translation).

3. Clair Hughes, *Dressed in Fiction* (Oxford: Berg, 2006), 132.

4. Frédéric Monneyron, *La sociologie de la mode* (Paris: Presses Universitaires de France, 2006), 77.

5. François-Marie Grau, *Histoire du costume* (Paris: Presses Universitaires de France, 1999), 5.

6. Hughes, *Dressed in Fiction,* 2, 3.

7. See Friedrich Nietzsche, "The Wanderer and His Shadow," in *Human, All Too Human: A*

Book for Free Spirits, trans. R. J. Hollingdale (Cambridge: Cambridge University Press, 1997), 301–95.

8. Elizabeth Wilson, *Adorned in Dreams* (London: Virago: 1985), 3.

9. See Anne Hollander, *Sex and Suits: The Evolution of Modern Dress* (New York: Knopf, 1994).

10. Christopher Breward, "The Dandy Laid Bare: Embodying Practices and Fashion for Men," in *Fashion Cultures: Theories, Explorations, and Analysis,* ed. Stella Bruzzi and Pamela Church Gibson (London: Routledge, 2000), 224.

11. Wilson, *Adorned in Dreams,* 180.

12. Ellen Moers, *The Dandy* (London: Secker and Warburg, 1960), 17.

13. See Thorstein Veblen, *The Theory of the Leisure Class* [1899] (London: Allen and Unwin, 1957).

14. A recent study by Hajo Adam and Adam D. Galinsky shows how our wardrobe influences our thinking and behavior. This internal dynamic is called "enclothed cognition" to parallel "embodied cognition," which examines the ways bodily sensations influence thoughts and emotions. See "Enclothed Cognition," *Journal of Experimental Social Psychology* 48, no. 4 (2012): 918–25.

15. See Georg Simmel, "Fashion" [1895], in *On Individuality and Social Forms* (Chicago: University of Chicago Press, 1971).

16. See René König, *Menschheit auf dem Laufsteg: Die Mode im Zivilisationsprozess* (Munich: Hanser, 1985). This idea was first promulgated by Rudolph von Jhering in his 1883 *Der Zweck im Recht* where he noted that the upper classes look "for new designs in the sewer of the Parisian demi-monde." Quoted in Walter Benjamin, *The Arcades Project,* trans. Howard Eiland and Kevin McLaughlin (Cambridge, Mass.: Belknap Press of Harvard University Press, 1999), 74–75.

17. Charlotte Perkins Stetson, "The Body and the Dress," *Pacific Rural Press,* July 11, 1891, 26.

18. Cristina Giorcelli, "The Power of Clothes: 'The Dress of Women,'" *Letterature d'America* 31, no. 134 (2011): 23–41.

19. Charlotte Perkins Gilman, "The Dress of Women," in *The Forerunner* (New York: Greenwood Reprint, 1968), 20.

20. Ibid., 80.

21. Ibid., 249.

22. Oscar Wilde, "Woman's Dress," in *Miscellanies* (London: Metheun, 1908), 48.

23. See John C. Flügel, *The Psychology of Clothes* (London: Hogarth, 1930).

24. Giovanni Boldini was born in Ferrara (Italy) in 1842; from 1871, he lived and worked primarily in France. He died in Paris in 1931.

25. Nathaniel Hawthorne, *Twice-Told Tales* (Boston: John B. Russell, 1837), 56.

26. Katherine Joslin, *Edith Wharton and the Making of Fashion* (Durham: University of New Hampshire Press, 2009), 7.

27. See Plato, *The Republic,* trans. D. Lee (London: Penguin, 1987), 316–25.

1

PSYCHOANALYTIC VIEWS OF
CROSS-DRESSING AND TRANSVESTISM

Bianca Iaccarino Idelson

DRESSING AND CROSS-DRESSING:
SIGN, SYMPTOM, SPECTACLE

Among the greatest achievements of Freudian theory has been the invention of a new language capable of giving shape, through images, to the subjective and private experiences of the unconscious. It is a figurative and imaginative language with a terminology of its own and an ability to play various roles within and between one's psychology. In doing so, it succeeds in creating a true dramatization of consciousness. That Sigmund Freud repeatedly turned to literature in his search for confirmation of his metapsychological theories indicates his awareness of the problem he was leaving unresolved in establishing the implicit equation between (cultural) sign and (individual) symptom. By contrast, the fact that we, his followers, think we have an interpretive method that can make sense of several types of cultural output is, in my opinion, a consequence of a sometimes unsatisfactory and arbitrary combination of psychoanalysis and academia.

The themes of cross-dressing and transvestism (in Italian *travestimento* and *travestitismo*), because of their links to the enormous and myriad dimensions of the subject's external appearance, serve as interfaces between public and private, sign and symptom. To understand the distinctions between cross-dressing and transvestism as they move from psychoanalysis to social theory, we need a more accurate way to differentiate between the pathological domain and diverse modes of cultural expression. At the same time, psychoanalytical thought needs to be pushed beyond a shallow way of reasoning that, with the loss of its emotional and interpretive power, has slid from intellectual adventure to received knowledge.

To clarify the essential distinction between transvestism and cross-dressing: Transvestism, in pyschoanalysis, belongs to the category of suffering and psychological unease. It involves a masquerade, a mimesis that implies the use of a particular type of language, that of clothing and appearance, in order to cover up the anxiety created by the void in the field of possible identifications. Cross-dressing, by contrast, pertains to the social category of play and to the dynamics of culture. Through double entendre, it alludes to the need to keep the enigma and mystery of sexual *difference* alive (despite the prescriptive function of language that establishes and validates the sexual *division* that orders the world). The true enigma, in fact, is not femininity but sexual difference.

Thus, it is my belief that when the subject falls in love, true desire doesn't involve possessing the loved one. True desire lies in the universal aspiration to deceive oneself, to cross the real boundary imposed on every human being—the Pillars of Hercules that are inevitably shattered when any great act of falling in love takes place, be it heterosexual or homosexual. The boundary may not be death as finality, as we are used to thinking; instead death represents the impossibility of looking, feeling, perceiving the world, life, and love as at once masculine and feminine together.

In psychoanalytical theory, perversion is considered to be a psychological form established as a way of avoiding the Oedipal complex and its associated fear of castration. On an intrapsychological level, psychoanalysis has considerably deepened the understanding of the psychopathological nature of perversion. However, it is also true that this deeper understanding has been unsuccessful in accounting for the intersections between the individual unconscious and what, to paraphrase Carl Gustav Jung, could be called the collective unconscious. The question that remains to be solved is this: what are the forms of thought or consciousness (and therefore, of desire) organized automatically by social and cultural life that might cause the pathological structure of desire known as transvestism?

What is crucial to an understanding of perversion is its basis in a developmental regression at the pregenital stage, which occurs at an inappropriate developmental age of the child and causes in the infant feelings of guilt and anxiety when s/he should be experiencing pleasure. Regression, indeed, is a central feature of perversion, but not the only one. In order for a perversion to exist (as opposed to a neurosis, for example) the feeling of guilt must be accompanied by an element of eroticization. In other words, guilt, instead of being confronted and resolved along the usual lines of adjustment to the needs of the superego, is avoided through a libidinal eroticizing mechanism that denies it as such and transforms it into a way of achieving libidinal pleasure. From this point of view, given that the structure of the personality turns to the denial of anxiety and guilt (which is assumed as a condition of being), perversion represents a form of defense not so much from neurosis but from an altogether terrifying psychosis.

This brief synthetic description of a psychoanalytic point of view brings two things clearly to light: on the one hand, an extreme articulation of the explanatory principle of the psychopathology of perversion (especially when compared, for example, with prior purely biological models) combined with a coherent and representative picture of the unhealthy personality in general; and on the other hand, an acceptance of the current cultural norm of heterosexuality where sexual division and evolution is naively considered to be the only biologically valid norm for sexual reproduction. Freudian thought does not appear to have been affected by the plethora of anthropological observations contradicting this argument: Australian tribes where incest between brother and sister forms part of the social-religious structure; many tribes in New Guinea where homosexuality is accepted as one of the norms of life; or the case of the Siberian shamans who, besides being homosexual, assume all the outward appearance of the other sex, leading true and authentic transvestite lives. It should be noted, incidentally, that in all these societies homosexuality and cross-dressing are integral to normal everyday life. Moreover, these various cultures adapt social functionality and behavior not to conform to biological imperatives but rather to help maintain a stable social structure.

Considered closely, the Freudian model seems useful and convincing as a means of understanding and perhaps even curing individual pathologies (even if therapies addressing perversions are among the most difficult), that is, those situations in which the deviation from the norm manifests as a symptom that produces the suffering subject. Psychoanalytic thought is less convincing, however, when it attempts to make sense of the broad range of behaviors and social phenomena that are countermarked, for example, by the act of cross-dressing and are thus classified as cultural signs: Mardi Gras carnivals, male–female cross-dressing in theatrical contexts, authors' use of opposite-sex pseudonyms, some institutionally imposed forms of dress, and so forth.

When we move from the unconscious level to the realm of appearance, a purely aesthetic (and cultural) dimension, psychoanalytic discourse falters. To examine this context, a more suggestive and exciting approach requires us to take a step back in time and return to the prepsychoanalytic language of traditional psychiatry. The greatest narrator of clinical cases in the period prior to Sigmund Freud is still Richard von Krafft-Ebing who, in his *Psychopathia sexualis,* collected an immense number of stories relating to clinical perversions that he gathered from the minutes of court hearings. The language he uses is essentially descriptive and phenomenological, precisely because of the absence of any strongly interpretative thought or model. At the same time, it is a language of high literary and poetic value.

Moreover, Krafft-Ebing centers the main problem of transvestism, using a very accurate methodology, within the ambit of the dynamic relationship between attraction and repulsion founded on aesthetic values.

[Henry] Havelock Ellis fought hard against the expression "transvestite instinct" because the subjects in question do not in fact want to cross-dress. Rather, they select clothing that reflects their entire sensibility that they, of course, wish to express. The people in question do not want to hide the external aspect of their sexuality behind different clothes. Quite the opposite. They want to dress in accordance with their deepest instinct. Havelock Ellis chose the phrase "aesthetic-sexual inversion" for his subjects fully aware that this was not entirely accurate either.

He justified the expression in relation to concepts that belong to aesthetic doctrine. Philosophers engaged in aesthetics maintain, in fact, that in our imagination we imitate the beauty we see and we identify with it sentimentally. According to Karl Gross, the central phenomenon of aesthetic enjoyment comes from the play of internal imitation, of intimate participation in the life of the admired object. . . .

[Theodor] Lipps . . . maintains that imitation and identification generally meet in aesthetic sensations. But when sex comes into play, there is less of a meeting. "We cannot explain," he says, "the influence of female beauty on imitation, given that a man does not want to have a woman's breasts, for example."

Nonetheless, while differentiating the two drives, identification and imitation, Gross maintains that when it comes to aesthetics, identification always plays the main role. Now, according to Havelock Ellis, . . . the subject affected by this anomaly (the drive to wear clothes of the opposite sex) does not necessarily have an inverse instinctual drive on the level of sexuality. On the contrary, one in fact would have reached an emotional state, fundamentally aesthetic, in the sexual sphere.

In the admiration for the loved person, one is not satisfied with limiting oneself to the normal aspect of identification but lives the entire aesthetic process because one is also involved in the need to imitate.[1]

Krafft-Ebing's psychopathological frame of transvestism might be called into question especially if we take into account other consequent psychoanalytical findings. However, in this phenomenological approach, either on its own or in relation to cross-dressing as a cultural phenomenon, what is significant is the position of the problem within the game of "aesthetic" signs (i.e., visual ones) as opposed to biological drives. Krafft-Ebing seems to have understood the central nub of cross-dressing better than anyone: as a universal aspiration toward metamorphosis.

CROSS-DRESSING AS A CULTURAL PHENOMENON
AND THE ENJOYMENT OF METAMORPHOSIS

In the play of oscillation between identification and imitation, Krafft-Ebing captures the key distinction between normality and pathology. But more interesting for the problem posed here is the angle from which he approaches the topic of cross-dressing. The methodological error of applied psychoanalysis lies in its implied equation between the psychobiological organism (governed by instincts, drives, and desires) and the cultural being, an error that becomes obvious in the sterile repetitiveness of research on the great authors and their work. By contrast, Krafft-Ebing's method of investigation is to choose a topic (e.g., aesthetic emotion and the way it is articulated in pathology) that does not force him into a reductionism, which, when applied to instinct, might be interpreted as genetic (people are born homosexual or transsexual) or psychoanalytic (people become homosexual or transsexual through a deviation of the instinct). In both of these versions, the true meaning of exhibited behavior lies in a scenario other than what appears on the surface. I would argue, following Krafft-Ebing, that cross-dressing, whenever it is the focus of literary, theatrical, or other forms of cultural expression, remains in the designated field of aesthetic appearance and, therefore, of cultural signs; one need not search for some other scenario from another order.

At this point, we must look further afield—to the illusionary world of theater—to adequately articulate the issue. The topic of cross-dressing requires and indeed demands a more sophisticated analysis than that based on a deterministic explanation of the world through cause and effect. Elsewhere, the mechanism for linking the language of appearance to that of the unconscious seems much more mysterious. If the sense of pretense, be it in fiction or theater, comes from allowing what goes on in the world of the imagination to become the standard for reality (even if it is a particular kind of reality), pretense within the pretense, as in cross-dressing, adds to this illusion the principle of secrecy. In the typical plot in which cross-dressing is crucial to the main character (often so as to win the love of a woman against the wishes of an authoritarian father figure who must be deceived), the witness and guardian of the cross-dressing secret is the spectator. The character who cross-dresses significantly transforms the paths of the unconscious between spectator and play, blocking the processes of identification and making them impossible.

The spectator can no longer identify with a he who is a she or vice versa except at the expense of confusing his/her own sexual identity, which might be potentially psychotic and from which s/he must then retreat. But, as everyone knows, the spectator watching a play based on cross-dressing does not become either bored or ill, nor does s/he leave the theater midperformance; instead s/he can actually enjoy the show, sometimes very much. What causes this enjoyment?

With the appearance on stage of the character who cross-dresses and takes on traits of the opposite sex, the spectator loses the possibility of merging with his or her unconscious emotional world since s/he acquires the role of custodian of the secret. This guarantees a collaborative role in the play, which is the real source of pleasure. In effect, introducing cross-dressing displaces the traditional position of the unconscious between the dualism of spectator and play. Instead, it produces a kind of role-playing game involving three players: the play, the spectator, and the secret that, through language, often generates and depends on double entendre. Thus the spectator's function seems to take on a particular importance. S/he is no longer a passive participant but actively takes part in the process of producing meaning, which is the most enjoyable part of all. The mechanism of the unconscious (to paraphrase Freudian terminology about dream-work) pulls back from the spectator-character dyad and infiltrates the very heart of language, which is not merely a vehicle for communicating meaning but becomes, in effect, the creator of a double entendre, inducing the spectator's pleasure.

This mise-en-scène with its traditional game of hide-and-seek developing around pretense becomes hyperinvested in signifying and produces its own effects especially in those ambiguous areas of language bound up in sexual identity. This language no longer has the simple communicative function, enclosed within the system of signs that represent it, of transmitting the meaning of a plot and arousing emotions. It is a language instead that seems to become a stranger to itself and assigns a new task to the spectator. The freedom of staged pretense gives rise to another kind of freedom for the spectator: a game that does not only consist in projecting and introjecting the images and fantasies of the individual and collective unconscious, but is transgressive and ironic about the restrictive nature of intentional language. In other words, the spectator does not transgress within the pretense of the scene of make-believe or abandon his/her own gender identity to the power of the game and freely enjoys the ludic dimension without anxiety. Rather, this type of transgressive pleasure is impossible due to a strong anxiety created by the absence of a stable sexual identity.

In my opinion, this is a pleasure played out within the double meaning contained in language through a scenario limited and defined by the reassurance provided by pretense and performance. Language as unconscious carrier drives its conventional and prescriptive nature (by attributing meaning) into a void. In this way, the work of the unconscious is displaced and its functioning operates from within the core of language, which in some ways could be said to be the principle behind gender division.

According to Jacques Lacan, for example, the error or fundamental naïveté of much psychoanalysis is that it maintains the secret as the explanatory key to the subject's interior world within the unconscious. If this point of view can be challenged when the discourse is confined to the clinical and the psychopathology of the symptom, when this topic extends itself to linguistic and cultural output, it makes sense. The secret of meaning is certainly no longer considered to be in the author's unconscious (if it were, an infinite series of contradictions would emerge) or in the viewer's subconscious, either separately or in direct relationship to one another. Rather, it must be looked for outside of these two figures, in the forms and functions with which language itself establishes, governs, and connects these two actors into a threesome that has suggestive—and perhaps they are only suggestive—resonances with the keystone of Freudian metapsychology: the Oedipal triangle.

By contrast, and incidentally, a more precise connection could be found with another figuration from the Freudian model: wit. In wit, two language segments come together. This meeting is casual and unconscious: if each segment stood alone there would be no meaning and wit could not arise. But the combination of the two, governed by the force of language itself that drags them along an unknown logic incomprehensible to them, produces a meaning otherwise unthinkable: a joke.

But leaving aside this psychoanalytic digression and returning to the problem of the intersection between the logic of meaning and the logic of double meaning, it seems to me that the spectator's real pleasure when faced with cross-dressing lies in the possibility of occupying the zones of ambiguous language offered by the text through the pleasure of metamorphosis. This not-possible pleasure encoded in language as a law is the natural setting for psychological structure and functioning. And it is with this that the double entendre of a cross-dressing context plays hide-and-seek. The process ensures the immutability of the division of the sexes, guaranteeing social order and the freedom to put into play the fixity of sexual identity that limits, rather than ensures, one's belonging to the world of symbols. Within the pathological or suffering subject, the enigma of sexual difference animates fantasies of total possession of the other, jealousy and the tremendous destructive force of hatred; wishing for impossible metamorphosis downgrades to symptom.

In the realm of language and culture in which theatrical cross-dressing is an apt example, the double entendre hidden in the folds of language surrounds identity, shattering the authority of the law, and shifts the enigma of sexual difference from symptom and pathology to the playful pleasure of metamorphosis.

NOTE

1. "Havelock-Ellis ha pure combattuto l'espressione 'istinto di travestimento,' perché i soggetti in questione non vogliono affatto travestirsi, ma anzi scelgono un abito che corrisponda a tutta la loro sensibilità, la quale, appunto, essi vogliono esprimere. Le persone in questione non vogliono nascondere sotto un altro abito l'aspetto esterno proprio al loro sesso, ma, vice-versa, vogliono vestirsi conformemente a quello che è il loro intimo istinto. Havelock-Ellis ha scelto per i suoi casi l'espressione 'inversione-sesso-estetica,' pure rendendosi perfettamente conto che neppure essa è proprio esatta. Egli ha giustificato tale espressione con concetti propri delle dottrine estetiche. I filosofi che si occupano di estetica ritengono, infatti, che nell'immaginazione noi imitiamo la bellezza che vediamo e in essa ci immedesimiamo sentimentalmente. Secondo Karl Gross il fenomeno centrale del godimento estetico è dato dal giuoco dell'imitazione interna, dell'intima partecipazione alla vita dell'oggetto. . . .

"L'imitazione e l'immedesimazione si incontrano generalmente, secondo Lipps . . . nella sensazione estetica, ma quando entra in giuoco il sesso, tale incontro viene meno. 'Noi non possiamo,' egli dice, 'spiegare l'influsso della bellezza della donna con l'imitazione, poiché un uomo non desidera avere, per esempio, il seno di donna.'

"Nondimeno Gross, sempre distinguendo i due stimoli, ritiene che quello all'immedesimazione esplichi sempre la parte principale. Ora, secondo Havelock-Ellis . . . il soggetto affetto da questa anomalia (stimolo a portare abiti dell'altro sesso) non avrebbe, semplicemente, invertita una tendenza generale appartenente alla sfera sessuale: al contrario, egli avrebbe invece raggiunto, in realtà, uno stato emozionale specificamente estetico nella sfera sessuale.

"Nell'ammirazione della persona amata egli non si contenta di limitarsi all'elemento normale dell'immedesimazione, ma vive tutto il processo estetico in quanto risente anche lo stimolo all' imitazione." Richard von Krafft-Ebing, *Psychopathia sexualis,* ed. Albert Moll, trans. Piero Giolla (Milan: Carlo Manfredi Editore, 1957), 643–44 (my translation). This passage, as such, does not appear in the English-language edition.

2

OUR JOB IS TO CREATE BEAUTY
A PERSONAL MEMOIR OF LA PERLA

Anna Masotti

Bologna 1954. With the enthusiasm and the spirit of enterprise typical of the postwar era, my grandmother, Ada Masotti, opened a small corset and lingerie workshop that had as its first address her kitchen, equipped with a cutting table and two Singer sewing machines. For this new enterprise, my grandfather, Antonio, handled the administration, and with the help of an assistant my grandmother created garments in lace, silk, and tulle that were in keeping with the very best classic tradition and also special styles made with a new material that came from the United States: nylon.

Bologna already had a four-centuries-long tradition of silk milling and refined textile manufacturing firms that had given rise to a well-known artisan school for crafting female undergarments. My grandmother, in her turn, was the daughter of an embroiderer and spent her childhood surrounded by needles, threads, and pieces of cloth. As a girl, she completed her training with the city's best atelier and became a skilled corset maker. This was at a time when the wearability of an item of underclothing could not yet be entrusted to elastic fibers but only to skillful modeling on the body. Thanks to this craftsman's training, my grandmother laid the foundations for that unique know-how that is still today an integral part of what she would call the La Perla philosophy.

She, together with my grandfather, chose the lucky name La Perla, inspired by this perfect creation of nature, the pearl, to suggest a precious and harmonious feminine style. In fact, the case in which the first creations were transported, lined with red velvet, resembled a jeweler's case. My grandmother received her first financing from two people who then became lifelong friends: one was the mother of a school friend of her son—my father, Alberto—and the other a minor supplier of textiles from Milan who was among the first to install a loom for the production of nylon fabrics.

Within this family network lies the secret of my grandmother's success: on the one hand, her creativity, business skills, and boundless energy—which allowed her to reconcile work commitments with the care of a small son—but, on the other, her instinct for adopting new techniques in the field, new yarns, and new machinery as well as her attention to the rapid changes in clothing styles typical of those times. A few years later, driven by the enthusiasm of a collaborator, Ubaldo Borgomanero—who would become her partner—she decided to incorporate the business. This change immediately met with great success: by 1965, the company had 150 employees.

Among the most important innovations that Grandma brought to her lingerie collections was certainly the introduction of fashion colors, aimed at the 1960s generation that had begun to enjoy the climate of postwar economic recovery and appreciate (and indulge in) the small luxuries of a consumer society. Indeed the 1960s marked a radical change in the history of clothing and especially in women's fashion. In London, Mary Quant launched the miniskirt, fashion magazines offered bright colors and optical patterns, and in general, a new type of female model could be seen: one who, compared to those of the past, was younger, uninhibited, and unconventional.

FIGURE 2.1 La Perla, stockings (Collezione 1991). Courtesy of Anna Masotti.

Ada sensed that the entire perspective on underwear was also destined to change and created a new concept of lingerie, where underwear left the confines of practicality to become an essential element in the style of every woman: it was subject to the changes in fashion, and it was ready to become, in itself, a fashion item for all intents and purposes. On the wave of this intuition, my grandmother decided to launch coordinates in brightly colored lace that met with immediate success in the Italian market. Within this new reality, she continued to offer creations that were in tune with the fashion and clothing phenomena of the era: bra and pantie sets in cotton with gingham checks inspired by the Brigitte Bardot look, tartan slips like the London miniskirts, and girdles printed with colorful flowers like those created by Ken Scott.

In the early 1970s, the company began to expand, moving into new product categories such as swimwear and sleepwear, where my grandma was able to extend and use the know-how that she had gained about design, modeling, and fabrics for lingerie. In parallel, my father Alberto, after having obtained his degree in medicine, became more involved in the family business. Grandma Ada handed complete management of the company over to him in 1990, although she remained a constant presence until her death in 1992. She was a reference point, above all, in the training of designers and pattern makers and passed on to them her wealth of experience. My father was helped in his job by my mother, Olga, who became the chief designer of beachwear fashion and later supervisor of the La Perla ready-to-wear collection. Through 2006, I also worked full-time in the company as director of communications and branding. In August 2007, the company contracted a strategic alliance with JH Partners, the San Francisco company established in 1986 that specializes in the consumer segment for medium-sized businesses with high growth potential. La Perla is no longer a family business.

One day my grandmother was asked for a definition of her job, and she replied with a phrase that would become the true company mission: "Our job is to create beauty." The most important legacy she left to those of us who followed are those strengths that we consider to be the chromosomes in the La Perla DNA: the technical background, the importance given to the design phase, the thorough knowledge of the female body, the

FIGURE 2.2 [LEFT] La Perla, tap pants (Collezione
2001). Courtesy of Anna Masotti.

FIGURE 2.3 [ABOVE] La Perla, bra, garter belt,
and stockings (Collezione 2005–6). Courtesy
of Anna Masotti.

blend of innovation and tradition, the Italian identity and international orientation, the
ethics of total quality. During the evolution from its first small workshop to its industrial
reality, she decided, for example, to use only Leavers lace from Calais, France (a type of
lace that even now is still produced on mechanical looms dating back to the 1800s), for
La Perla lingerie. What is more, her great experience in design and pattern-making led
her to teach her collaborators to create pieces of lingerie by constantly trying them out
on the female body. Even into the new millennium, in keeping with this practice, every
new creation is born this way, revealing that almost maniacal attention to detail she considered the real mark of quality. The company continued to use the most precious materials that contributed to our fame, in addition to Leavers laces, the very best embroidered tulle and different kinds of silk, but we also sought out new-generation textiles
that guarantee excellent performance in terms of comfort and lightness.

Always, inspiration for our creations came from the most varied sources. We usually began by thinking about a historical moment, a film, a type of woman, or an artistic era, and on the basis of this reflection, we elaborated a concept for the collection that also considered the technical problems linked to materials and to patterns. I am a tireless explorer of vintage stores and markets all over the world where I would find new ideas to include in our collections. We also return to our past by reinterpreting it in a contemporary way; we therefore take inspiration from the creations of my grandmother that were developed over a period of fifty years. In fact, in 2004 La Perla celebrated its fiftieth birthday!

The pleasure of being different, of wearing a distinctive detail, and of carrying an individual style seems to be one of the fashion obsessions of the new millennium. In perfect tune with such a need for uniqueness, we have produced the La Perla Limited Edition characterized by an exclusive range of creations with special workmanship primarily done by hand. This fashion exploration took us on a journey to discover precious materials and rediscover traditional techniques interpreted in a contemporary manner. One of these is the *soutache* where a strip of fabric, made from silk for our lingerie or from Lycra for our swimwear, is held by tiny stitches to create curls and arabesques that seem to appear out of nowhere. Another special technique is *frastaglio* (beveling), in which lace is applied by hand to a base of silk and then patiently clipped along the edges with scissors until the outlines of the pattern emerge in all their harmony. These exclusive creations have been the real features of the house together with some garments that have remained cult pieces, such as the Sculpture bra launched in 1994 and reworked in 2007 or the *brassière-bretelle* of 2001: a bra that is made up of two strips of lace that cover the central part of the bust just like a pair of men's suspenders. The same type of bra was also included in the La Perla Swimwear Spring/Summer 2001 collection where it became the *chain-kini*: a swimwear treasure covered with golden metal chains, which was also produced in a super-limited version in eighteen-carat gold. And more gold is in the Midas bra launched in Autumn/Winter 2008 as part of the Filigrane Collection, which revived a kind of workmanship inspired by goldsmiths' filigree technique.

Far from being bound by the limits of pure functionality, underwear today takes its own place in the world of fashion and increasingly shares those details, materials, and colors that were once reserved for outerwear. At the same time, because of its close bond with the body, it enjoys an aura of sensuous potential and emotion that cannot easily be shared by other kinds of clothing. I think that, at the moment, underwear is increasingly likened to an accessory thanks to both its ability to identify the self—and therefore express the personality of the wearer—and for its power to offer a unique and special touch that also ends up by distinguishing the garments that cover it. Undergarments have indeed become one of the key elements, a compass of style for every woman. That is why our philosophy wishes to communicate the emotions associated with a product that is not only to be worn but also to be imagined and, above all, to be dreamed about.

La Perla has become a comprehensive enterprise that, beginning with its core business tied to undergarments and swimwear, has evolved by extending its concept of style to outerwear, to baby clothing collections, to the world of perfumes and of hosiery. My hope would be to continue in the creation of new emotions by exploring the language of the senses, by seeking ideas and suggestions in the worlds of music, art, and design. Through my family's commitment, the La Perla brand has become a sensual experience beyond the confines in which it was born, retaining, however, its prerogative to uniqueness as a characteristic of the most exclusive tradition.

3

MODERNITY CLOTHING
BIRTHING THE MODERN ATLANTIC/
BIRTHING THE MODERN REPUBLIC

Carroll Smith-Rosenberg

Clothing is the great marker of social categories. It distinguishes classes, castes, nations, regions, occupations, religions, and genders. It conveys multiple often conflicting meanings. Carefully arranged, clothing can signify social compliance; in disarray, political or social protest.[1] And always clothing is performative, always involving acts of self-display. During times of fundamental transformations, of economic, demographic, or political revolution, clothing takes on increased significance. Graphic representations of clothing—and its negation, nakedness—played important roles at two key moments in the evolution of Atlantic modernity. The first marks what many consider the birth of European modernity: Europe's expansion into the Atlantic. Sailing down the coast of Africa, boldly crossing the Atlantic, Europeans came face to face with a superabundance of riches: gold, silver, rare spices, wood, and other tropical goods. Exploiting these goods, trading in them, made possible the development of modern capitalism, modern imperialism, and the modern state. But Europeans also came face to face with a variety of peoples radically unlike themselves in appearance, culture, religion, and, yes, clothing. The sheer expanse of space, the richness of the lands they saw for the first time, the variety of peoples they found there radically transformed Europeans' sense of their world and of themselves. Simultaneously tempted by and fearful of such superabundance, they strove to establish a sense of order and control over a world they barely understood. Two centuries later, the birth of the United States as the first modern republic marks the second moment in this inquiry that focuses on the ways the United States struggled to break free of European modes of representing America and to present itself as new people, independent, liberty-loving—and the political and cultural equal of a watching Europe. During these two critical moments of Atlantic history and the development of economic and political modernity, clothing served as a critical medium through which the modern subject and the modern nation-state were represented.

DISCOVERING DIFFERENCE/AFFIRMING ORDER

As Europeans ventured further and further into the Atlantic, the new continents, peoples, and cultures they found there transformed their sense of self. Distinguishing themselves from these others, they began to think of themselves as Europeans. (But what did it mean to be European at a time when thinking of oneself as English, French, or Spanish was itself new?) Novelty caused confusion, and so did the sheer superabundance of human and natural variety that circumnavigating the Atlantic revealed. Differences, never before imagined, had now to be conceptualized and categorized. The allure of new riches had to be balanced by systems of order, new desires by restraint. And most of all, the threat that an infinity of raw, turbulent nature posed had to be contained. Modern imperialism, political structures, and most critically of all, the modern European and the modern colonized subject were born in the process of positioning new lands and peoples within a hierarchic and increasingly racialized grid of sameness and difference.[2]

Cartography played a key role in the process of categorization and containment. At the cutting edge of navigational science, literally mapping Europe's imperial ventures, cartography was central to Europe's efforts to contain the human diversity those imperial ventures revealed.[3] And as maps were central to imperial ventures, so bodies, clothed and naked, were central to early modern maps. While carefully charting coastlines and safe harbors, early cartographers filled the unknown interiors of newly found islands and continents with imaginary monstrous bodies. Drawn from Herodotus and Ovid, dragons and centaurs, men with dogs' faces, men covered with feathers, and wild amazons crowded these domains, symbolizing the threatening unknown. Gradually, however, early mapmakers added figures based on voyagers' observations. Now images of naked Native American hunters and gatherers joined dragons and monstrous men, all mixing promiscuously with images of cannibals munching on dismembered human bodies.[4]

Unassimilated difference, however, was not allowed to govern the new worlds unchallenged. Guarding their maps' edges, cartographers arranged densely populated borders of richly garbed, authoritative European figures—English, Spanish, and Italian noblemen, Dutch burgers, English countrymen and their wives—their rich costumes signifying a known and reliable social order capable of containing the advance of headless men and naked cannibals.[5] Indeed, clothing and its related term "habit" became the principle means by which early modern cartographers marked distinctions between the civilized and the savage, modernity and the primitive, Christian and heathen, order and disorder.

In medieval times the term "habit" was a synonym for clothing and apparel. By the early modern period, however, the term "habit" had assumed an additional meaning, being used to indicate internal character, disposition, and mental association. External covering and internal nature fused in "habit's" new meaning, coming, early modernist Valerie Traub tells us, to "synthesize . . . the separate, yet closely related concepts, costume and custom, manners and morals." And all, grafted onto early modern maps, came to mark gradations in the culture and civilization to which different peoples could lay claim. Thus long before modern forms of European racism centering on phenotype and skin color had become the principle markers of the difference and inferiority of peoples outside of Europe, the term "habit" served this end. Re-presented as "habit," clothing marked a people's ability to transform raw nature into objects of utility and beauty. It demonstrated a people's ability to participate in the productive, consuming world of modernity. Nakedness, in contrast, signified the inability to do so. In this way, nakedness and the primitive fused in the early modern European *imaginaire*.[6]

A closer look at the borders surrounding early modern world maps reveals the centrality of habit as a marker of difference and inferiority. Figures of richly clothed Europeans only bordered the northern reaches of world maps. As the eye moved south along the maps' meridians, exotically garbed easterners appeared—Arabian, Persian, and Egyptian potentates and their richly garbed wives and catamites. But further south, as the eye follows the coast of sub-Saharan Africa or moves west to the Caribbean or Brazil, naked figures emerge. No longer neatly paired with their wives and consorts, these figures form polymorphous groupings of women and men. We have entered the world of the savage and the heathen—a world that cries out to be conquered, exploited, and enslaved. As Roxanne Wheeler argues, "The significance of clothing to identifying European difference from savages should not be underestimated; its absence or scantiness signified a negation or paucity of civilization." This was especially true when those bodies were displayed along the maps' meridians with the precise purpose of encouraging comparative viewing and categorization. Thus differences in clothing, and most specifically the negation of clothing, morphed imperceptibly into early modern racist categories.[7]

The contrast between richly clothed Europeans and naked Africans and Americans ripe for colonization becomes even clearer when we examine the cartouches that decorated early modern wall maps and atlases. For instance, in the 1628 title page to Mercator's atlas, *Historia Mundi*, Africa and Mexico appear naked, recumbent above the boundary containing a chaste-looking (and dressed) Asia and Europe. A decade later, in the 1639 edition, the continental relationships are even clearer. Positioned within these cartouches, looking down from Olympian heights, the four continents—portrayed as voluptuous and richly endowed women who embodied the material riches and superabundance of the lands they represented—reinscribed a hierarchical and racialized order upon the rapidly changing and challenging world. And again, clothing, the marker of habit, is the telling sign of difference. Europe, richly garbed, a royal scepter in one hand, the Christian cross within a T-circle instrument (astrolabe) in the other, governs all. Scenes of cities, palaces, and courtly

FIGURE 3.1 [ABOVE LEFT] Engraved
title page, Abraham Ortelius, *Theatrum
Orbis Terrarum* (1570). James Ford
Bell Library, University of Minnesota,
Minneapolis, Minnesota.

FIGURE 3.2 [ABOVE] Engraved title
page, Gerhard Mercator, *Atlas/Historia
Mundi* (1628). James Ford Bell Library,
University of Minnesota, Minneapolis,
Minnesota.

FIGURE 3.3 [LEFT] Frontispiece
engraving, Gerhard Mercator, *Historia
Mundi or Mercators Atlas*. London,
printed for Michaell Sparke, 1639.
William L. Clements Library,
University of Michigan, Atlas W-2-C.

processions, the world transformed by science and the arts, lie behind her. Asia, her economies far richer in reality than early modern Europe's, is also represented as richly, but far more exotically, clothed, a censor of rare perfumes in her hand, camels behind her bearing the riches of the silk and spice trade. Below these two regally costumed figures and subject to their gaze, two naked continents languidly recline, lacking the industry and skill to even clothe themselves: dusky Africa, a burning sun behind her head, a lion by her side; a feathered America, surrounded by cannibals, exotic plants, and animals. No cities suggest the arts and sciences. There is no sign of trade or industry—only nature unadorned and unimproved.

In still other engravings, Europe, represented by those twin icons of modernity, the scientist and the imperial monarch, observes America and Africa from the high ground of reason, objectivity, and Renaissance perspective. On one level, these engravings seem to speak for themselves. But nakedness has multiple meanings. It symbolizes not only sloth and barbarism, but also Adam and Eve before the fall, their nakedness revealing their innocence of evil. By the mid-eighteenth century, it could also stand for man in a state of nature, uncorrupted by clothes, artificiality, and unearned status. But nakedness can also stand for nature untamed, threatening man's puny efforts at control. To explore the complex meanings the contrast of clothing to nakedness carried in early modern European iconography, let us look at one of the most widely distributed, and studied, early modern engravings of America as a naked American woman—Theodore and Phillip Galles' copy of *America: Americus Rediscovering America* (1638), which itself was recycled, having appeared in numerous earlier publications, including Jan van der Straet's *New Discoveries* that contained engravings first issued by Stradanus in the 1580s.[8]

Most obviously, this engraving represents America as a sexualized primitive, surrounded by exotic creatures, living outside of time and progress, waiting to be awakened by European science and military might. Behind her, we see the telltale sloth and that ultimate sign of barbarism, a cannibal feast and a human leg carelessly dropped in a ditch. Exotic, America is also erotic and vulnerable to Europe's male gaze, the intense gaze of the classic humanist-cum-European scientist/explorer, Americus Vespucius (Amerigo Ves-

AMERICA—*Americus rediscovers America,—He called her but once and thenceforth she was always awake.*

Americus Vespuccius, the Florentine, followed Columbus to America landing on the South American coast in 1497. He is shown here debarked, holding a banner with the Southern Cross (which he was the first to see) and an astronomical ring. Before him, upon a native hammock, is awakened America. On the landscape are the earliest representations of American fauna including an anteater in the right foreground, a tapir, and a sloth on the tree. In the background natives are practising cannibalism.

FIGURE 3.4 *America: Americus Rediscovers America,* engraving by Stradanus (ca. 1580). Reprinted in Jan van der Straet, *New Discoveries.* James Ford Bell Library, University of Minnesota, Minneapolis, Minnesota.

pucci). Doubly garbed in a suit of armor topped by early modern scholarly robes, with an astrolabe in one hand, the cross of imperial conquest in the other, and his warship immediately off shore, Vespucci exemplifies European scientific, naval, and commercial drive and power, in short, modernity as Europe understood the term. Significantly, America is presented holding out her arm invitingly to this penetrating humanist presence. In the painting from which the engraving comes, we not only see the reclining and naked America holding out her welcoming hand, we witness the moment when Europe names America, giving the "new" continent the European scientist/explorer's (and mapmaker's) own name—appropriately feminized from Americus to America. The engraving thus captures the essence of the European imperialist venture: its colonization, feminization, and sexualization of the exotic and desirable other, its bifurcations of the world into the civilized and the primitive, its constitution of the primitive other as a fiction of the European *imaginaire*. But the bucolic setting, America's nakedness, Vespucci in the act of naming her in his own image also recall the Garden of Eden with Adam entrusted by God with naming the creatures of the world—Eve being the first. Certainly across the Atlantic, explorer-scientists like Vespucci claimed as God-given their right to name all that was previously unknown to them.

But is this all that is going on in this engraving—an expression of the power of modernizing Europe to subject the rest of the world to its imperial vision? Or do European fears of the exotic and barely known shadow this bold self-presentation? Looking carefully we realize that this is not a simple Garden of Eden, and this American Eve is far from innocent. While she welcomes Vespucci with an inviting move of her hand, that same movement gestures toward the cannibal feast that lurks over her shoulder. Beckoning Vespucci to enter her kingdom, is she simultaneously inviting him to attend her feast, perhaps to become that which she will feast upon? The engraving balances the image of the European warship with the image of the cannibal feast, pitting one form of power against another. This early in European penetration into the unknown, was it altogether clear which form of power would prevail? How many white men would disappear into America's or Africa's uncharted depths, seduced by their desires for newly revealed riches? The fact that the engraving presents Eve as far larger than Vespucci encourages these questions. Does her naked voluptuousness bespeak not simply America's natural riches but European men's fears of enveloping nature and, more pointedly, the power untamed nature poses? The home of hurricanes and cannibals, of the deep inner reaches of the Amazon, can savage America ever be trusted?

FIGURE 3.5 Detail from Henry Overton, *America*, 1727. William L. Clements Library, University of Michigan, Maps 2-B-11.

As the seventeenth century evolved, engravings of America as a naked Indian Princess became one of Europe's most common representations of primitive lands just opened to European settlement—of their lack of clothing, habit, civility. But as a result of such settlements and the economic development they represented, America and its image began to change. Less and less an emblem of the primitive and exotic, the image of the Native American "Eve" increasingly came to stand for the continent's great exportable riches, produced by the commercial development of the Caribbean and Brazil.

In the cartouche of a 1727 map of the Americas, for example, we see a semi-naked America surrounded by slaves bent nearly double with the weight of sacks and casks of the riches produced in America, which they carry to awaiting ships. No longer surrounded with sloths and cannibals, America now stands for the sugar, coffee, chocolate, tobacco, and spices produced by the plantation slave economies first of Brazil and, by the late seventeenth century, of the Caribbean, Surinam, and the Carolinas. It is her cornucopia of marketable riches that now whets European desire. Yet she herself remains naked. Able to produce riches for others, she still lacks the "habit" to clothe herself.

This cartouche points to a second significant change in representations of America. She has become black. This America figures not unknown and exotic lands but Atlantic slavery. Iconographic representations of America thus fuse with fetishistic representations of the imperial wealth slavery and the slave trade made possible.

The earliest engraving of naked black America that I have found was printed in Amsterdam and then reprinted in London in 1671. That Dutch engravers were the first to represent America as black should not surprise us. The Netherlands had been a pioneer of the plantation slave production of sugar in Brazil. It was the Dutch who helped British planters introduce sugar production to Barbados in 1643, and after 1667, they made Surinam one of the most profitable and cruel of the sugar colonies.

In this engraving America is still represented as a naked Indian woman. But all the other traditional iconic markers have changed. Rather than resting supinely in an exotic setting unchanged by human productivity, this America is regally borne through a busy commercial scene. Stevedores labor with heavy burdens; European ships lie at the harbor's mouth. European merchants and soldiers, pikes aloft, watch in a scene reminiscent of a mid-seventeenth-century painting of Amsterdam—except that to the side of this busy harbor scene we see a heavily armed fortress, suggestive of the slave forts the Dutch had constructed along the coast of Ghana and Angola as early as the 1640s. This engraving thus fuses African and American scenes. There is one other addition we must note. America, in a regal gesture, rains gold coins and goblets upon her subjects. This gesture is copied directly from Peter Paul Rubens's painting *The Benefits of the Regency of Marie de Medici* of France, but now it is the naked African American who, displacing the richly clothed European princess, enriches Europe, just as the Dutch engraver/artisan appropriates neoclassical imagery to represent not European royalty but the new commercial imperialism and its riches. But further questions suggest themselves. Has European desire for the riches

FIGURE 3.6 [LEFT] Jacob van Meurs, *America,* in John Ogilby, *America: Being the Latest . . . ,* 1671. James Ford Bell Library, University of Minnesota, Minneapolis, Minnesota.

FIGURE 3.7 [BELOW] Map of America with cartouches. John Ogilby, *America: Being the Latest . . . ,* 1671. James Ford Bell Library, University of Minnesota, Minneapolis, Minnesota.

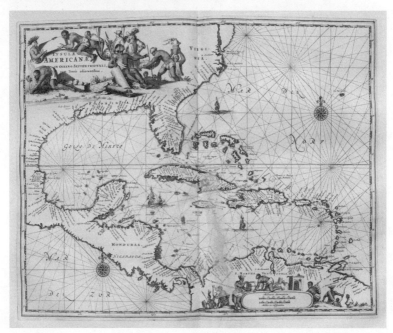

plantation slave economies made possible eroded the clear distinctions Europeans drew between themselves and their others, fusing and confusing images of the European and the American, civilization and barbarism? Do these conscious and unconscious conflations hint at the barbarism Atlantic slavery melded into the European soul?

The ways neoclassical and Renaissance imagery rise as pentimenti through eighteenth-century engravings of America awaiting European exploitation brings us to what may well

FIGURE 3.8 *The Voyage of the Sable Venus from Angola to the West Indies,* in Bryan Edwards, *The History, Civil and Commercial, of the British Colonies in the West Indies* (London, 1794). James Ford Bell Library, University of Minnesota, Minneapolis, Minnesota.

The VOYAGE of the SABLE VENUS, from ANGOLA to the WEST INDIES.

be the ultimate inscription of the naked female body as commodity, fetish, and mystification. *The Voyage of the Sable Venus from Angola to the West Indies* appeared in Jamaica planter Bryan Edwards's highly influential *History, Civil and Commercial, of the British Colonies in the West Indies*, first published in 1794.

Self-consciously appropriating Botticelli's *Birth of Venus*—and even more obviously Raphael's *Galatea*—to fetishize the Middle Passage, the so-called Sable Venus aestheticizes the millions of African bodies carried to the Caribbean, Brazil, and Britain's thirteen mainland colonies, layering femininity, sexual consent, and passivity with commodification, fetishization, and violence.[9] The Sable Venus is clothed only in a girdle of pearls. Her neck, wrists, and ankles are encircled with gold bangles, which at the same time suggest the shackles used to confine slaves on the Middle Passage. A muscular and powerful Neptune represents the virile, colonizing white male slaver who impels her passage to the West Indies. His gaze, directed at her barely concealed genitals, further eroticizes the picture. Here the Sable Venus, goddess of beauty, bedecked in gold and pearls, consenting to be carried across the seas into slavery, mystifies the violence and brutality of the slave trade and the plantation slave economy it made possible. In this way, the new Atlantic world appropriates and refigures the classical Mediterranean world and at the same time permits white settlers in those lands—author and plantation-owner Bryan Edwards in this case—to humorously assert their mastery of neoclassical culture. America may be a savage Indian or a Sable Venus, but white settlers remain cultured and richly clothed Europeans.

NATIONAL TRANSPOSITIONS: FROM NAKED INDIAN PRINCESS TO ROMAN MATRON

This blackening of America clearly served the interests of Europeans, their economies made prosperous by the trade in goods and bodies from Africa and the Americas and still desirous of establishing their superiority to their enriching colonies. With equal clarity, images of America as a Sable Venus or a naked Indian Princess were directly opposed to the semiotic needs of the founders of the newly independent United States, who during the very years that Bryan Edwards fantasized his Sable Venus worked to constitute a coherent national identity for their first modern republic. The new nation's press therefore had to create a radically different figure for America, one that emphasized not America's savage exoticism or her enslavement by Europeans but rather her independence, love of liberty, civic virtue—and cultural equality with Europe. The founding generation sought to establish their new Republic as the heir of Enlightenment political theories and culture. It had, therefore, to replace America's feathers with classical European symbols and images suggesting political independence and national sovereignty. As early as 1778, when the new nation was but a ragtag group of insurgents struggling against Europe's most powerful empire, the French engraving *L'Amérique Indépendante* did precisely that.

It was one of France's first gifts to the new Republic. True, an Indian Princess, naked and with feathers, still holds center stage, but she is overshadowed by two powerful figures: Liberty, in Roman garb and liberty cap, and Benjamin Franklin, similarly wearing a toga, who compels the Indian Princess to kneel, his hand upon her shoulder, his rod pointing to her as to an object in an anatomical exhibit, though given Franklin's rakish reputation, the phallic implications cannot be ignored.

In fascinating ways, the engraving mimics the earlier, sixteenth- and seventeenth-century representation of America circulated in the versions by Stradanus/Straet/the Galles as a naked Indian Princess—now, however, she is bowed rather than newly awakened. The bourgeois European-American settler Franklin replaces the European Vespucci, Franklin's rod, Vespucci's astrolabe, Franklin's Roman garb and laurel wreath, Vespucci's seventeenth-century armor. In place of the ships of discovery and the scenes of cannibalism the Galles had deployed to inscribe America as a new and exotic land, this later engraving is filled with the familiar figures of classical European allegory. Minerva, plumed and armored, valiantly defends Liberty. Hercules, symbolizing the new nation's bravery, drives Britannia into the sea. Mercury, representing commerce, and Demeter, goddess of agriculture, watch approvingly. The bowed Indian continent is made subject to Franklin the new European-American scientist and diplomat, the self-made man from a self-made na-

FIGURE 3.9

Jean Charles Le Vasseur,
L'Amérique Indépendante,
1778. Engraving on paper,
image: 43.2 × 35 cm; sheet:
51 × 38.3 cm. National
Portrait Gallery, Smithsonian
Institution, NPG 78.74.

tion. New, but not primitive or culturally inferior. Garbed in a Roman toga, crowned with laurel, Franklin's ties to a classic European heritage could not be more graphically represented. We should note as well that in this engraving the Indian Princess has become white again.

References to both Roman gods and goddesses, along with the presence of Liberty crowned with a Phrygian cap, underscore the importance those classical emblems of republican virtue, the Athenian and Roman republics, held for the United States' founding generation. Classic republican rhetoric, rooted in Aristotle's *Politics* and imbued with Scottish and Continental Enlightenment concepts of equality and inalienable right, had inspired European Americans' revolution against Great Britain.[10] The founding generation searched for a national emblem that would speak to this classical republican heritage. The result? America as naked Indian Princess was transformed into the modestly clothed Columbia, a pure, white republican matron, the mother of virtuous republican sons. How better to represent the new American Republic? Modeled after the simply clothed Cornelia, mother of the Gracchi (whose jewels were her valiant sons), Columbia, draped in a Roman toga, maintained America's ties to European republican ideals and classical cultural heritage. She was ideally designed to evoke the heroic patriotism of her manly republican sons and reaffirm their civic virtue. Of equal importance, she effaced the earlier image of a naked and primitive America and insisted that European Americans were heirs to European culture.

Columbia, however, had a much shorter life span than the earlier Americas we have examined. She failed to satisfy the new Republic's need for an emblem that stressed its ties to a European republican heritage while proclaiming the new nation's independence from and moral superiority to Europe. Why? Following European iconographic traditions that made the emblems of continents and nations women (Britannica being the most obvious example), the founding generation had chosen a female icon for the new Republic. But the virtuous republican political body, as constituted in Western political discourses from Aristotle to the Enlightenment, had to be male. The United States' self-fashioning as an independent and united nation rested on its celebration of manliness, virility, and *virtus*. The new Republic's political press held up images of virile male citizens, renowned for their Spartan stoicism, Roman bravery, and statesman-like self-control, as emblems of republican virtue. Endless essays glorified George Washington's military prowess and Franklin's phallic powers over the lightening-streaked heavens—and British tyranny. In sharp contrast, women, degraded into voluptuous, seductive, and physically frail, threatened to corrupt heroic republicans and pollute pure, virile republics.[11] They could not embody a virtuous republic, no matter how classically garbed. In following European iconographic traditions and choosing the image of Columbia, the founding generation had transgressed republican ideology in deeply disruptive ways. The result was a confused, unstable, and short-lived national icon.

To illustrate what I mean, simply look at the first two volumes of the new nation's most fashionable political journal, the *Columbian Magazine, or Monthly Miscellany*. The editors of the *Columbian Magazine* inaugurated their first issue with a frontispiece of the magazine's namesake, Columbia, blessed by Minerva, representing the victorious American Republic. Mature and highly respectable women dominate this engraving. Minerva, clothed in military garb, her arm resting on a pedestal, holding a staff of office, her other hand stretched forth blessing Columbia and her children, occupies the authoritative and authorizing position. Republican mother and son, in Roman garb, evoke classical republican images. Only Columbia's young son, the smallest figure in the central grouping, and a diminutive farmer plowing his fields in the far distance represent the virtuous and powerful male citizen. Given the centrality the virile citizen played in the symbolic construction of the new nation, his absence underscores the problems the choice of Columbia as icon posed for the new Republic.

FIGURE 3.10 "While Commerce spreads her canvas . . ." Frontispiece engraving. *Columbian Magazine, or Monthly Miscellany*, volume 1, September 1786. William L. Clements Library, University of Michigan.

While Commerce spreads her canvass o'er the main
And Agriculture ploughs the gratefull plain
Minerva aids Columbia's rising race
With arms to triumph and with arts to grace

But look again. Do men really play such a secondary role—or are they an absent presence? Our two principal figures, Columbia and Minerva, are clearly women. On the other hand, they are women who refer back, forcefully, unmistakably, to men. Columbia is a feminized version of Christopher Columbus. Minerva, born from Zeus's head, is the motherless goddess who both championed the matricide Orestes and accomplished the downfall of the Furies, the three primal female deities. For all their engraved softness, we cannot ignore the male references shadowing these two central figures. This is especially true because men resurface in critical ways in the engraving. When reexamined, the diminutive white farmer far in the back of the engraving emerges as its fulcrum, the center point upon which all else balances. Since Homer, plowing has suggested sexual as well as agricultural productivity. To read this engraving we must see through its surfaces to its underlying pentimenti. Women only appear to dominate the picture. Like married women under coverture, they draw their true meaning from the men whose names or patrimony they represent. And, in the end, it is a man, generatively engaged, who centers and stabilizes the scene.

But in a multiplied layered engraving can we be sure that even this reading exhausts the meanings? Does the deployment of classical iconic figures reaffirm the underlying maleness and virility of the new United States? Or does the engraving further problematize that identity? Do we see women referencing and valorizing men, making men the source of national identity? Or do we see the fusion, the inseparability of male and female identities? Still, other, more disruptive readings suggest themselves. If Columbia and Minerva are vehicles for the mediated display of male identities, are they truly female figures, or rather are they feminized male subjects—men in drag? Can we ever be sure of what we see? Fusing male and female, indeterminate and divided figures, do Minerva and Columbia figure the ways gender divides and renders uncertain the new United States' national identity?

The frontispiece for the *Columbian Magazine*'s second volume reiterates the ambivalence of America's iconographic feminization. Again female figures dominate. Two classically garbed feminine figures occupy the foreground, addressed by a highly androgynous adolescent putto, his front demurely shielded from our view. In the background is a Greek temple crowned by three guardian female figures: Liberty, Justice, and Peace. Father Time,

FIGURE 3.11 "Behold, a Fabric new to Freedom rear'd . . ." Frontispiece engraving. *Columbian Magazine, or Monthly Miscellany,* volume 2, January 1788. William L. Clements Library, University of Michigan, Serials 1 Co.

again quite diminutive and distant, appears as the only male present, other than the putto—neither icons for untroubled virile masculinity.

But again, does this fully describe what can be seen? The publishers included a subtext beneath the engraving. Reading, rather than looking, we learn that the central figure in the triad before the temple is not a female after all but "Concord, fair Columbia's son." This information raises still more questions. Why did the engraver represent "fair Columbia's son" in such a feminine manner? Neither his dress nor his physique distinguish him from Clio, the female muse of history, who kneels, pen in hand, at his side. Concord's form is slender, almost frail. His hair is dressed exactly as is Clio's; his pelvis is thrust slightly forward, again in a feminine manner. At this point, the magazine's editors and publishers added yet one more layer of confusion, multiplying our questions and uncertainties. Apparently they did not feel that the engraving's subtext adequately represented their intention. In an "Address to the Public" that followed the title page and the engraving, they provided a further gloss. Here "fair Columbia's son" is transformed back into a woman, CONCORD, and invited by the "winged youth" to enter the temple that is the American Republic. A woman, even if identified as "Concord," invited into the pure temple of virtuous republican government! into the public political arena! Such an image threatened the new Republic with corruption and decay caused by a too close identification with women.

Twice-told tales hold multiple meanings. What deep ambivalence surrounds the iconographic representations of the virile and virtuous American Republic! Did Columbia, as s/he stood hesitatingly before the temple of the new American government, represent not simply a typographer's error or even the editors' own gendered ambivalence but the mutability of gender itself and hence of national and political identities?

And what about thrice-told tales? The founding fathers were never able to efface either Columbia or her semiclothed black double. Far into the nineteenth century, images of classic Roman Columbia (albeit always waving an American flag and accompanied by images of Washington and other male patriots) appeared with small black children at her side. Their presence, never explained, leads one to ask if America's eighteenth-century iconic and seminaked blackness was ever truly erased or if it was simply displaced onto those children—sometimes represented as black Native Americans, sometimes as pensive slaves. Still later, in twentieth- and twenty-first-century protest art, such as the posters of a Black Statue of Liberty by Michael Ray Charles, *Forever Free: Established a Long Time Ago,* or Faith Ringgold's *Welcome to America: The American Collection #1,* the Sable Venus again returns, a weapon of anger for the marginalized and the repressed. Significantly now a defiant slave, she is garbed in the classic robes of the Statue of Liberty. It would seem that America without her black sister is unimaginable—that at her core America relentlessly entwines black and white as she fuses Europe and America.

1. If we think of the series of colonial congresses held during the opening decades of the twentieth century, this pattern will become clear. Most delegates from the colonized world very selfconsciously dressed in a European manner. Gandhi, as part of his protest against British imperialism and to argue that the colonized world had as great a right to civilized status as Europe, wore his simple white loincloth.

2. There is an extensive literature on Europeans' "discovery" of difference—of lands, climates, and peoples. For a few examples of the wealth and diversity of approaches to Europe and its Others, see, for example, Stephen Greenblatt, *Marvelous Possessions: The Wonder of the New World* (Chicago: University of Chicago Press, 1991); Louis Montrose, "The Work of Gender in the Discourse of Discovery," and Mary C. Fuller, "Raleigh's Fugitive Gold: Reference and Deferral in the *Discovery of Guiana*," both in *Representations* 33 (Winter 1991): 1–41 and 42–64; Walter D. Mignolo, *The Darker Side of the Renaissance: Literacy, Territoriality & Colonization* (Ann Arbor: University of Michigan Press, 1995); Peter Hulme, *Colonial Encounters: Europe and the Native Caribbean, 1492–1797* (London: Metheun, 1986); Mary Louise Pratt, *Imperial Eyes: Travel Writing and Transculturation* (New York: Routledge, 1992).

3. For a discussion of the emergence of modern European cartography, see, for example, J. B. Harley, "Meaning and Ambiguity in Tudor Cartography," in *English Map-Making, 1500–1650: Historical Essays*, ed. Sarah Tyacke (London: British Library, 1983), 23–40; Harley and David Woodward's multivolume *History of Cartography* (Chicago: University of Chicago Press, 1987), especially their essay "The Map and the Development of the History of Cartography," in vol. 1. I am particularly indebted to Valerie Traub's generative study of early modern cartography, "Mapping the Global Body," in *Early Modern Visual Culture: Representation, Race and Empire in Renaissance England*, ed. Peter Erickson and Clark Hulme (Philadelphia: University of Pennsylvania Press, 2000), 44–97. This essay has shaped my exploration of the relation between maps, bodies, and modernity.

4. See, for example, Jennifer L. Morgan, " 'Some Could Suckle Over their Shoulder': Male Travelers, Female Bodies, and the Gendering of Racial Ideology, 1500–1770," *William and Mary Quarterly*, 3rd. ser., 54 (January 1997): 167–92; John Gillis, *Shakespeare and the Geography of Difference* (Cambridge: Cambridge University Press, 1994). Peter Hulme connects European obsession with the prevalence of cannibalism among indigenous Americans and the way it marked a shift from a

classical and Mediterranean perspective to an Atlantic and colonizing perspective in *Colonial Encounters,* chs. 1 and 2.

5. Traub, "Mapping the Global Body," 61–77, analyzes these borders at length, arguing that "Miming the grammar of latitudes and longitudes that organized the cartographic idiom itself, maps of this period began to imply that [not only lands but] the bodies [inhabiting them] may be a terrain to be charted" (49, 59–71).

6. Traub, "Mapping the Global Body," 51. To trace the change in the meaning of "habit" from the Middle Ages to the early modern period, see the *Oxford English Dictionary.* Roxanne Wheeler concurs with Traub on the importance of "habit," arguing "Two of the most important ways that Europeans conveyed difference between themselves and Others were with reference to religion and clothing." In her lengthy treatment of the emergence of racialized categories during the eighteenth century, Wheeler also points to Europeans' deployment of commerce, social organization, the treatment of women, and respect for private property when representing both themselves and their others. Roxanne Wheeler, *The Complexion of Race: Categories of Difference in Eighteenth-Century British Culture* (Philadelphia: University of Pennsylvania Press, 2000), especially "Introduction," 1–48. See also David Theo Goldberg, *Racist Culture: Philosophy and the Politics of Meaning* (Oxford: Blackwell, 1993), especially ch. 3, 4–57.

7. Wheeler, *Complexion of Race,* 72. Traub argues: "The exuberant deployment of cartographic bodies along the map edges enable two related changes. On the one hand, it made possible a more pronounced differentiation of skin color and clothing, as peoples across the globe are placed according to their physical location and display so as to represent a particular culture," while laid out along the map's edges these clothed and naked bodies "articulate gradations of status and rank from the top to the bottom of the social scale"; placement from the top to the bottom of world maps thus reinscribes a people's position at top or bottom of the scale from civilization and modernity to barbarism and primitivism ("Mapping the Global Body," 49–50).

8. Widely distributed in the seventeenth and eighteenth centuries, this engraving is as widely studied by postcolonial theorists today. It is read both as marking the beginning of history and as the epitome of early modern allegory and paradox. See, for example, Michel de Certeau, *The Writing of History,* trans. Tom Conley (New York: Columbia University Press, 1988), esp. "Preface," xxv–xxvii, and José Rabasa, *Inventing A-M-E-R-I-C-A: Spanish Historiography and the Formation of Eurocentrism* (Norman: University of Oklahoma Press, 1993), esp. ch. 1. "The Nakedness of America?" 3–48.

9. I am grateful to art historian Celeste Brusati for suggesting the parallels between Raphael's *Galatea* and the Sable Venus. I am grateful as well to Caribbean literary scholar Leah Reade Rosenberg for pointing out to me the ways in which the Sable Venus's musculature differs significantly from that of Renaissance depictions of white goddesses. She argues that the Sable Venus is far more muscular and less feminine than Donatello's or Raphael's goddesses, pointing out that her differences as an enslaved African laborer rise as pentamenti to the surface of the engraving. Leah Reade Rosenberg, *Nationalism and the Formation of Caribbean Literature* (New York: Palgrave, 2007).

10. The universally acknowledged analysis of classic republican rhetoric is J. G. A. Pocock's *Machiavellian Moment: Florentine Political Thought and the Atlantic Republican Tradition* (Princeton, N.J.: Princeton University Press, 1975). See as well Bernard Bailyn, *The Ideological Origins of the American Revolution* (Cambridge, Mass.: Harvard University Press, 1967). A number of scholars have begun to question the dominance of republican rhetoric as the new republic took form and the growing importance of both Lockean and Continental liberalism. See, for example, Joyce Appleby, *Liberalism and Republicanism in the Historical Imagination* (Cambridge, Mass.: Harvard University Press, 1992). Carroll Smith-Rosenberg in *This Violent Empire: The Birth of an American National Identity* (Raleigh: Printed by the University of North Carolina Press for the Omohundro Institute of Early American History and Culture, Williamsburg, Virginia, 2009), suggests the ways these disparate rhetorical systems fused and confused one another, destabilizing the new nation's political self-image.

11. For a discussion of the role of gender in the construction of a new American national identity, see Smith-Rosenberg, *This Violent Empire*.

4

GARMENT OF THE UNSEEN
THE PHILOSOPHY OF CLOTHES IN CARLYLE AND EMERSON

Giuseppe Nori

> *It is written, the Heavens and the Earth shall fade away like a Vesture; which indeed*
> *they are: the Time-vesture of the Eternal. Whatsoever sensibly exists, whatsoever represents*
> *Spirit to Spirit, is properly a Clothing, a suit of Raiment, put on for a season, and to be*
> *laid off. Thus in this one pregnant subject of Clothes, rightly understood, is included all*
> *that men have thought, dreamed, done, and been: the whole External Universe and what*
> *it holds is but Clothing; and the essence of all Science lies in the Philosophy of Clothes.*
>
> THOMAS CARLYLE, *Sartor Resartus*

"If *Sartor Resartus* had not been published," an Ohio correspondent wrote the Boston *Christian Register* in March 1837, "we should not have had *Nature*, such as it now is." And "it is not improbable," the correspondent went on to say, "that Professor Teufelsdröckh suggested Mr Furness' work on miracles."[1] Acknowledging the influence of Carlyle's book on "Clothes" and of its extravagant, brooding hero, the anonymous Midwestern observer was calling attention to some notable publishing events of the previous year, 1836, the annus mirabilis, as it came to be canonized, of early American romanticism. Besides William Henry Furness's *Remarks on the Four Gospels*, among the other works that contributed to the rise of what Convers Francis called the "German School" in New England, Carlyle's *Sartor Resartus* and Ralph Waldo Emerson's *Nature* were destined to remain as two outstanding examples of intellectual exchange and cultural transaction that took place across the waters in the first half of the nineteenth century.[2]

The "book about nature" that Emerson had on his mind since his journey back from Europe in 1833 had come out in Boston, published by James Munroe and Company, on September 9, 1836.[3] Five months before, on April 9, the same publisher brought out *Sartor Resartus* in book form, with Emerson actively seeing it through the press. The editio princeps was not only the transatlantic fruit of Emerson's personal friendship,[4] it also represented New England's spiritual affinity, "the enthusiasm felt for Carlyle, in those days, by so many of the younger men and women," for whom the Scottish writer, as transcendentalist James Freeman Clarke recalled years later, had made "a new heaven and a new earth, a new religion and a new life."[5] The Boston edition of *Sartor Resartus* was addressed to the "discerning reader" by Emerson himself, with an unsigned preface attributed to anonymous "American Editors"—an edition "induced," to recall the communal effort of the venture, "by the express desire of many persons." In such a kindred spirit Carlyle himself thought of his early admirers in the New World as "Transoceanic Brothers" and "Transoceanic Sisters."[6]

In this double capacity, Emerson may be said to have launched his literary career with the publication of two books, entering the New England cultural scene, at age thirty-three, as an anonymous vicarious author, or transatlantic agent, with Carlyle's *Sartor Resartus* on one side, and as an ambitious, though still anonymous, New World author with *Nature*, a few months later, on the other. Reviewing the early Emerson from this double standpoint, one may revisit his "little book"[7] with the romantic and idealist assumptions of Carlyle's eccentric German hero, Diogenes Teufelsdröckh, and his "Philosophy of Clothes" (5–6).[8] Reading *Nature* with *Sartor Resartus* in the context of the so-called Atlantic double-cross opens its theoretical poignancy if Teufelsdröckh's "Clothes-Philosophy" comes to be understood, specifically, as "Life-Philosophy" (58).[9] This is how the Professor's system of thought is named, almost casually but significantly, at a crucial moment of structural transition of the book, though no explication is given by the narrator for such a conceptual equivalence. Once understood as a romantic "philosophy of life" *(Lebensphilosophie)*, Teufelsdröckh's "Clothes-Philosophy" discloses itself as a "philosophy of nature" (*Naturphilosophie*, in the terminology of romantic idealism). As such, it casts light on the "theory of nature" that Emerson elaborates in the first work of his long career (7): "the first document" of "that remarkable outburst of Romanticism," as James Elliot Cabot noted in his memoir of Emerson, "on Puritan ground."[10]

CLOTHES-PHILOSOPHY AND LIFE-PHILOSOPHY

Carlyle entrusts the narration of *Sartor Resartus* to an unnamed speaker who announces himself to the reader as "Editor" of Teufelsdröckh's book, a strange dissertation "on the subject of Clothes," allegedly titled "*Die Kleider ihr Werden und Wirken* (Clothes, their Origin and Influence)," that he has just received from Germany (3, 6). Within this narrative frame, *Sartor Resartus* can be read as "a collection of philosophic fragments, biographical narrative, and editorial comment."[11] In book 1, the central topic of clothes is introduced in relation to Teufelsdröckh's treatise as well as to the "editorial difficulties" it raises for a possible English version. While the Editor is waiting for crucial biographical documents from one Hofrath Heuschrecke, the "Professor's chief friend and associate" in Germany, he fills the chapters with personal "reminiscences" about the author, fragments of his "Transcendental Philosophies," a description of his "style," occasional probings into his "moral feeling," and a "cursory" glance over the contents of his "remarkable Volume" (8, 9, 12, 23, 24, 25, 29, 26). In book 2, as soon as the "unimaginable Documents" arrive and are painfully deciphered, the Editor tells the story of Teufelsdröckh's life. This biography is in fact a bildungsroman in its own right, a small book within the book, tracing Teufelsdröckh's evolution from his birth ("Genesis") to maturity and affirmation ("The Everlasting Yea"). In book 3, the Editor goes back to the topic of clothes ("Garments"), further illustrated with Teufelsdröckh's speculations, both funny and moving, sarcastic and apocalyptic, about the various social, political, religious, and cultural issues of the European and the British world of the time (61, 63, 140, 157).

At the end of book 1, before turning to Teufelsdröckh's story in book 2, the Editor refers to the Professor's "Clothes-Philosophy" as "Life-Philosophy": "however it may be with Metaphysics, and other abstract Science originating in the Head *(Verstand)* alone, no Life-Philosophy *(Lebensphilosophie)*, such as this of Clothes pretends to be, which originates equally in the Character *(Gemüth)*, and equally speaks thereto, can attain its significance till the Character itself is known and seen" (58). In this apparently random use of the term, *Lebensphilosophie* stands out against other sciences or systems "originating in the Head," rendered by *Verstand*, "Understanding," a concept that in Coleridge's and Carlyle's version of German idealism stands opposed to *Vernunft*, "Reason."

FIGURE 4.1

Edmund Joseph Sullivan, "The Bedlam of Creation." Illustration depicting Diogenes Teufelsdröckh in Monmouth Street, 1898. Illustrated edition of Thomas Carlyle's *Sartor Resartus.*

Coleridge had explained this dichotomy over the course of two decades, from *The Friend* (1809–10) through his *Biographia Literaria* (1817) and *Aids to Reflection* (1825, 1831). "Reason is the Power of Universal and necessary Convictions," he states in *Aids to Reflection*, "the Source and Substance of Truths above Sense, and having their evidence in themselves. Its presence is always marked by the *necessity* of the position affirmed: this necessity being *conditional*, when a truth of Reason is applied to Facts of Experience, or to the rules and maxims of the Understanding; but *absolute*, when the subject matter is itself the growth or offspring of the Reason."[12] *Aids to Reflection*, in particular, would exert a significant impact on American readers, thanks to a New England edition published in 1829 with a "Preliminary Essay" by James Marsh. About the same time, before the rhapsodies of *Sartor Resartus*, Carlyle had also expounded this philosophical distinction in some of his most striking essays, especially "State of German Literature" (1827) and "Novalis" (1829).[13] This dichotomy became the object of reflection among transcendentalists in Cambridge and Boston in the early 1830s and "permitted Emerson a 'two truth' theory of knowledge": while understanding was viewed as "the logical and practical intelligence" that apprehends and deals with "empirical truths," reason was exalted as the "intuition" that perceives "absolute truths, transcending sense experience."[14] "Reason is the highest faculty of the soul," Emerson tells his brother Edward in a well-known letter (May 31, 1834); "it never *reasons*, never proves, it simply perceives; it is vision."[15]

Besides having his fictional Editor use this distinction in *Sartor Resartus* to characterize Teufelsdröckh's work as "Life-Philosophy," Carlyle—at the time a busy editor and reviewer himself—was much aware of contemporary works that could be included, in a general or special sense, under the heading "Philosophy of Life." In fact, after his first and unsuccessful attempts in August 1831 to find a publisher for *Sartor Resartus* in London, he contemplated a critical essay "grouping" some of these remarkable (and less remarkable) works together. In a letter of October 8, 1831 to Macvey Napier, editor of the *Edinburgh Review*, he wrote:

Hope's Book *on Man* is also a subject I might have something to say upon; works of that sort are a characteristic of our era, and appear in great numbers: Godwin has published one (of little merit); Coleridge also has lately set forth a fragmentary Philosophy of Life; and I read a very strange one by Friedrich Schlegel, which he died while completing. It struck me that by grouping two or three of these together, contrasting their several tendencies, and endeavouring, as is the Reviewer's task, to stand peaceably in the middle of them all, something fit and useful might be done.[16]

While the book on clothes was to wait two more years before it started to appear in the pages of *Fraser's Magazine* from November 1833 through August 1834, the proposed article on the "Philosophy of Life" for the *Edinburgh Review* appeared in December 1831 as "Characteristics." Carlyle limited himself to Thomas Hope's *Essay on the Origin and Prospects of Man* and Friedrich Schlegel's *Philosophische Vorlesungen,* his course of lectures on *The Philosophy of Language,* a "publication" that, according to the German editor's preface, "throws much light and more fully carries out the views advanced by Schlegel in the Lectures delivered two years before, at Vienna, on the Philosophy of Life."[17]

"Characteristics" echoed the speculative turns and philosophical inquiries of the still unpublished masterpiece on clothes:

In the perfect state, all Thought were but the Picture and inspiring Symbol of Action; Philosophy, except as Poetry and Religion, had no being. And yet how, in this imperfect state, can it be avoided, can it be dispensed with? Man stands as in the centre of Nature; his fraction of Time encircled by Eternity, his handbreadth of Space encircled by Infinitude: how shall he forbear asking himself, What am I; and Whence; and Whither?[18]

In *Sartor Resartus* the genesis of Teufelsdröckh's system of thought as "Life-Philosophy" is dramatized in a similarly interrogative fashion. In book 1, when the Editor moves from the "Descriptive-Historical Portion," discussing the rise and subsequent improvement of clothes, to the "Speculative-Philosophical Portion," Professor Teufelsdröckh's "higher and new" philosophy takes discernible form (41). As he recalls the deep, meditative experience in which his vision had originated, Teufelsdröckh starts exactly from the same ontological question posited in the essay "Characteristics," the "question" that, "in wonder and fear," all "men of a speculative turn" inevitably come to ask themselves: "Who am I; the thing that can say 'I' *(das Wesen das sich Ich nennt)*?"; "Who am I; what is this Me?" This question, apparently "unanswerable," involves a philosophical exercise in vision. While the "world, with its loud trafficking, retires into the distance," the inquirer's eye must pierce through "all the living and lifeless Integuments" that surround his "Existence," until his "sight reaches forth into the void Deep." Then man is "alone with the Universe, and silently commune[s] with it, as one mysterious Presence with another" (42).

If the I's question ("Who am I; what is this Me?") has been somehow answered by modern philosophy (the "Cogito ergo sum" mockingly quoted by Teufelsdröckh), that answer proves unsatisfactory and generates more questions: "Alas, poor Cogitator, this takes us but a little way," adds the Professor. "Sure enough, I am; and lately was not: but Whence? How? Whereto?" Out of the I's silent communion with the universe, and beyond the inadequate reflections of modern philosophy, the "answer lies all around" in nature itself (42), resting upon another fundamental dichotomy of post-Kantian idealism: the distinction between "Me" and "Not-me," or "*Ich* and *Nicht-Ich* (I and Not-I)," that Carlyle had explained a few years earlier in his essay on "Novalis" through a synopsis of Johann Fichte's philosophy of the subject.[19] The Not-I holds and returns the answer to the I's question when both matter and the world of nature dissolve as transparent vestments, to disclose the spirit and the "reflex" of the I himself: "So that this so solid-seeming World, after all, were but an air-image, our Me the only reality: and Nature, with its thousand-fold production and destruction, but the reflex of our own inward Force, the 'phantasy of our Dream'; or what the Earth-Spirit in *Faust* names it, *the living visible Garment of God*" (44). Nature is "*the living visible Garment of God*," as Goethe's Erdgeist puts it in *Faust*.[20] "It was in some such mood," Teufelsdröckh comments, "that I first came upon the question of Clothes" (44). Besides Goethe's *Faust,* with Fichte's *Science of Knowledge* looming in the background, intertextual traces such as Jean Paul Richter's "inward Force" and Novalis's "phantasy of our Dream" enrich the crucial epiphanic genesis of the Professor's thought, placing his "question of Clothes" and, consequently, its related Clothes-Philosophy within a whole literary and speculative tradition: a tradition that was part of Carlyle's apprenticeship and that he himself had popularized and made accessible for the British and American reader.[21]

The Editor reiterates Teufelsdröckh's illumination at the end of book 2, in "The Everlasting Yea," when the hero's evolution reaches its positive climax through conversion: "Or what is Nature? Ha! why do I not name thee GOD? Art thou not the 'Living Garment of God?' O Heavens, is it, in very deed, HE, then, that ever speaks through thee; that lives and loves in thee, that lives and loves in me?" (143). In the next chapter, "Pause," the Editor wraps up what he calls the "outline" of such philosophical views, again associating "all Nature and Life" in Teufelsdröckh's "almost magic Diagram of the Universe": "How all Nature and Life are but one *Garment,* a 'Living Garment,' woven and ever a-weaving in the 'Loom of Time': is not here, indeed," asks the Editor, "the outline of a whole *Clothes-Philosophy;* at least the arena it is to work in?" (155). The transcendental tenets firmly place the Professor's philosophy of clothes, even as a simple "outline" perceived by the Editor and, hopefully, by his readers, within the life-philosophical and nature-philosophical romantic tradition of post-Kantian idealism.

THE LIVING GARMENT OF GOD

In the chapter entitled "Characteristics," the Editor had already assumed that the Professor's "peculiarity" in regarding men and objects with a "strange impartiality," or a "strange scientific freedom," could descend from his "Transcendental Philosophies," namely from his "humor of looking at all Matter and Material things as Spirit" (23). In the subsequent chapters, he confirms the assumption. Whether "despicable" or "honourable," "Matter . . . is Spirit, the manifestation of Spirit." Similarly, the "thing Visible, nay the thing Imagined, the thing in any way conceived as Visible, what is it," Teufelsdröckh asks, "but a Garment, a Clothing of the higher, celestial Invisible?" (52).

A few years earlier, in his Viennese lectures on *The Philosophy of Life,* followed by his lectures on *The Philosophy of Language* reviewed by Carlyle in the essay "Characteristics," Friedrich Schlegel had stated that "the whole sensible world is to be looked upon as nothing else than an almost transparent, and at all events, a very perishable veil of the spiritual world," thus relating the latter to "nature" and "life," to nature as a "living force" that, in its "divine order," cannot be "self-subsisting," that is, "independent of its Creator."[22] In this mature work, the German thinker defines "philosophy of life": a philosophy that speaks "words of life," and announces itself as "a simple theory of spiritual life, drawn from life itself, and the simple understanding thereof."[23] He echoes shared positions and common ideas of the early Romantics, from the philosophy of nature that Friedrich Schelling had worked out between 1797 and 1804 to the mysticism of nature that their disciple Novalis had partly outlined in those years. "Life," Novalis says in one of his notes, "is absolutely only to be explained from life itself."[24]

"Nature must be visible spirit, spirit invisible nature," Schelling had maintained in the introduction to his *Ideas for a Philosophy of Nature.* Sara Coleridge takes up and quotes Schelling's insight in her "Notes" to the 1847 edition of her father's *Biographia Literaria,* almost reiterating and justifying—beyond or against the charge of "conscious intentional plagiarism," as she says in her introduction—Coleridge's more or less openly acknowledged "obligations to the great German Philosopher." "Here then in the absolute identity of the spirit in us, and of nature out of us," Schelling continues in the passage quoted by Coleridge's daughter, "must the problem, how a nature without us is possible, be solved."[25] In *The Disciples at Saïs* Novalis builds upon this solution when he states that "Nature would not be Nature had she no spirit." And without spirit "she would not be that unique counterpart of Humanity." "What is Nature?" he asks in one of his fragments, translated by Carlyle in his essay: "An encyclopedical, systematic Index or Plan of our Spirit."[26]

Following this philosophy of "absolute identity" and its crucial belief that matter is spirit, Teufelsdröckh applies the central idea of clothing to nature, human life, and all their activities. If matter is spirit, then man is a spirit too, while the clothes he wears are manifest emblems of his spiritual nature. "A Soul, a Spirit, and divine Apparition," man has a body, Teufelsdröckh argues, that "under all those wool-rags" is also a piece of clothing, "a Garment of Flesh (or of Senses), contextured in the Loom of Heaven," wrapped "round his mysterious ME." In addition, if man himself is "an Emblem; a Clothing or visible Garment for that divine ME," then language too must be envisaged as a garment. "Language," Teufelsdröckh maintains, "is the Flesh-Garment, the Body, of Thought" (51, 57). Similarly, for Emerson, language is also one of the primary functions of his nature in the service of man. In a concentric pattern, up to the largest circle, nature—namely the world, the whole external universe, or the Fichtean *Nicht-Ich* or Not-Me, rekindled by spirit—is a "Vesture," the "Time-vesture of the Eternal" (57) or "Time-vesture of God" (200), all-encompassing, in the face of the *Ich* or Me, but within which the *Ich* or Me is bound to rediscover himself.

In *Sartor Resartus,* Carlyle puts forward a definition of nature that he had already illustrated and ascribed to Novalis. For the poet-philosopher "the material Creation is but an Appearance, a typical shadow in which the Deity manifests himself to man." In Carlyle's eyes Novalis embodied the evolution of post-Kantian idealism at its most original and concise, from Fichte's philosophy of the subject, through Schelling's philosophy of nature, to the philosophy of life that he himself had partly worked out together with his friend and mentor Friedrich Schlegel. Thus he traces a steady outline within Novalis's fragmentary work in which he illustrates not only the "far-famed" dichotomy "*Ich* and *Nicht-Ich* (I and Not-I)," but also the opposition between "Reason" and "Understanding":

> We allude to the recognition, by these Transcendentalists, of a higher faculty in man than Understanding; of Reason *(Vernunft)*, the pure, ultimate light of our nature; wherein, as they assert, lies the foundation of all Poetry, Virtue, Religion; things which are properly beyond the province of the Understanding, of which the Understanding *can* take no cognisance, except a false one.[27]

Idealism's fundamental principle (matter is spirit) reflects the distinctions between one "Manifestation of Power" and another ("Me" and "Not-Me"), and between one faculty of the mind and another ("Reason" and "Understanding"). As such, already formulated by the German transcendentalists, anglicized by Coleridge, and rehearsed by Carlyle, this principle travels across the Atlantic to the New England transcendentalists.

On the grounds of the distinction between "I and Not-I," matter can be perceived as spirit—and therefore man's body can be seen as the garment of the soul, language as the flesh-garment of thought, nature as the living garment of God, and the whole external universe as a vesture of the eternal—only to the eye that is able to see and to the ear that is able to hear, that is, to those privileged organs that can discern according to the intuitive dictates of "reason." Thus Teufelsdröckh invokes "the cunning eye and ear" (42), or, more philosophically, "the eye of Pure Reason" (51), in opposition to the "Head" or "Understanding," a faculty that, as the Editor argues when he refers to Teufelsdröckh's *Lebensphilosophie,* is unable to found a "Life-Philosophy . . . such as [that] of Clothes pretends to be" (58).Thus one must learn how to look, and therefore to know, with the eye of pure reason, through intuition and transparency: "The beginning of all Wisdom is to look fixedly on Clothes, or even with armed eyesight, till they become *transparent*" (52). As one is introduced to Teufelsdröckh's "views and glances," one discovers that for him "Nature [is] not an Aggregate but a Whole," where God, whom man knows "only by tradition" (as Emerson will point out, too, in the opening of *Nature*), is everywhere a "FORCE": "knowest thou," he asks of the "cultivated reader," "any corner of the world where at least FORCE is not?" (55). As Novalis states in a note, "No matter without force and vice versa."[28]

Teufelsdröckh roams on transcendental journeys into the Not-Me and looks at matter with such a purified eye. Thus, as night falls, and he rides through the Black Forest, the Professor meditates on a "star-like" flame, shimmering in a breathing world of undisclosed and connected energies. His horse ride stands as a symbol of the romantic philosophy of life for which nothing in nature "is motionless; without Force, and utterly dead." The "little fire" burning in the smithy across the moor is a glowing rite that cel-

ebrates nature's vital forces and universal affinities in the womb of a comprehensive totality (55–56). This rhapsodic view of a joined and all-inclusive world is taken up verba-
tim from Novalis, a poet-philosopher, Carlyle remarks in his essay, who "consider[s] Nature rather in the concrete," namely "not analytically and as a divisible *Aggregate*," but
"as a self-subsistent universally connected *Whole*" (emphases mine). "All the forces of
Nature are active in the flame of a light," Novalis states in a similar passage of *The Disciples at Saïs;* "she represents and transforms herself perpetually everywhere." If Teufelsdröckh shares Novalis's outlook and language, then he, too, may be said to regard nature
as "no longer dead, hostile Matter," as Carlyle observes in his piece, but as "the veil and
mysterious Garment of the Unseen." Hence, in the transition from book 2 to book 3, as
if he were speaking of Novalis himself, the Editor again emphasizes the significance of
Teufelsdröckh's "somewhat peculiar view" of the external world, pointing to "the decisive Oneness he ascribes to Nature" (155). For Emerson, too, "every thing in nature," as
he writes in "Compensation," "contains all the powers of nature."[29]

   This view perceives every individual, in all its multifarious manifestations, as a part
reflecting the whole, an epitome of totality. "The drop," Emerson says in "The American
Scholar," "is a small ocean." "A man," he continues, "is related to all nature." Through an
inverted process, by the same principle, or "doctrine of omnipresence," as he argues in
"Compensation," the "world globes itself in a drop of dew."[30] The part and the whole
may be said to correspond and proceed reciprocally. If the former is never severed from
the latter, then the single part, within that spiritual interconnection that grounds it and
ties it to the whole itself, is and works, Teufelsdröckh points out, as "a little ganglion, or
nervous centre, in the great vital system of Immensity. . . . Detached, separated! I say
there is no such separation: nothing hitherto was ever stranded, cast aside; but all, were
it only a withered leaf, works together with all; is borne forward on the bottomless, shore-
less flood of Action, and lives through perpetual metamorphoses" (56). Though inalien-
ably unique and individual, every particular is vibrantly and indissolubly bound to the
whole universe and vice versa. The "universe," Emerson says in "Compensation," "is represented in every one of its particles," or, in "The Over-Soul," "is represented in an atom,

in a moment of time."[31] By virtue of this mutual dependence, life in all its possible forms is neither diminished nor stagnant but accomplished and inexhaustible. Nothing is lost, but everything, Carlyle's German hero stresses, works and lives simultaneously in the "bosom of the All." Thus Teufelsdröckh's "philosophic eye," Carlyle maintains, re-iterating an insight from his 1831 essay on "Schiller," redeems even the "meanest object" from any possible depreciation:[32]

> The withered leaf is not dead and lost, there are Forces in it and around it, though work-ing in inverse order; else how could it *rot*? Despise not the rag from which man makes Paper, or the litter from which the Earth makes Corn. Rightly viewed, no meanest object is insignificant; all objects are as windows, through which the philosophic eye looks into Infinitude itself. (56)

Schlegel affirms the same copresence and exuberance of force and life in nature. In "the natural world," he claims, "every object consists of living forces," and "properly noth-ing is rigid and dead, but all replete with hidden life." These living powers are at work even where life seems to contract, decay, and vanish. "Putrefaction is loathsome," Emer-son says in "The School"; "but putrefaction seen as a step in the circle of nature, pleases." And it is exactly within this "circle of nature" that things represent a universe—a uni-verse that, in turn, embraces them, and that, reciprocally, the parts enclose and reflect out. As such, any single object is a witness and an individual agent of what Emerson in *Nature* calls "central Unity" (56) or, in later essays, "central and wide-related nature," "central life," and "central identity": the "centre" that is "everywhere," as he says at the beginning of "Circles," recalling Augustine's description of "the nature of God," and "its circumference nowhere." "For every object has its roots in central nature," he explains in "Art," "and may of course be so exhibited to us as to represent the world."[33] Thus in *Nature* he illustrates poetically and philosophically this vital correspondence of every particular. "A leaf, a drop, a crystal, a moment of time is related to the whole, and par-takes of the perfection of the whole. Each particle is a microcosm, and faithfully renders the likeness of the world" (29–30).

This conflation of life philosophy and nature philosophy was the tradition on which Schelling, going back to the "ancient idea" of a *World Soul* (Emerson's "universal soul" in *Nature*, his "Over-Soul" in his 1841 *Essays*), founded the concept of "organism," which implies the active presence of "spirit" and "life."[34] Novalis theorized this fundamental "operation" of "romantic philosophy" along a vertical axis of "elevation" (small to large, low to high) and "abasement" (large to small, high to low). In what was to become one of his most celebrated fragments, he called it *Romantisieren*, "romanticizing," the world.

> The world must be made romantic. . . . By endowing the commonplace with a higher meaning, the ordinary with mysterious respect, the known with the dignity of the unknown, the finite with an appearance of the infinite, I am making it Romantic. The operation for the higher, unknown, mystical, infinite is the converse. . . . Romantic philosophy. *Lingua romana*. Raising and lowering by turns.

Romantisieren, the finite becoming infinite, the infinite finite, was also part of Carlyle's transoceanic lesson: "He taught us . . . to see divine truth and beauty and wonder everywhere around," says James Freeman Clarke, recalling the momentous advent of "the new prophet" in the late 1820s in New England; to "see the divine in the human, the infinite in the finite, God in man, heaven on earth, immortality commencing here, eternity pervading time."[35]

This romantic "operation" clearly reverberates in the writings of Carlyle's new friend across the Atlantic: "I embrace the common, I explore and sit at the feet of the familiar, the low," Emerson says in "The American Scholar." "The near explains the far." Besides his preromantic and romantic literary heroes, from Oliver Goldsmith, Robert Burns, and William Cowper to Johann W. Goethe, William Wordsworth, and Carlyle, Emerson invokes Emanuel Swedenborg too, explicitly calling this romantic vision a "philosophy of life." In his 1850 essay on the Swedish mystic in *Representative Men*, he will call it "Identity-philosophy."[36] So Emerson "romanticizes" the world—and his New World in particular—filling his writings with idealistic fragments, echoes, and reflections that "spiritualize" matter. "There is no miracle," Novalis says in a fragment, "without a natural event and vice versa." Vice versa, there is no natural event that is not, at the same time, a miracle. In keeping with his "operation" of "reciprocal" raising and lowering, Novalis speaks of "the elevation of all phenomena to the *state of wonder.*"[37]

In *Nature,* Emerson reiterates Novalis's romantic operation. He emphasizes the poetic "power . . . to dwarf the great, to magnify the small," namely the "transfiguration" of "all material objects," explicitly calling the "relation between the mind and matter" a "miracle" (35, 25). And "to see the miraculous in the common," he says before closing his book, is the "invariable mark of wisdom" (47). "The existence of the merest atom, when we duly consider it, is an unspeakable miracle," Emerson's childhood friend and schoolmate William Henry Furness states in his *Remarks on the Four Gospels,* a book fittingly defined a "prosaic *Nature.*" "The universe—all being—is miraculous. There is no presumption therefore against the truth of any fact upon this ground. The presumption would seem to be in the opposite direction, for all things are wonders, all are miracles." Whether or not directly influenced or "suggested" by Professor Teufelsdröckh, as conjectured by the anonymous Ohio correspondent in the pages of the *Christian Register,* both Emerson's *Nature* and Furness's *Remarks,* along with all the other notable works that the "spiritualists" produced in that annus mirabilis 1836, were destined to remain as the "wonders" of early American romanticism.[38]

SARTOR IN NATURA

In the wake of his return from Europe—through his apprenticeship years, so to speak, leading to the Munroe editions of *Sartor Resartus* and *Nature*—Emerson continued to elaborate and refine his theory of aesthetic vision centered on "eyesight": from what he had already and variously called the "new eye" of the priest (or "prophetic eye," "omniscient Eye," "inward eye") to the "anointed eye" of the traveller on his Old World journey.[39] In his journals and early lectures, this theory is often dramatized as an education of the organ of vision, whose potential importance, as much as its actual lack in the New

World, Emerson pronounced upon for more than twenty years. Such an education consists in teaching the eye, poetically as well as philosophically, to look on the Not-Me, the world, until its surfaces—namely, in Teufelsdröckh's terminology, its "Integuments," "vestments," "tissues," "wrappages," "rags," "hulls and garnitures," or more simply "clothes"—become transparent. "To an instructed eye," Emerson states in an entry for November 3, 1833, later used in *Nature*, "the universe is transparent. The light of higher laws than its own shines through it." Echoing Teufelsdröckh, Emerson calls this educable organ "Reason's eye," aware as he is, though, that one does not easily raise its "lids" and acquire that higher and sharper vision praised by Carlyle's hero. In a journal entry for August 8, 1835, he in fact speaks of "the iron lids of Reason's eye," which are hard and sluggish to open, an image he uses again some months later, in January 1836, in "Modern Aspects of Letters," the last lecture of the series *English Literature*. Thus, in a striking passage that partly anticipates the argument of his first book, inviting an ideal "relation" between man and nature, Emerson attests at once the efforts and the difficulties, and therefore the importance, of the opening eye. "A virtuous man is in keeping with the works of Nature and makes the central figure in the visible sphere . . . men open the eye of the sense, but the iron lids of the Reason are slow to unclose."[40] This distinction between the "eye of the sense" and the heavy "lids of the Reason" comes back in *Nature* as an opposition between the "animal eye" and the "eye of Reason": an I/eye, the latter of which Emerson lightens and enlightens, dramatizing it in the landscapes and vistas of the *American* Not-Me, more memorably and poetically, as a "transparent eye-ball."

In the first paragraph of his "Introduction" to *Nature*, Emerson is driven by the antinomian impulse of the radical tradition of New England Protestantism. He moves from a position of protest and refusal, set against an arid and ghostly present in which man, oppressed by the past and excessively preoccupied to make it monumental, has slackened and has lost, as he says and repeats often in his writings, the "erect" or "upright position."[41] "Our age is retrospective," he begins. "It builds the sepulchres of the fathers. It writes biographies, histories, and criticism." Like Teufelsdröckh, he rebukes man for knowing God and nature through "tradition" only. "The foregoing generations beheld God and nature face to face," he says; "we, through their eyes." As he hopes to reestablish "an original relation to the universe," a culture of "insight," and "a religion" founded on "revelation" and not on its own "history," he focuses on a regenerative present of glowing fullness and revitalizing promise. "The sun shines to-day also. There is more wool and flax in the fields," he adds, to call attention to natural and living fibers and tissues for new and luminous garments, to be woven in the loom of time, to replace the "faded wardrobe" of the present generation and their "masquerade." "There are new lands, new men, new thoughts," he states, reassuring his reader, confirming such adversarial spirit of transformation and renewal (7).

In biblical language, Emerson frames a speculation and strives to "interrogate" nature, the "great apparition," he says, echoing Teufelsdröckh, "that shines so peacefully around us": "Let us inquire, to what end is nature?" If the "one aim" is "to find a theory of nature" (7), then that theory must rest upon a solid philosophical premise. This premise for the early Emerson, according to the rigorous terms of German idealism, is the distinction between Me and Not-Me. "Philosophically considered, the universe is composed of Nature and the Soul. Strictly speaking, therefore, all that is separate from us, all which Philosophy distinguishes as the NOT ME, that is, both nature and art, all other men and my own body, must be ranked under this name, NATURE" (8). To enter into *Nature* means to follow Emerson into "Nature," as the first chapter is symptomatically titled, as if he wanted to duplicate and explicate, through the concrete example of a romantic excursion, the title of the book itself. In the four subsequent chapters, Emerson adopts an outline that he had traced some months earlier in his journal, through a "classification" of the many "uses" of nature by man. "Thus through nature is there a striving upward," reads his entry for March 27, 1836: "Commodity points to a greater good. Beauty is nought until the spiritual element. Language refers to that which is to be said. . . . Finally; Nature is a discipline, & points to the pupil & exists for the pupil."[42] He devotes a section to each one of these "classes" (chapters 2 to 5: "Commodity," "Beauty," "Language," and "Discipline"), then pursues a reflection and a critique of the "Ideal theory" itself in chapters 6 and 7 ("Idealism" and "Spirit"), to conclude his argument with a final chapter, "Prospects," recalling the last and crucial "Prospective" chapter of book 1 of *Sartor Resartus*. At the end of *Nature* he unfolds a redemptive, apocalyptic view of the world. This not only implies a new vision ("So shall we come to look at the world with new eyes") as opposed to the old one of the "foregoing generations" and "their eyes." It also calls for action ("Build, therefore, your own world"), in order to inhabit a "kingdom" where the new man ultimately establishes his sovereignty over nature (48, 49).

As one interprets Emerson through the sequence of these chapters, the philosophical territory becomes familiar and can be explored with the tenets and the insights of Carlyle's "wonderful Professor."[43] Besides the dichotomy between Me and Not-Me, Emerson invokes the altogether crucial opposition between reason and understanding. In the chapter "Discipline" he draws the distinction between the two faculties and apprentices them to nature. All the elements of nature as discipline ("space, time, society, labor, climate, food, locomotion, the animals, the mechanical forces") "give us sincerest lessons," he says, and "educate both the Understanding and the Reason":

Every property of matter is a school for the understanding,—its solidity or resistance, its inertia, its extension, its figure, its divisibility. The understanding adds, divides, combines, measures, and finds everlasting nutriment and room for its activity in this worthy scene. Meantime, Reason transfers all these lessons into its own world of thought, by perceiving the analogy that marries Matter and Mind. (26)

The "analogy that marries Matter and Mind" perceived by reason reproposes the idealist equivalence that assumes that matter exists only spiritually. The "uniform effect of culture on the human mind," namely of the idealist culture of reason, Emerson states in the next chapter, "Idealism," is "to lead us to regard nature as a phenomenon, not a substance; to attribute necessary existence to spirit; to esteem nature as an accident and an effect" (33). Nevertheless, Emerson elaborates a philosophical objection that becomes part of a larger transatlantic critique of idealism itself. When "Idealism saith: matter is a phenomenon, not a substance," Emerson feels that "the ideal theory" answers only the first of the three "questions" that "are put by nature to the mind": "What is matter?" The other two Teufelsdröckh-like questions—"Whence is it?" and "Whereto?"—remain unanswered (40). "Idealism is a hypothesis to account for nature by other principles than those of carpentry and chemistry. Yet, if it only deny the existence of matter, it does not satisfy the demands of the spirit. It leaves God out of me" (41).

Emerson implies that to limit oneself to the premise of the ideal theory, namely to "deny the existence of matter," is in itself *idealistically* reductive or incomplete, unless one energizes matter, as one learns from the post-Kantian idealist tradition, with the living forces of "spirit, that is, the Supreme Being." Through these powers, Emerson explains in terms of philosophy of life and nature, the Creator "does not build up nature around us, but puts it forth through us, as the life of a tree puts forth new branches and leaves through the pores of the old" (41). Again: "Nature," "God," "me." This trinity recalls Teufelsdröckh's transcendental vision of the vital coalescence of God and his operations ("speaks," "lives," and "loves") in and through nature and man, which, in turn, recalls Novalis. A "shadow in which the Deity manifests himself," the material creation for the German poet-philosopher, Carlyle points out, is also "the Voice with which the Deity proclaims himself to man."[44] Similarly, for Emerson, if "the noblest ministry of nature," as he says in the "Spirit" chapter, "is to stand as the apparition of God," then nature is also "the organ through which the universal spirit speaks to the individual, and strives to lead back the individual to it" (40). When nature appears and speaks as God, and God appears and speaks as nature, man finds himself, both receptively and creatively, in that "absolute identity" advanced by Schelling as the solution to the "problem" of idealism. So man must be taught to see the correspondence and hear the language of spirit, to go beyond the boundaries of the senses and the understanding, right into the realm of the Not-Me, and be "part or particle" of the trinity (41, 33, 10). To "satisfy the demands of the spirit" the American transcendentalist aspires to a complete application of the ideal theory.

As a poet-philosopher and educator, privileging the organ of vision, Emerson enjoins man to see through the medium of transparency. "To speak truly," he says, "few adult persons can see nature" (10), a phrase that Henry David Thoreau will often reiterate and dramatize in his writings. The chief agency in this transcendental school of vision is the faculty that, through a synecdoche, against the "animal eye," he personifies as the "eye of Reason" (33), a direct duplicate of Teufelsdröckh's "eye of Pure Reason." When this eye opens, "outlines and surfaces become transparent, and are no longer seen; causes and spirits are seen through them. The best moments of life are these delicious awakenings of the higher powers, and the reverential withdrawing of nature before its God" (33).

This a posteriori comment may explain those ecstatic "moments of life" that Emerson had already dramatized in the first chapter of the book with its beautiful and peaceful landscapes and commons, with its fields and woods and wilderness. Speaking of nature with "a distinct but most poetical sense in mind," he teaches how to reach and treasure, aesthetically, the "integrity of impression made by manifold natural objects." This "integrity" enables man to distinguish, even as one looks at the same identical object, between "the stick of timber of the wood-cutter," on one side, and "the tree of the poet," on the other, as much as it allows one to draw a distinction between a possessed environment, which is the object of the "animal eye," and an organic whole, which only the poetic "eye," beyond what Emerson calls "a very superficial seeing," can contemplate and therefore truly own (9–10). Even by morning light, a "charming landscape" reminds the beholder that the external world of nature is also and "indubitably" a series of private properties. A prosaic land division implies a prosaic list of owners: "Miller owns this field, Locke that, and Manning the woodland beyond," Emerson points out. "But none of them," he adds starkly, "owns the landscape. There is a property in the horizon which no man has but he whose eye can integrate all the parts, that is, the poet. This is the best part of these men's farms, yet to this their warranty-deeds give no title" (9). As he then crosses a "bare common, in snow puddles, at twilight, under a clouded sky," or as he walks through the sacred "woods" of the Not-Me, one learns to enjoy "a perfect exhilaration" or cast off the wrappages of time, "as the snake his slough." Here and now he can see God in nature, be one with nature, and be with God himself:

> In the woods too, a man casts off his years, as the snake his slough, and at what period soever of life, is always a child. In the woods, is perpetual youth. . . . In the woods, we return to reason and faith. . . . Standing on the bare ground,—my head bathed by the blithe air, and uplifted into infinite space,—all mean egotism vanishes. I become a transparent eye-ball; I am nothing; I see all; the currents of the Universal Being circulate through me; I am part or particle of God. (10)

An ordinary walk across a town common or through the woods of New England, no less than a ride through the Black Forest of Romantic Germany, can become an ideal experience that returns a person to the sublime of "exhilaration" and "fear," to the pristine innocence of the "child" and "perpetual youth," to "reason and faith." This experience of abandonment to the "higher agency" that makes objects transparent makes the self a transparent object, too, the very organ of vision: the "transparent eye-ball." Teufelsdröckh's "eye of Pure Reason" has become Emerson's eye of pure vision, the "aesthetic" consciousness that in Novalis's "operation" romanticizes the world. The "lower self" or "mean egotism" expands and fades away into brightness through vertical "elevation." Brought to the pinnacle of self-transparency, "uplifted into infinite space," at once magnified and dissolved to the point of being nothing and yet seeing all, the Emersonian I/eye obliterates the concreteness of facts and givens, rises above social interactions and conflicts, and therefore makes history itself, if only for a brief, ecstatic moment, irrelevant or totally unnecessary. "The name of the nearest friend sounds then foreign and accidental: to be brothers, to be acquaintances,—master or servant, is then a trifle and a disturbance. I am the lover of uncontained and immortal beauty" (10). Kinship and brotherhood, individual acquaintances and communal bonds, racial antipathies and class struggles seem to vanish as much as the solid I/eye vanishes in self-transparency through aesthetic rapture, a carnal and spiritual intercourse with absolute beauty.

At the climax of these visionary experiences, Emerson may be said to end up, para-doxically, obscuring the historicity of life, perhaps even its facticity. Within the horizon of the dichotomy drawn by the "integrity of impression," the "timber of the wood-cutter," in all its actual and potential materiality, cannot vie with the immaterial "tree of the poet." By the same principle, the land divided into private property makes a sorry spec-tacle in the face of that open "property in the horizon." Emerson wants man spiritually to repossess the world of the Not-Me, even though it will continue to be a material object of land fragmentations and transactions. In the same fashion, he urges him to retrans-form the commons and the woods of New England into original "plantations of God." There, he shows, it may still be possible to commune with the "Universal Being" and, by that communion ("part or particle"), disrobe oneself of the constraints of society and the encumbrances of history.

These transcendental strategies by an idealist whose declared purpose is to "interro-gate" nature as the "apparition of God" should not be read as ideological mystifications or obfuscations of empirical reality. Beyond the exhilarating moments, Emerson is very much aware of the transitoriness of any transcendental experience and of the many "problems to be solved" in the relation between man and nature (43). Among them, with all their economic, geographic, political, ideological, social, and racial ramifications, there remain the ethical and aesthetic problems "of restoring to the world original and eternal beauty"—no less real and American than the other problems in a young republic that, a decade after sanctifying the first jubilee of her existence, began to lament, almost systematically, its dire lack of a visible culture and a national literature (47).

The "Prospects" that Emerson unfolds in the final chapter of *Nature* are apocalyptic horizons of renewal and recovery, collapsing as they do the separation—by distance, resistance, opacity, even conflict—between man and the world, the soul and nature, Me and Not-Me. In this view, the final chapter reiterates the presence of human limits such as carelessness (we ignore the "wonderful congruity which subsists between man and the world"); unbelief and disowning ("We distrust and deny inwardly our sympathy with nature"); degeneration and degradation ("man is a god in ruins" or "the dwarf of himself"); slothfulness and perversion ("man applies to nature but half his force") (46–47). In short, it indicts a spiritual barrenness whose effect is blindness. "The problem of restoring to the world original and eternal beauty, is solved by the redemption of the soul. The ruin or the blank, that we see when we look at nature, is in our own eye. The axis of vision is not coincident with the axis of things, and so they appear not transparent but opake" (47). If the "problem" lies in the I/eye/soul, and is caused by a "not coincident" relation with the Not-I/matter/nature, then to restore beauty to the world, turning its opacity into transparency, one needs to realign the "axis of vision" with the "axis of things."

Such a redemption may happen, as Emerson thinks, in those "best moments of life" (33) that occur through ordinary experience, when man's attainment of pure vision, in Novalis's terms, his "qualitative potentiation," brings him into a perfect communion with nature, and through nature, as "the garment of the Unseen," with God or the "Universal Being." So the "new eyes" with which "to look at the world" of the Not-Me should hopefully and always be transparent eyeballs. Then he will be sure to discover, as Emerson states with the prophetic voice of his "Orphic poet" at the end of *Nature,* that "the world exists for [him]," and for him "is the phenomenon perfect," to the point that he can and shall build therefore his "own world" (48), to enter it, messianically, and inhabit it, regenerated, as lord of a kingdom: "The kingdom of man over nature, which cometh not with observation,—a dominion such as now is beyond his dream of God,—he shall enter without more wonder than the blind man feels who is gradually restored to perfect sight" (49).

This "kingdom" recalls the kingdom "within" of the Gospel of Luke (17:20–21) that Emerson the preacher had often invoked in his sermons.[45] And to this "kingdom" Emerson the orphic poet-prophet of *Nature* now foresees that man shall have access, as by a miracle, with a mended and therefore new I/eye, as the "perfect phenomenon" of the garment of God must need a "perfect sight" that, through a gradual restoration, will reach and disclose the fullness of the unseen behind the garment itself. In this sense, nature "receives the dominion of man," a "dominion" that is both material and spiritual, secular and sacred, "as meekly as the ass on which the Saviour rode" (28). The Christo-logical title of this new man, compared with Jesus, is as eloquent as is his redemptive role within the salvation history of American nature. In this renewed lordship, man is to deliver nature as Christ delivered humanity. The Protestant doctrine of *sola scriptura* becomes "the Romantic doctrine of *sola natura*." In a fragment that Carlyle translated in his 1829 essay, and then readapted in *Sartor Resartus*, Novalis illustrates this romantic and symbolic version of salvation. "Man has ever expressed some symbolical Philosophy of his Being in his Works and Conduct; he announces himself and his Gospel of Nature; he is the Messiah of Nature."[46] Reelaborating Novalis's "symbolical Philosophy" through Teufelsdröckh's "Clothes-Philosophy," Carlyle, in the "Symbols" chapter of *Sartor Resartus,* calls this "Gospel of Nature" a "Gospel of Freedom," thus further empha-sizing man's mission and expectation, through "the mystic god-given Force that is in him," as natural deliverer. It is this "Gospel of Freedom," Teufelsdröckh claims, as he had already rhapsodized in the Black Forest (55–56), that man, "the 'Messias of Nature,' preaches, as he can, by act and word" (167). From Novalis through Carlyle to the early Emerson, in the New World, too, man must be a "Saviour," a natural redeemer, though acting and speaking in a larger sacred-secular world-historical context, both national and universal, of "process and fulfillment" combined.[47] For Emerson man is the "Mes-siah of Nature" in his latter-day, namely American and therefore ultimate, advent and apparition.

After the enthusiasm of such an apocalyptic moment, romantically fulfilling a whole European spiritualist or idealist tradition on the transatlantic stage of the new continent, to the Emerson of the subsequent two decades, as well as to those writers who were to make a national culture fully visible through what a century later was to be assessed as the "American renaissance," would fall the job of rematerializing, namely of reclothing and darkening, the universe of the Not-Me. This inverted "operation," to recall and over-turn Emerson's transoceanic application of Novalis's theory, would imply a redefinition and a contraction of the spiritualized relation between man and nature itself.

From Young America's manifest destiny and expansionism through the Compromise of 1850 and Civil War, this idealist relation was to be increasingly called into question. It came to be complicated by the doubts of skepticism or the uncompromising positions of adversarial individualism as well as unsettled by racial and gender hierarchies and sexual pressures and preferences. It was shaken by the "living forces" of the "great apparition" itself, that on the oceans of the globe or on the prairies of the continent were not so peaceful and transparent as they would appear in the microcosm of the drop of dew or in the wildflower of the mystics of nature. It was split and rehistoricized through race and class conflicts and the epic clashes of nations, to the point of turning the New World into an expansive arena teeming with hostilities. If, on the one hand, this inverted operation must be viewed as one of the most enduring and disturbing accomplishments of classic American literature at midcentury, then, on the other, it may be said to have paved the way for the further and final transformation of the romantic universe of the Not-Me by the naturalist writers of the second half of the nineteenth century. A deromanticized inheritance, the "living visible garment of God" was ultimately turned back into a primitive and obscure place and force. Nature reemerged as the inscrutable battlefield of man's struggle against circumstances and necessity and, at the same time, as man's "pitiless enemy" itself. It was a "dead land" of "persistent toil" and "suffering," as Stephen Crane put it, as well as an agency of "strange and unspeakable punishment" beyond the reach of any possible gospel of liberation and human restitution: "the massive altar of the earth" upon which humanity was again destined to be ritually, and always incomprehensibly, "offered in sacrifice to the wrath of some blind and pitiless deity."[48]

NOTES

1. Robert E. Burkholder and Joel Myerson, eds., *Emerson: An Annotated Secondary Bibliography* (Pittsburgh: University of Pittsburgh Press, 1985), 13.

2. Francis's comments on the "German School" are in John Weiss, *Discourse Occasioned by the Death of Convers Francis, D. D., Delivered before the First Congregational Society, Watertown, April 19, 1863* (Cambridge, Mass.: Welch, Bigelow, 1863), 28. For the "annus mirabilis" of American tran-

scendentalism, see Perry Miller, ed., *The Transcendentalists: An Anthology* (Cambridge, Mass.: Harvard University Press, 1950), 106–56. Both Joel Myerson's *Transcendentalism: A Reader* (New York: Oxford University Press, 2000) and the literary histories by Barbara Packer, "The Transcendentalists," in *The Cambridge History of American Literature*, ed. Sacvan Bercovitch, 8 vols. (New York: Cambridge University Press, 1994–2005), 2:329–604, and Philip F. Gura, *American Transcendentalism: A History* (New York: Hill and Wang, 2007), also call due critical attention to the several works produced in the "year of wonders," 1836. Besides Emerson's *Nature* and Furness's *Remarks on the Four Gospels* (Philadelphia: Carey, Lea, and Blanchard, 1836), the other works that according to Miller's definition constitute the canon of the "annus mirabilis" are Convers Francis's *Christianity as a Purely Internal Principle* (Boston: Bowles, 1836), Orestes A. Brownson's *New Views of Christianity, Society, and the Church* (Boston: Munroe, 1836), George Ripley's *Discourses on the Philosophy of Religion* (Boston: Munroe, 1836), A. Bronson Alcott's *Conversations with Children on the Gospels* (Boston: Munroe, 1836), as well as the second edition of Elizabeth Palmer Peabody's *Record of a School: Exemplifying the General Principles of Spiritual Culture* (Boston: Russell, Shattuck, 1836). To all these one could safely add the 1836 Boston edition of *Sartor Resartus*.

3. *The Journals and Miscellaneous Notebooks of Ralph Waldo Emerson*, ed. William H. Gilman et al., 16 vols. (Cambridge, Mass.: Harvard University Press, 1960–82), 4:237.

4. On the Boston edition as the editio princeps of Carlyle's work, see Charles Frederick Harrold, introduction to Carlyle, *Sartor Resartus: The Life and Opinions of Herr Teufelsdröckh* (Indianapolis: Odyssey Press, 1937), xiii–lxxvi, and, for a more recent and comprehensive discussion, Rodger L. Tarr, introduction to Carlyle, *Sartor Resartus: The Life and Opinions of Herr Teufelsdröckh in Three Books* (Berkeley: University of California Press, 2000), xxi–xciv.

5. James Freeman Clarke, "The Two Carlyles, or Carlyle Past and Present," *Christian Examiner* 77 (1864): 215.

6. Emerson's unsigned preface (titled "Preface of the American Editors") appears in the 1836 and 1837 Boston editions of *Sartor Resartus*. Later, simply titled "New-England Editors," it was included by Carlyle "as the fourth and final item in the 'Testimonies of Authors' . . . attached as a preface to the [British] editions of 1838, 1841, and 1849, and as an appendix to the editions of 1869 and 1871." See Tarr, introduction to Carlyle, *Sartor Resartus*, ciii. *The Collected Letters of Thomas and Jane Welsh Carlyle*, ed. Charles Richard Sanders et al., 40 vols. to date (Durham, N.C.: Duke University Press, 1970–), 7:265; 10:87–90.

7. That is how Emerson refers to his first work, "nearly done," in a letter to his brother William

on June 28, 1836, in *The Selected Letters of Ralph Waldo Emerson,* ed. Joel Myerson (New York: Columbia University Press, 1997), 165.

8. Thomas Carlyle, *Sartor Resartus,* ed. Kerry McSweeney and Peter Sabor (Oxford: Oxford University Press, 1987). Ralph Waldo Emerson, *Nature* in *Essays and Lectures,* ed. Joel Porte (New York: Library of America, 1983). Citations appear in the text.

9. For the "Atlantic double-cross" and recent studies of transatlantic romanticism in general, see, among others, Robert Weisbuch, *Atlantic Double-Cross: American Literature and British Influence in the Age of Emerson* (Chicago: University of Chicago Press, 1986); Susan Manning, *The Puritan-Provincial Vision: Scottish and American Literature in the Nineteenth Century* (Cambridge: Cambridge University Press, 1990); Richard Poirier, *Trying It Out in America: Literary and Other Performances* (New York: Farrar, Straus and Giraux, 1999); Richard Gravil, *Romantic Dialogues: Anglo-American Continuities, 1776–1862* (New York: St. Martin's Press, 2000); Armin Paul Frank and Kurt Mueller-Vollmer, *The Internationality of National Literatures in Either America: Transfer and Transformation. British America and the United States, 1770s–1850s* (Leipzig: Wallstein Verlag, 2000); Patrick J. Keane, *Emerson, Romanticism and Intuitive Reason: The Transatlantic "Light of All Our Day"* (Columbia: University of Missouri Press, 2005); Susan Manning and Andrew Taylor, eds., *Transatlantic Literary Studies: A Reader* (Baltimore: Johns Hopkins University Press, 2007); and the numerous studies by Paul Giles: *Transatlantic Insurrections: British Culture and the Formation of American Literature, 1730–1860* (Philadelphia: University of Pennsylvania Press, 2001), *Virtual Americas: Transnational Fictions and Transatlantic Imaginary* (Durham, N.C.: Duke University Press, 2002), *Atlantic Republic: The American Tradition in English Literature* (Oxford: Oxford University Press, 2006), *The Global Remapping of American Literature* (Princeton, N.J.: Princeton University Press, 2011). For philosophical studies of Emerson in a transatlantic romantic context, see the various contributions by Stanley Cavell, gathered in his *Emerson's Transcendental Etudes,* ed. David Justin Hodge (Stanford: Stanford University Press, 2003).

10. James Elliot Cabot, *A Memoir of Ralph Waldo Emerson,* 2 vols. (Boston: Riverside, 1887), 1:248.

11. Harrold, introduction to Carlyle, *Sartor Resartus,* xxx.

12. Samuel Taylor Coleridge, *Aids to Reflection in the Formation of a Manly Character: On the Several Grounds of Prudence, Morality, and Religion* (London: Taylor and Hessey, 1825), 208.

13. James Marsh, "Preliminary Essay" to *Aids to Reflection* (Burlington: Goodrich, 1829), vii–liv;

Thomas Carlyle, "State of German Literature," in *The Works of Thomas Carlyle,* ed. H. D. Traill, 30 vols. (London: Chapman and Hall, 1896–99), 26:26–86; Carlyle, "Novalis," in *Works,* 27:1–55.

14. Stephen E. Whicher, ed., *Selections from Ralph Waldo Emerson* (Boston: Houghton Mifflin, 1957), 470.

15. Emerson, *Selected Letters,* 133.

16. Carlyle, *Collected Letters,* 6:13.

17. Friedrich Schlegel, *The Philosophy of Life, and Philosophy of Language in a Course of Lectures,* trans. A. J. W. Morrison (London: Bohn, 1847), 349. The lectures on the *Philosophy of Life* were delivered at Vienna in 1827 and published in 1828; those on the *Philosophy of Language* were delivered at Dresden in 1828–29 and published in 1830.

18. Carlyle, "Characteristics," in *Works,* 28:25.

19. Carlyle, "Novalis," 25.

20. Johann Wolfgang Goethe, *Faust,* ed. Walter Kaufmann (Garden City: Anchor Books, 1963), 102.

21. Carlyle's and Teufelsdröckh's German obligations have been studied and discussed by Charles Frederick Harrold, *Carlyle and German Thought: 1819–1834* (New Haven, Conn.: Yale University Press, 1934), and, more recently, by Elizabeth M. Vida, *Romantic Affinities: German Authors and Carlyle. A Study in the History of Ideas* (Toronto: University of Toronto Press, 1993).

22. Schlegel, *Philosophy of Life,* 90, 118.

23. Ibid., 21.

24. Novalis, *Notes for a Romantic Encyclopaedia: Das Allgemeine Brouillon,* ed. David W. Wood (Albany: State University of New York Press, 2007), 104.

25. Friedrich Wilhelm Joseph Schelling, translated and quoted by Sara Coleridge in Samuel Taylor Coleridge, *Biographia Literaria; or, Biographical Sketches of My Literary Life and Opinions,* ed. Henry Nelson Coleridge and Sara Coleridge, 2 vols. (London: Pickering, 1847), 1:267, v–vi, 267. For a modern English edition of Schelling's work, see *Ideas for a Philosophy of Nature,* trans. Erroll Harris and Peter Heath (Cambridge: Cambridge University Press, 1988).

26. Novalis, *The Disciples at Saïs and Other Fragments,* ed. Una Birch (London: Methuen, 1903), 126 (translation slightly modified); Carlyle, "Novalis," 39.

27. Carlyle, "Novalis," 27, 25, 27.

28. Novalis, *Notes for a Romantic Encyclopaedia,* 104.

29. Carlyle, "Novalis," 28; Novalis, *Disciples,* 131; Carlyle, "Novalis," 29; Emerson, *Essays and Lectures,* 289.

30. Emerson, *Essays and Lectures,* 69, 289.

31. Ibid., 289, 400.

32. Carlyle, "Schiller," in *Works,* 27:199.

33. Schlegel, *Philosophy of Life,* 86; Emerson, "The School," in *The Early Lectures of Ralph Waldo Emerson,* ed. Stephen E. Whicher et al., 3 vols. (Cambridge, Mass.: Harvard University Press, 1959–72), 3:49; Emerson, *Essays and Lectures,* 256, 412, 433, 631, 403, 676.

34. Iain Hamilton Grant, "F. W. J. Schelling, 'On the World Soul': Translation and Introduction," *Collapse* 6 (2010): 58–95; Emerson, *Essays and Lectures,* 383–400.

35. Novalis, *Philosophical Writings,* ed. Margaret Mahony Stoljar (Albany: State University of New York Press, 1997), 60; see also Novalis, *Fichte Studies,* ed. Jane Keller (Cambridge: Cambridge University Press, 2003), xxxiii; and Novalis, *Notes for a Romantic Encyclopaedia,* xvi; Clarke, "The Two Carlyles," 215.

36. Emerson, *Essays and Lectures,* 68–69, 69, 668.

37. Novalis, *Philosophical Writings,* 25; Novalis, *Notes for a Romantic Encyclopaedia,* 160.

38. Furness, *Remarks on the Four Gospels,* 129; the definition of Furness's work as a "prosaic *Nature*" is Miller's, *The Transcendentalists,* 124; Weiss, *Discourse,* 28–29.

39. Emerson, *Journals,* 3:152, 166, 167, 172; 4:113.

40. Emerson, *Journals,* 4:96; 5:85; Emerson, "Modern Aspects of Letters," in *Early Lectures,* 1:385.

41. Emerson speaks of a "philosophy of the erect position" or "upright position" in several journal entries of the early 1830s (see, among others, *Journals,* 4:333; 5:43, 302), and then elaborates it in some of his greatest essays of the 1840s, such as "Self-Reliance" and "Circles."

42. Emerson, *Journals,* 5:146–47.

43. This is how Emerson calls *Sartor Resartus*'s astonishing German hero in his second letter to Carlyle, November 20, 1834, in *Selected Letters,* 135.

44. Carlyle, "Novalis," 27, 29.

45. *The Complete Sermons of Ralph Waldo Emerson,* ed. Albert J. von Frank et al., 4 vols. (Columbia: University of Missouri Press, 1989–92), 4:121, 275.

46. Carlyle, "Novalis," 40.

47. Besides this readaptation of Novalis's "symbolical Philosophy" in *Sartor Resartus*, see also Carlyle's 1832 essay "Boswell's Life of Johnson," in *Works*, 28:90, where he quotes and uses again the phrases "Gospel of Freedom" and "Messias of Nature" in relation to Nature's life-philosophical twin, that is, "Life" itself, and its related literary genre "Biography." For a discussion of Carlyle's allegedly limited understanding of Novalis's vision of man as redeemer of nature, see Carlyle, *Sartor Resartus*, ed. Harrold, 220n, and, more extensively, Vida, *Romantic Affinities*, 117–24. On the possible differences between Emerson's interpretation of the self "through the medium of American nature" (in the context of "the Romantic doctrine of *sola natura*" and the "teleology" of "process and fulfillment") on one side, and the views of Carlyle and "the European symbolist" in general on the other, see Sacvan Bercovitch, *The Puritan Origins of the American Self, with a New Preface*, 2nd ed. (New Haven, Conn.: Yale University Press, 2011), 148–63.

48. Stephen Crane, "Nebraska's Bitter Fight for Life," in *Poetry and Prose*, ed. J. C. Levenson (New York: Library of America, 1984), 689, 690, 694.

5

AN EMBLEM OF ALL THE REST

WEARING THE WIDOW'S CAP IN VICTORIAN LITERATURE

Dagni Bredesen

Early in Charlotte Yonge's best-selling novel *Magnum Bonum* (1879), her heroine, the still young Caroline Allen Brownlow, loses her older physician husband to an epidemic.[1] Devoted to him while he lived, committed to carrying on his medical legacy (the Magnum Bonum of the title), and deeply invested in the care of their children, Caroline nevertheless conforms with difficulty to the sartorial conventions and social restrictions imposed on widows. Her implicit rebellion is signaled by her carelessness about her cap: "'Oh, that wretched cap!' she cried, jumping up, petulantly, and going to the glass to set it to rights, but with so hasty a hand that the pin became entangled in her hair. . . . 'It's just an emblem of all the rest of it'" (133–34).

By "all the rest of it" Caroline refers to the code of conduct expected of her now that she is widowed. She has moved her family to the country at her late husband's behest so that her brother-in-law and his wife can better assist and, it turns out, keep an eye on this youthful, bohemian wife of the late city doctor. With her cap askew on her head, if on at all (frequently she runs out of the house without it), Caroline is subjected to the repeated admonitions of her sister-in-law, Ellen: "Caroline, your cap!" (61). Ellen's policing takes effect. Caroline begins to internalize the strictures; she starts to monitor herself, self-consciously checking the status of her cap (88). Tellingly, the pressures of widowhood that the cap represents manifest somatically in the headaches that afflict her only after the death of her husband. Yet when her children entice her away from the world of social expectations into "the land of fairy," as they refer to the fields near their rural home, she leaves her widow's cap behind (99–100).

In Victorian literature, the widow's cap frequently acquires meanings that transcend its overt purpose as a requisite accessory to a complete mourning ensemble. It not only signifies a woman's bereaved status; it often marks the negotiations she makes between her private grief (or relief) over her husband's death and public expectations. Different concepts are communicated by the widow's cap in various Victorian narratives. But to grasp these fully, I discuss widowhood as a category of Victorian womanhood and, specifically, the widow's cap as part of societal prescriptions regarding mourning dress: what to wear and how long to wear it. What might be considered transgressive uses of the cap in literary narratives complicates the emblematic meanings of the cap that identifies a widow; they are problematic because paradoxical. The widow's cap that cloaks and circumscribes a woman' s sexuality also calls attention to it, for wearing the widow's cap indicates that the ostensibly bereaved has been married, and if married, then, presumably, she has had sexual experience. Similarly, the headdress meant to function as a tribute to the dead husband simultaneously signals his absence. Hence, the wearing of the widow's cap can be directed toward ends that evade prescriptive norms of mourning. Narrative attention to the widow's cap, even when that cap is worn in a normative fashion by a genuine and, one might say, model widow, creates an opportunity for a critique of the conventions and codes that constrain widows specifically and women more generally.

COVERING THE FEME DISCOVERT

In nineteenth-century Great Britain, women were considered "relative creatures"; that is, a woman's status was determined by her relationship to her male relatives (father, son, and husband). The term "widow" signified the loss of what had been for that woman a primary relationship and, at that time, the primary legal means of constituting her identity. To be *sous couverture* meant that upon marriage a wife came under the covering of her husband and surrendered effectually a legal existence distinct from her spouse's. The law considered the *feme covert,* as a married woman was termed in English common law, incapable of managing her own property, making contracts, or having a will of her own, political or otherwise.[2] When a husband died, his wife became not *feme sole* (literally a woman alone, which is the designation for a spinster) but *feme discovert,* that is, a woman uncovered. Her civil identity no longer submerged into that of her husband, the widow in nineteenth-century Britain experienced a legal resurrection of sorts. Not only did she recover her single status, she also potentially discovered an increased range of activities and wider economic and legal scope.[3] At the same time, the widow was expected to conform to an elaborate etiquette of clothing and conduct that served to impress her exceptional status on herself and her community. Literary texts often portray the widow as anomalous, someone who disrupts the gender formula, a wild card. Consequently, much concern is expressed over regulating the widow's behavior and dress. The widow wears too much mourning (or not enough); she wears her "weeds" for too long (or not long enough); she cries too much (or not enough). Figurations of widowhood run in at least two directions. The widow is, on the one hand, a marker of the gap left by the husband, an absence that needs to be filled. On the other, she is a figure of excess. Her agency itself is the product of her excess in that, given the cultural mandate of coverture, she is a reminder and remainder of the husband she has buried and, therefore, needs to be recontained, re-covered. This entrenched impression that women needed to be under a husband's covering may explain the British cultural mandate for the conspicuous re-covering of the widow in crepe veils, bonnets, and the widow's cap.

In Victorian mourning dress, the most visible sign of a widow's bereaved status is her headgear. According to Anne Hollander, "the general use of black clothing for formal wear in the nineteenth century demanded that widowhood be signalized by such a widow's cap—black with a thick veil and later sometimes white with a veil, in the style

Mourning Dress 1800–1910

FIGURE 5.1 This image combines a mourning bonnet, about 1840–50, from the Royal Pavilion and Museums (Brighton and Hove) with a black crepe veil from the Worthing Museum and Art Gallery. Photograph reproduced with the kind permission of the Royal Pavilion and Museums (Brighton and Hove) and the Worthing Museum and Art Gallery.

adopted and popularized by Queen Victoria."[4] Women of the poorer classes who could not afford the conventional dress of crepe (the matte, generally black fabric adopted by the middle and upper classes) contrived, at the very least, a semblance of a widow's cap. But for those who could afford it, respectable mourning required a more rigid adherence to a formidable regimen. In *Mourning Dress* (1983), her rich study of mourning costumes and customs, Lou Taylor specifies that widows wore three kinds of caps: white crepe indoor caps, black outdoor caps, and white caps that covered the hair and were worn underneath outdoor hats.[5]

Taylor notes that "Both indoor and outdoor caps shared one common feature and that was a V-point shaped down over the centre forehead and described always as the Marie Stuart style" (137–38). Though scarcely a fashion trendsetter, Queen Victoria revived the style worn by Mary, Queen of Scots, which, in turn, was widely adopted by her widowed subjects, after the prince consort's death in 1861. Articles on mourning etiquette cite the queen's example in the wearing of caps, as in the column on "The Etiquette of Mourning" found in *Myra's Journal of Dress and Fashion:*

Widows' caps are, and are likely to remain, *de rigueur.* The example set by Her Majesty is not likely to be forgotten by those ladies who, like their gracious Queen, are mourning their loved and lost; but widows' caps are no longer the heavy, unsightly coiffures of olden days, but are made in simpler shapes, and may be found in our leading West End mourning establishments, in styles suited for every age. For lightening a widow's mourning, caps of tulle, with long lappets, are worn; these caps cannot be worn with propriety during the first eight months of mourning, nor is any other coiffure needed than the cap of fine muslin, so harmonious with the rigid simplicity of a widow's mourning.[6]

Anne Buck observes that "the cap, of white crape, was worn for a year and a day, but by many widows, amongst them Queen Victoria, for half a lifetime. This with its long white

FIGURE 5.2 From a copy of an 1864 portrait of Queen Victoria found in the *Ladies Field*, February 2, 1901. Permission of Lou Taylor.

streamers was the most distinctive feature of the widow's mourning, but the different shapes worn during the period quietly reflect contemporary fashion in hats and capes."[7]

In her study *The Hat* (1990), Madeleine Ginsburg situates the widow's cap in relation to the rest of the mourning dress for Victorians:

> The rules of mourning had been set by the early 15th century and confirmed in the following centuries. Colorless garments, black and white, with a dull finish were the norm and especially for the widow; the custom was complete segregation, modified in modern society to concealment under caps, hats, and veils. . . . The white widow's cap, tight around the face with pendant lappets, sometimes also called weepers, and the black widow's bonnet, surmounting the acres of sepulchral crêpe, became symbols of an age in which women took responsibility for making social statements on behalf of the family.[8]

As Ginsburg and others point out, historically and cross-culturally, women rather than men have carried the burden of mourning. At no time does this burden seem heavier than in the second half of the nineteenth century when Queen Victoria raised mourning to cult status after the death of the prince consort. John Morley notes that "at the high point of Victorian mourning when even a bride could appear in black . . . the figure of the widow embodied the convention in the most exaggerated form: she was self-consciously set apart in grief."[9] The mourning regimen, which prescribed what clothes to wear and how long to wear them, in effect cordoned a woman off from the world, turning her into a living symbol of her dead husband, a kind of memento mori, as well as a showpiece of her family's wealth and respectability.

Given the complexity of the mourning codes and the subtle censure that infractions might incur, one can understand the frequent delineations of correct mourning found in ladies' magazines such as the *Englishwoman's Domestic Magazine,* which begins its two-page spread, also called "The Etiquette of Mourning," noting "We are constantly receiving inquiries respecting both the depth and duration of mourning which it is correct to wear for relatives of different degrees." The article continues with a description of the prescribed mourning apparel, one that emphasizes the significance of the widow's cap, the length of time one wears it, and once again, invokes the widowed Queen Victoria as exemplar:

> The first degree of mourning is of course that of a widow; the dress is always of para-matta entirely covered with crape to within an inch or two of the waist, the crape being in one piece, not in separate tucks, for the first nine months. If after this period it requires renewing it may be put on in two deep tucks, with about an inch space between them, but must come up as high on the skirt as before. The sleeves are tight to the arm, the body entirely covered with crape, and deep lawn cuffs and collar are worn. . . . The cap was formerly constructed so as almost entirely to conceal the hair and to fasten under the chin; but this severe style is now considerably mitigated, and many different shapes are worn, the Marie Stuart, so familiar to us in the portraits of Her Majesty, being the most general. It must be worn for a year and a day. . . . The bonnet is entirely crape, with a widow's cap tacked inside it, and with a crape veil with a deep hem. . . . Of course during the first year of mourning a widow can neither accept invitations nor frequent places of public amusement; a widow's cap in such scenes has a most incongruous appearance. After the year has elapsed she may, if so inclined, gradually return to society.[10]

The comparable set of instructions found in *Myra's Journal of Dress and Fashion* ends with the admonition, "Good taste and feeling will always point the course to be taken. Young widows will do well to err upon the side of over-strictness and severity of costume, than to be in haste to throw aside the outward signs of respectful regret" (3).

John Morley notes that "Twenty-one months after bereavement crape could be left off entirely—this was known as 'slighting' the mourning—and plain black worn; two years after the bereavement the widow could go into half mourning for six months. The colours worn in half mourning were grey, lavender, mauve, violet, or black, grey and white stripes; the change should be gradual." Morley adds that "the widow's dress was uncomfortable. The streamers on the cap, because of their weight and roughness (they caught on the dress) made it difficult to turn the head. The dress was said also to be 'un-hygienic,' and exercise was 'impossible.'"[11]

The contemporary criticism of mourning indicated by words such as "unhygienic" and "impossible" in reference to the widow's mourning garb found formal expression in movements both on a national level and within the Anglican Church that began in 1875. While these funeral and mourning reform associations turned their attention to issues such as coffin construction, burial procedures, and sanitation, they expressed concern as well toward expensive and ostentatious mourning apparel. Over time the work of these organizations and rational dress societies seemed to have an effect on mourning fashion. Anne Buck cites the emergence of a more radical, feminist critique of mourning garb by the late 1880s in journals such as the *Woman's World* (1889). In one article a writer points out the gendered expectations in mourning dress, noting that for men, a seven-inch crepe band around the crown of their hat was the deepest expression of mourning in their required apparel whereas, "In all cases the nearer the relative, the more cumbrous becomes the dress of the female mourner, but the widow's dress positively amounts to a mild form of suttee."[12]

These contemporary discourses on mourning as an institution, on mourning etiquette, and on fashion—widow's weeds in general and the widow's cap specifically—manifest the pressure and desire for respectability competing with the currents of modernity and rationality. Contemporary advice columns responded to anxiety over the widow's conduct and dress, especially the young widow's behavior and clothing. This anxiety seeped into literary texts in which the widow's cap becomes the flashpoint for much of the potential scandal inherent in the *feme discovert*'s legal uncovering. In novels, the subversive aspects of the widow's status become readily apparent in at least two specific cases: when women who are not widowed appropriate a new identity by donning the widow's cap, and when women who are widowed use the cap to advertise their marital availability instead of their deep grief.

A 1903 compendium of quotations about widows contains a poem that runs:

> Her mourning is all make-believe;
> 'Tis plain there's nothing in it:
> With weepers she has tipp'd her sleeve,
> The while she's laughing in it.[13]

Although it does not mention the widow's cap, in this ditty ascribed to "Burns," the widow clothes herself in mourning garb but literally laughs up her sleeve. In both literary narratives and sartorial conventions of Victorian widowhood, apart from tears, there is nothing specific to a woman's body that marks her as widowed. Only her clothing signals a woman's widowed status to those around her. But while dress and cap confirm to the world the widow qua widow, her clothing proves to be an unstable signifier. The eye notes the widow's weeds—her cap, her veil, her black crepe dress—and the ear records the title "Mrs." Yet the props of widowhood—the costumes, as well as much of the script —are always available for appropriation by the woman who has other ends in mind than mourning the death of her husband. In Victorian literature, in such cases where the so-called widow's identity and behavior is suspected, her cap functions as an emblem of potential impropriety, as can be seen in Elizabeth Gaskell's *Ruth* (1853) and Anthony Trollope's *Can You Forgive Her?* (1864–65).[14]

In *Ruth*, the adoption of a widow's garb and status is an act fraught with ambivalence. A dissenting clergyman and his spinster sister—the Bensons—encourage the pregnant teenaged heroine, an abandoned victim of seduction, to assume a widow's identity because it appears to them as the only way of legitimizing the presence of a child and granting the fallen woman entrance into a community. On the one hand, the narrative voice decries Faith Benson (who proposes the scheme) as a "tempter! unconscious tempter!" and her proposition as "a way of evading the trials for the poor little unborn child . . . the decision—the pivot, on which the fate of years moved" (121), thus suggesting that the better path would be to brave society's rejection. On the other hand, the story con-demns a system that turns away the repentant magdalen and persecutes her innocent offspring. Ambivalence manifests further in the multiple perspectives of the three char-acters who conspire in the deception: in Mr. Benson's distress over lying, in his sister Faith's satisfaction with the neat fiction that will conceal so much, and in Ruth's passive complicity in the "pious fraud."[15]

Although Ruth allows Faith to buy her a black gown and to introduce her as a cousin, Mrs. Denbigh, "early left a widow," the fiction of widowhood prompts immediate suspi-cion (130). Ruth's performance—rather, her lack of a good or thorough performance—provokes Sally, the Bensons' housekeeper, to ask "Is this chit a widow. . . . If I'd been her mother, I'd ha' given her a lollypop instead of a husband" (134). Sally's sharp eyes note the missing props: the wedding ring that Faith only belatedly supplies and the widow's cap. Handing Ruth "two widow's caps of commonest make and coarsest textures," Sally declares:

> Missus—or miss, as the case may be—I've my doubts as to you. I'm not going to have my master and Miss Faith put upon, or shame come near them. Widows wears these sort o' caps, and has their hair cut off; and whether widows wears wedding-rings or not, they shall have their hair cut off—they shall. . . . I'll not see this family disgraced by any one's long curls. (143)

Although haircutting and head shaving as a sign of mourning operate in other times and cultures, Sally's concern over Ruth's long curls seems more motivated by her sense of the unseemliness of long curls in conjunction with mourning (and as she suspects disgrace) than by a specific contemporary mandate to cut one's hair. Sally's intervention makes clear that a black dress and the designation "widow" are not enough to ensure communal recognition and acceptance of a woman identifying herself as widow. The widow's complete outfit crucially requires a cap, most especially for a working-class woman, who might not be able to afford the entire mourning ensemble prescribed in women's magazines of the day.

Ruth's acceptance by the community is conditioned by the pretense of respectable widowhood, and for the first ten years of her son's life, her reputation is unblemished by rumors of her past. Eventually, her "vital secret" is uncovered, but the thoroughly reformed Ruth finds a new way of working out her self-redemption as a sick nurse (386). This position, like the widow's, places Ruth in a contiguous relation to death: "She was so often in connection with Death that something of the superstitious awe with which the dead were regarded . . . surrounded her" (388). Having replaced her widow's cap with that of a nurse, Ruth—like Helen Graham of Anne Brontë's *Tenant of Wildfell Hall* (1848), who, though married, also passes in respectable society as a widow—is called to the sickbed of the man who betrayed her.[16] Unlike Helen Graham, however, Ruth suffers for her complicity in her seduction. In the logic of the mid-Victorian novel, even one as progressive as Gaskell's—or perhaps because the novel in its criticism of society's double sexual standards is in so many other ways progressive—the fallen woman must die. As a result of nursing her seducer back to health, Ruth contracts typhus fever and dies.

The equivocal status of widowhood in *Ruth* has received little critical attention. Widowhood is either overlooked completely because, after all, Ruth is not actually widowed when she passes as such, or it serves as an invisible lens through which to view the specific social ill of fallenness. To examine widowhood in this novel by way of the widow's cap, then, is to focus on the mechanism that conditions perception itself, not as a transparent lens, but as a filter that colors the way this woman and her movements are perceived. The widow's cap supplies a cover that allows Ruth to recover from the sins of her youth, while the fiction of widowhood provides the pretext for the presence of a fatherless child. Even though Ruth adopts the widow's cap and identity on her son's behalf, the act is judged to be powerfully transgressive because she does so in order to subvert conventional morality. The offense of using the widow's cap as a means of evading patriarchal structures and strictures is compounded when one remembers that the widow's garments are donned ostensibly in honor of the husband through whom her identity was supposed to be constituted.

When Gaskell's Ruth adopts the widow's cap, she gains a new, if temporary, identity. In Anthony Trollope's *Can You Forgive Her?* the actual status of the widow is not in doubt so much as the authenticity of her grief. Citing Lou Taylor, Pat Jalland writes that the widow's "drab, uncomfortable attire symbolized the perception that a wife's identity and sexuality were subsumed in her husband's and died with him. . . . It helped to place her beyond the marriage market."[17] In *Can You Forgive Her?*, however, Trollope's recently widowed Arabella Greenow contravenes the conventions of mourning and uses her widow's weeds, especially her cap, to advertise her availability. Though the novel shows the Widow Greenow conforming to the conventions of mourning dress "to the letter," it wryly notes that she throws "the spirit of it to the winds" (426). Underlying all that satirizes the figure of the widow in literary history is the idea that sooner or later she will find surcease for her sorrow in the enjoyment of her freedom, her inheritance, and perhaps a new lover with whom to share her good fortune. Arabella Greenow most certainly conforms to the stereotype of the remarrying widow that reaches back into ancient Rome's Widow of Ephesus and stretches into the twenty-first century in fiction and in real life.[18]

The Widow Greenow is introduced into the novel by way of a conversation between her nieces, Alice and Kate, in which they comment on her foibles. Kate objects most strongly to her aunt's charade of mourning the death of her elderly husband and her strategic deployment of widow's weeds:

> I wouldn't have her laugh; but neither would I have her cry. And she's quite right to wear weeds; but she needn't be so very outrageous in the depth of her hems or so very careful that her caps are becoming. Her eyes will be worn out by their double service. They are always red with weeping, yet she is ready every minute with a full battery of execution for any man she sees. (90)

Kate's umbrage underscores that, far from representing Arabella Greenow's devotion to her deceased husband, the widow's cap broadcasts her availability on the very marriage market from which decorum demands she exempt herself. In addition to alerting readers to the Widow Greenow's intention to remarry, Kate's critique of her aunt calls attention to Arabella's demonstrable command over the rhetoric of the devoted relict and the semiotics of grief, which, at the time of the novel's serialization, were being played out for the public by Queen Victoria, already several years into the decade of deep mourning following the death of Prince Albert. Having married for money, the Widow Greenow manufactured the requisite devotion to her elderly husband until his death and, now, revels in mourning for him even as she positions herself to attract a second husband. In order to move through the stages of mourning with alacrity, though with some semblance of propriety, Arabella keeps adding months to her account of the postmortem period. In all other respects, she strictly adheres to the elaborate mourning regimen prescribed for widows. Nevertheless, the wry narrator describes her thus:

> The widow was almost gorgeous in her weeds. I believe that she had not sinned in her dress against any of those canons which the semi-ecclesiastical authorities on widowhood have laid down as to the outward garments fitted for gentlemen's relicts. The materials were those which are devoted to deepest conjugal grief. As regarded every item of the written law her suttee worship was carried out to the letter. There was the widow's cap, generally so hideous, so well known to the eyes of all men, so odious to womanhood. Let us hope that such headgear may have some assuaging effect on the departed spirits of husbands. . . . here were the trailing weepers, and widow's kerchief pinned round her neck, and somewhat tightly over her bosom. But there was a genius about Mrs. Greenow, that she turned every seeming disadvantage to some special profit, and had so dressed herself, though she obeyed the law to the letter, that she had thrown the spirit of it to the winds. Her cap sat jauntily on her head, and showed just so much of her rich brown hair as to give her the appearance of youth which she desired. . . . Her weepers were bright with newness, and she would waft them aside from her shoulder with an air which turned even them into auxiliaries. (425–26)

Here, as in *Ruth,* the wearing of the widow's cap and gown generates ambivalence, though the ambivalence, in this case, appears to be authorial. On the one hand, Anthony Trollope despised the etiquette imposed on widows, a disdain that is apparent in his facetious reference to a widow's doleful attire as "suttee worship" and articulated else-where.[19] On the other hand, obviously he finds fascinating the potential sex appeal of "weeds," which his characterization of Arabella Greenow fully exploits. The Widow Greenow exudes a vibrant physicality and deploys her weeds to make herself as sexually attractive as possible, an intent that the narrative voice all but applauds. At the same time, augmenting her sex appeal with the outfit that performs the social function of me-morializing a dead husband is clearly, if humorously, viewed as transgressive. Neverthe-less, although the "letter of the law" refers to the strict sartorial code that ostensibly quar-antines the widow socially and sexually for at least two years, Arabella manipulates other conventions and the rhetoric of mourning with easy flare. Her abandonment of the spirit of those laws is flagged first and foremost in the jauntiness of her cap.

The widowed Arabella's blithe disregard for the intended limitations of mourning comes as a relief when one thinks of all the female self-recrimination and self-repres-sion voiced in *Can You Forgive Her?*, which might be more aptly named *Can She Forgive Herself?* The representative single woman, Alice Vavasor, hates herself because of her romantic vacillations and ambivalence toward marriage; the representative married woman, Glencora Palliser, is ashamed of her apparent infertility and love for a man who is not her husband. By the end of the novel, these two characters reconcile themselves to the constraints imposed on Victorian womanhood (Alice marries her "worthy" suitor and Glencora learns to love her plodding politician husband and gives birth to his heir). At first glance, Arabella, too, seems to conform in that she soon "sets her cap" on and succeeds in capturing matrimonially the roguish Captain Bellfield, whom she success-fully domesticates. Yet Trollope conveys no sense that Arabella Bellfield has capitulated to the rules of patriarchy; she manages to maintain control of her wealth, and she puts her weeds in lavender "for future possible occasions," indicating that she can imagine outliving this second husband as well as her first (804). Hence the most subversive as-pect of the widow's cap is not its usefulness as a prop that enables one to pass in re-spectable society or to perform a grief one doesn't really feel; it is that wearing this emblem of closure (a husband's life ended, a married life over) opens new narrative pos-sibilities for the woman who wears it.

In the nineteenth-century novel, the widow's cap is not necessarily and always a marker of renegade female sexuality (à la Ruth's violated virginity or Arabella's robust appetites). In *Barchester Towers* (1857), Anthony Trollope creates a widowed heroine who conforms decorously to the dress code and calendar of mourning, as does Dorothea Brooke Casaubon in George Eliot's *Middlemarch* (1871–72).[20] The moral lives of both women are blameless, and they wear their widow's caps with propriety. Yet, in both novels, the widow's cap substitutes for a host of practices and conventions to which women are subject and gives rise to critiques of Victorian gender ideology and still, if inadvertently, calls attention to the young widow's sexuality.

Anthony Trollope introduces the heroine of *Barchester Towers,* Eleanor Bold, as "now alas a widow" (10). Three times in as many sentences the narrator says, "Poor Eleanor," an epithet that belies the fact that she has been left in prosperous circumstances.[21] Sandwiched between these appeals to the reader's sympathies is the invitation to note the attractiveness of Eleanor's headgear: "How well does that widow's cap become her, and the solemn gravity with which she devotes herself to her new duties" (12). These new duties consist primarily of raising her husband's posthumously born son and endeavoring to conserve and even augment the fortune she inherits from her husband in order to turn it over intact to John Bold junior when he comes of age.

As evinced early in the novel, the widow's cap, which should completely cover a woman's hair, with its very narrow border, crimped on each side to encircle her face, metaphorically and materially circumscribes her range of vision and, thus, facilitates Eleanor's focused attention on her baby son (14). Intriguingly, however, one of the most sexually provocative scenes occurs in the chapter entitled "Baby Worship" and begins with Baby Johnny pulling his mother's hair out from under her close-fitting cap. She is surprised by a visit from Obadiah Slope, one of her suitors, who immediately responds to the sexual charge that attends the exposure of her chestnut hair, hitherto covered by the cap. The loosed mane conjures up for Reverend Slope visions of conjugal bliss; the fortune-hunting clergyman decides that "irrespective of her fortune, she would be an inmate that a man might well desire for his house, a partner for his bosom's care" (130). Eleanor herself feels the unseemliness of being caught with her hair down and hurries from the room to confine her locks back under the cap that is supposed to discourage male attention.

Anyone who has read *Barchester Towers* knows that much of the novel's romantic intrigue stems from the attempts of three men to woo the lovely, well-endowed Widow Bold. When donned correctly (and in the proper spirit), the cap does indeed ward off male advances, like those of Bertie Stanhope, who, though initially attracted to the widow "with lots of tin" (124), finds that "the widow's cap prevents him from making a positive declaration" (212). Over time, though, the streamers on the cap shorten, and the cap itself diminishes in size, changes that register Eleanor's gradual passage from first to second to half mourning. The size of this "emblem of grief," as Trollope calls the cap, outwardly indicates the widow's emotional readiness to be courted. The transition, permitted if not encouraged, in the wearing of widow's weeds, corresponds to a shift in the level of her devotion to her husband's memory that the narrator observes in connection with the cap.[22]

> It was, after all, but a small cap now, and had but little of the weeping-willow left in its construction. It is singular how these emblems of grief fade away by unseen gradations. Each pretends to be the counterpart of the forerunner, and yet the last little bit of crimped white crêpe that sits so jauntily on the back of the head, is as dissimilar to the first huge mountain of woe which disfigured the face of the weeper, as the state of the Hindoo is to the jointure of the English dowager. (212)

This passage echoes the comparison between English mourning garments and Indian widow-burning made by Signora Neroni who, earlier in the novel, disparages Eleanor's attractions by calling her "a vapid, swarthy thing in a widow's cap" (124) and remarks "what woman on earth could look well with such a thing as that she had on her head . . . the death of twenty husbands should not make me undergo such a penance. It is as much a relic of paganism as the sacrifice of a Hindoo woman at the burning of her husband's body. If not so bloody, it is quite as barbarous and quite as useless" (125). The disruptive Signora unsettles the normative view of widowhood, for in repudiating the widow's cap, Signora Neroni also rejects the prescribed mourning conduct.

When her brother Bertie counters her criticism, "I fancy . . . that if I were to die, and then walk, I should think that my widow looked better in one of those caps than any other kind of head-dress," Madeline retorts:

> Yes—and you'd fancy also that she could do nothing better than shut herself up and cry for you, or else burn herself. But she would think differently. She'd probably wear one of those horrid she-helmets because she'd want the courage not to do so. . . . I hate such shallow false pretences. For my part I would let the world say what it pleased, and show no grief if I felt none—and perhaps not, if I did. (124–25)

Connecting the widow's cap to suttee both trivializes the material consequences for the Hindu woman who performs this act and intensifies the negative connotations of an Englishwoman's mourning as a living death.[23] For the Signora, the cap is yet another oppressive and retrogressive social expectation. Of course, we must consider the speaker. Madeline here is the ersatz Italian signora (the self-styled "mother of the last of the Neros") whose continental affectations, crippled condition, ambiguous marital status, and uncertain morals place her on the fringe of respectability. Signora Neroni's notoriety makes her more marginal than the widowed heroine and, thus, a fitting foil for the Widow Bold; her own outrageousness undermines her critique of "pagan" Victorian widowhood. Yet her outsider status enables her to critique the patriarchal fantasy of having a wife serve as "an animated gravestone" as well as the social expectations that pressure widows into wearing those "horrid she-helmets."[24] Her views receive only the weakest challenge and, incidentally, it is the Signora who provides Eleanor with the best advice concerning Francis Arabin, the man who eventually replaces John Bold in Eleanor's connubial affections.

A similar repudiation of mourning takes place in George Eliot's *Middlemarch*, when

Celia removes the widow's cap from her sister Dorothea's head. At first, Celia urges "Dodo" to "throw off that cap. I am sure your dress must make you ill." Dorothea, however, does not readily accede to this request: "I am so used to the cap—it has become a sort of shell. . . . I feel rather bare and exposed when it is off." In an age when married women were subject to the common law doctrine of coverture, for Dorothea, the widow's cap supplies a surrogate cover. Just as she allowed her initial visions of doing great work in the world to be curbed by prevailing gender conventions and bitter life experience, so too has Dorothea grown accustomed to having her sight curtailed by the "shell" of her cap. But Celia insists on releasing Dorothea from what even she understands is the bondage of widowhood:

> It was a pretty picture this little lady in white muslin unfastening the widow's cap from her more majestic sister, and tossing it on to a chair. Just as the coils and braids of dark-brown hair had been set free, Sir James entered the room. He looked at the released head, and said, "Ah!" in a tone of satisfaction.
>
> "It was I who did it, James," said Celia. "Dodo need not make such a slavery of her mourning; she need not wear that cap any more among her friends." (339)

As in *Barchester Towers*, there is a deflation of the symbolic value of the widow's cap; Celia tosses it cavalierly onto a chair. Here, too, the uncovering of the widow's hair has a dramatic effect on a male viewer. And like Signora Madeline Neroni, Celia identifies mourning conventions with a benighted practice, in this case slavery rather than suttee. The constraining effect of the widow's cap becomes evident when Celia comments to Dorothea, "Really, Dodo, taking your cap off made you like yourself in more ways than one. You spoke up just as you used to do, when anything was said to displease you" (340).

The removal of the widow's cap not only releases Dorothea's hair and liberates her personality, thus returning her to her prenuptial self, but its absence (like its presence) introduces into the minds of those around her the possibility of remarriage. Immediately, the conversation turns to the dress etiquette for a widow who remarries, much to Sir James's displeasure. Celia responds to her husband's disapproval by announcing that

"It all came out of Dodo's cap . . . a woman could not be married in a widow's cap" (340). A corresponding temporal shift, back in time and then forward into the future, occurs when Will Ladislaw encounters Dorothea sans widow's cap for the first time since Casaubon's death. Will thinks back to their first meeting: "her face looked just as it did when she first shook hands with him in Rome; for her widow's cap, fixed in her bonnet, had gone off with it" (390). With her cap off, Dorothea finally perceives that "it is really herself whom Will loved," and to catch a better glimpse of him as she departs in her coach, she throws back the "heavy weepers" attached to her cap that would ordinarily foreclose her view (392, 393). Despite Casaubon's codicil that aimed to thwart a future union between Dorothea and Will, both of them think of that future even if, at this point in the novel, it appears impossible. Comparable to the ways the shrinking dimensions of the widow's cap chart Eleanor's emotional receptivity to romance in *Barchester Towers*, in *Middlemarch* the doffing of the widow's cap connotes the possibility, indeed, for many the inevitability, of a widow's remarriage.

In *Middlemarch*, Dorothea's lady's maid, Tantripp, utters the last words concerning the widow's headgear:

"There's a reason in mourning, as I've always said; and three folds at the bottom of your skirt and a plain quilling in your bonnet—and if ever anybody looked like an angel, it's you in net quilling—is what's consistent for a second year. At least, that's my thinking," ended Tantripp, looking anxiously at the fire; "and if anybody was to marry me flattering himself I should wear those hijeous weepers two years for him, he'd be deceived by his own vanity, that's all." (486)

Once again there is a revulsion against the extravagancies of mourning. Like Signora Neroni, Tantripp identifies the roots of any prolonged display of grief in male vanity. Abandoning her widow's cap and weepers becomes for Dorothea a rite of passage in which she leaves the deep grief of her first marriage behind her. Earlier in *Middlemarch* the narrator comments that her first husband, Casaubon, "willingly imagined her toiling under the fetters of a promise to erect a tomb with his name upon it. Not that Mr.

Casaubon called the future volumes a tomb; he called them the Key to all Mythologies" (306). Only his sudden death frees Dorothea from "his cold grasp on her life" he had wanted to maintain from beyond the grave. Though she does not fulfill his desire that she continue with his work, in her exaggerated mourning and self-mortification, Dorothea nevertheless serves as an animated gravestone, until, that is, she signals a profound internal shift by moving out of her mourning garb, changing clothes and her headgear.[25] Recognizing that her life and capacity for love did not end with the death of her husband, she sees that she is "part of that involuntary, palpitating life, and could neither look out on it from her luxurious shelter as a mere spectator, nor hide her eyes in selfish complaining," or, indeed, under the widow's cap. Dorothea then asks Tantripp to "bring me my new dress; and most likely I shall want my new bonnet today" (486).

Although widow's caps played a role in Victorian life and literature, they receded as primary markers of widowhood toward the end of the nineteenth century; Lucie Heaton Armstrong observed in an 1896 article in the *Woman's Signal,*

> Widows do not make themselves as conspicuous now as formerly, or, at any rate, not for so long a time. It can scarcely be wondered at that so many women have lately "struck" against wearing this distressing form of head-gear, and have done away with the long veil with all possible speed. The widow's cap is not adopted at present by young people, but I can remember the time it was almost compulsory. As a matter of fact it was a survival of a time when women wore caps directly they were married. . . . The old-fashioned caps were terrible constructions.[26]

Armstrong's comment indicates that the widow's cap was on the same continuum as the caps worn by women "directly they were married," head coverings that demonstrated that a wife had come under the covering of her husband's authority. The decline in use of the widow's cap coincides suggestively with legal as well as social shifts of the time. The adjustments in women's legal positions through the series of Married Women's Property Acts that eventually gave married women control of their own property, as well as the earlier Matrimonial Causes Act of 1857 that in time made divorcees (known as

"Grass Widows") more common and, in consequence, more anxiety-producing than actual widows, combined with the movements to reform mourning and rationalize dress. The widow's cap may have been abandoned, then, not only because mourning fashions had been modernized, but also because coverture, the very aspect of marriage it symbolized, no longer defined women's legal position to the same extent. These changes thus suggest that the ambivalence we see in the novels discussed arises from the critique of marriage and mourning conventions as well as an admiration, indeed a nostalgia, for a posthumous wifely devotion the cap was supposed to represent. In literature, the widow's cap was indeed an "emblem" not only "of grief" but also "of all the rest of it," being the intersection of the tradition of coverture with changing attitudes and laws in England over the course of the nineteenth century.

NOTES

I wish to thank the Huntington Library for supporting the initial research of this essay through the Fletcher Jones Fellowship. Many thanks to Ruth Hoberman, Newton Key, and David Raybin for their insightful reading. Thanks as well to Lou Taylor for her helpful suggestions, and to Karen Whisler at Eastern Illinois University's Booth Library for help acquiring materials.

1. Charlotte Yonge, *Magnum Bonum* (London: Macmillan, 1879), 133–34. Further citations appear in the text.

2. "Feme" is Law French for "woman." J. H. Baker, *Manual of Law French* (Aldershot: Scholar Press, 1990), 114, supplies this definition: "feme 1. woman; 2. wife *(and sometimes used for a widow)* L. femina. Feme covert, married woman L. foemina copperta. Feme sole, single woman L. foemina sola." Baker states that the introduction of Law French in British law is attributed to the Norman Conquest and was in use until the reign of Charles II and even later.

3. Although, historically, widows were often left destitute or, at the very least, found their social and economic status reduced by the deaths of their husbands and providers, novelists such as Charles Dickens, Anthony Trollope, and others enjoyed mining the narrative possibilities of the widow uncovered and unleashed as evinced in the warnings uttered by Dickens's Tony Weller to

be "wery careful o' widders" in *The Pickwick Papers* (1837) and Trollope's many vivid depictions of widows.

4. Anne Hollander, *Seeing through Clothes* (New York: Viking, 1978), 382.

5. For a "complete list of clothes needed by a widow for correct and respectable first mourning" published in 1881 by *Sylvia's Home Journal,* see Lou Taylor, *Mourning Dress: A Costume and Social History* (London: George Allen and Unwin, 1983), 139. Further citations appear in the text.

6. "The Etiquette of Mourning," *Myra's Journal of Dress and Fashion* (London), February 1, 1875, 3.

7. Anne Buck, "The Trap Re-baited: Mourning Dress 1860–1890, High Victorian Costume 1860–1890," in *Proceedings of the Second Annual Conference of the Costume Society* (London: Victoria and Albert Museum, 1969), 33.

8. Madeleine Ginsburg, *The Hat: Trends and Traditions* (New York: Barron's, 1990), 84.

9. John Morley, *Death, Heaven and the Victorians* (Pittsburgh: University of Pittsburgh Press, 1971), 68.

10. "The Etiquette of Mourning," *Englishwoman's Domestic Magazine* (London), 134, February 1, 1876, 67.

11. Morley, *Death, Heaven and the Victorians,* 68.

12. Buck, "The Trap Re-baited," 37.

13. Cited in Cora D. Willmarth, *Widows Grave and Otherwise* (San Francisco: Peter Elder, 1903), 18. It should be noted that although Willmarth attributes this to "Burns," I have not been able to confirm what Burns it might be; I have not been able to find the poem in any of Robert Burns's published work.

14. Elizabeth Gaskell, *Ruth* (London: Dent, 1984) and Anthony Trollope, *Can You Forgive Her?,* ed. Stephen Wall (London: Penguin, 1972). Citations appear in the text.

15. From an unsigned review of *Ruth* in *Bentley's Miscellany,* February 1, 1853; see Angus Easson, *Elizabeth Gaskell: A Critical Heritage* (London: Routledge, 1991), 240.

16. Anne Brontë, *The Tenant of Wildfell Hall* (Oxford: Clarendon Press, 1992). For more on this topic, see my essay, "At the Drop of a Veil: Widow's Weeds and Fictions of (Dis)Coverture," in *Conference Proceedings Inter/National Intersections: Law's Changing Territories* (Vancouver: University of British Columbia Press, 1998), 200–210.

17. Pat Jalland, *Death in the Victorian Family* (Oxford: Oxford University Press, 1996), 301.

18. From the Widow of Ephesus to the Wife of Bath and on into the nineteenth century, the scandal of the widow lies in the perception and representation of her social and economic agency evinced in the widow's freedom to pursue her desires, especially her sexual desires. In the Victorian era, widows like Arabella Greenow emerge in novels as a potentially suspect category of renegade femininity, in part because of the long-standing comic and satirical literary associations that attend the figure of the "grieving" widow made glad by a new lover over her husband's dead body.

19. In the biography *Anthony Trollope* (New York: Knopf, 1993), Victoria Glendenning writes of Trollope's attitude toward mourning garments, "He hated too the ostentation of bereavement, particularly, widow's weeds—enveloping black crêpe garments which went rusty brown as the dye faded, and made women ugly" (177). In *Can You Forgive Her?*, the narrative voice seems to speak for Trollope, "Grief taken up because grief is supposed to be proper, is only one degree better than pretended grief. When one sees it, one cannot but think of the lady who asked her friend, in confidence, whether hot roast fowl and bread-sauce were compatible with the earliest state of weeds" (578). In *The Eustace Diamonds* (Oxford: Oxford University Press, 1873), Anthony Trollope's narrator correlates "widow-burning" or "suttee" *(sati)* in colonial India and the metropolitan widow's conspicuous mourning when he remarks that "Suttee propensities of all sorts, from burning alive down to bombazine and hideous forms of clothing, are becoming less and less popular among the nations" (193).

20. Anthony Trollope, *Barchester Towers* (London: Penguin, 1982); George Eliot, *Middlemarch* (New York: Norton, 2000). Citations appear in the text.

21. This epithet is reiterated throughout the novel. See pages 122, 149, 158, 177, 181, 370, 422, 468.

22. Taylor notes that, "After a year and a day, a widow could move on to the second stage of mourning. She was advised, however, not to do so on the very day she was entitled to, but, for the sake of good taste, to prolong the change for some time" (*Mourning Dress*, 141).

23. Here, as elsewhere, the trope of suttee/*sati* served Victorians as a vehicle for critique against practices and policies that victimized British women. Victorian writers found it particularly easy to draw comparisons between the condition of Indian widows and the practices of their English counterparts, especially the English widow's mourning clothing. Much has been written on *sati* as a justification for the British Imperial presence in India based on the intervention of "white men saving brown women from brown men": Gayatri Spivak, "Can the Subaltern Speak?" in *Marxism*

and the Interpretation of Culture, ed. Cary Nelson and Lawrence Grossberg (Urbana: University of Illinois Press, 1988), 297. See, for example, Lata Mani's "Contentious Traditions: The Debate on Sati in Colonial India," in Recasting Women: Essays in Indian Colonial History, ed. by KumKum Sangari and Sudesh Vaid (New Brunswick, N.J.: Rutgers University Press, 1990), 87–126, who describes representations of sati in both British colonialist and indigenous Indian texts. Also see Rajeswari Rajan, "Representing Sati: Continuities and Discontinuities," in Death and Representation, ed. Sarah Webster Goodwin and Elisabeth Bronfen (Baltimore: Johns Hopkins University Press, 1993), 285–311. For a discussion of the circulation of sati/suttee as a trope in Victorian Britain, see Sophie Gilmartin, "The Sati, the Bride, and the Widow: Sacrificial Woman in the Nineteenth Century," Victorian Literature and Culture 25 (1997): 141–58.

24. Stephen Collins discusses the disapprobation expressed during the sixteenth century and through to the nineteenth toward the remarrying widow and the widely held social expectations that a widow serve as an "animated gravestone" in "'A Kind of Lawful Adultery': English Attitudes to the Remarriage of Widows, 1550–1800," in The Changing Face of Death: Historical Accounts of Death and Disposal, ed. Peter C. Jupp and Glennys Howarth (London: Macmillan, 1997), 39.

25. See Clair Hughes, "'Mind and Millinery': Middlemarch," in Dressed in Fiction (Oxford: Berg, 2006), 89–114.

26. Lucie Heaton Armstrong, "On Widow's Mourning," Woman's Signal 5, no. 128 (1896): 378.

6

CLOTHING THE MARMOREAN FLOCK
SARTORIAL HISTORICISM AND THE MARBLE FAUN

Bruno Monfort

In the first half of chapter 14 of *The Marble Faun*, the topic of clothes and fashion turns up in the course of a discussion about the art of sculpture.[1] In a seemingly lighthearted, spirited, and rather flippant conversation, the sculptor Kenyon faces Miriam, the "dark lady" of the novel who ultimately will bear a heavy share of responsibility for the murder of the "model" committed by Donatello. This independent woman makes original work and paints figures of murderous women (Jael, Judith, Salome, Beatrice Cenci, and Charlotte Corday) who dispose of powerful men: "Over and over again there was the idea of woman acting the part of a revengeful mischief towards man" (*MF* 44). At this stage, she has come to Kenyon's studio for sympathy and counsel (as we understand from the previous chapter), but somehow, after seeing the new statue of Cleopatra Kenyon unveils for her, she realizes Kenyon's fascination with the dark energies of womanhood and reluctantly comes to recognize herself as the embodiment of them. Kenyon's Cleopatra is burning with repressed desire, "fierce, voluptuous, passionate, tender, wicked, terrible and full of poisonous and rapturous enchantment," "like a tigress," "cruel as fire," and capable of "lighting a tropic fire" (*MF* 127, 126) in the hearts of men. Miriam leads or, more accurately, manipulates Kenyon into unwittingly confessing that she could easily stand as the living counterpart to his Cleopatra. She more or less forces Kenyon to acknowledge that Hilda clearly cannot fit the description: this too ethereal and innocent creature is consistently associated with doves and, though born in the homeland of the Puritans, abdicates her culture and devotes herself to a private cult of the Virgin in Catholic Rome. Miriam waxes alarmingly passionate; as a result, Kenyon resists her repeatedly asserted desire to have him hear her confession of the burning secret in her heart. She rightly perceives or interprets Kenyon's embarrassment as reluctance. This is the evidence she needs: Kenyon's expressed willingness to hear her confession is the best reason for never confessing. To a certain extent Kenyon seems aware of being caught in a double bind as the narrator clearly privileges Kenyon's point of view and does not provide any insight into Miriam's. Kenyon's sincerity, his genuine readiness to hear her story, thus seems bound to be misinterpreted by Miriam. Nonetheless, the narrator provides a ready-made reading of the events he reports that cannot be fully trusted. The narrator's account of Kenyon's silent debate with himself is too analytic, too involved in the details of Kenyon's mental process calculating his moves, and may be unfair, prejudiced in favor of Kenyon. What the narrator's discourse says is not what it shows, and possibly means. This gap reveals that Kenyon is in effect once or twice removed from the unmediated sympathy his words proclaim, and therefore Miriam has been right not to trust him. The narrator's weakness becomes apparent when he notes that Kenyon has finally been ovecome by genuine emotion. On this particular occasion, no insight into Kenyon's thought process is required. Ironically, the narrator's straightforward statement comes too late: Miriam abruptly rejects Kenyon's proffered, and this time spontaneous, sympathy, flatly denying that she has any affinities with his Cleopatra. In effect, she abandons Kenyon to Hilda and relinquishes him as a friend. She has failed to bridge "the voiceless gulf" separating her from Kenyon and Hilda (*MF* 113).

This passage is a rare instance in a Hawthorne text in which clothes are debated at some length, though rather sarcastically. Not Miriam's clothes, but Cleopatra's. Not an article of fashion, but the idea of clothes and their significance and import for the relationship between art and life. As a rule, when clothes and fashion are mentioned in this novel and in other novels by Hawthorne, it is not just *"pour parler chiffons"* but with rather oblique purposes and most frequently in relation to statues and sculptures and also, which is less surprising, in relation to flesh-and-blood women. In other words, Hawthorne's novels or stories offer very few descriptions of clothes.[2]

The Blithedale Romance would be a case in point. On several occasions, such as when Zenobia visits Coverdale in his sick-chamber at Blithedale, he observes that she is a particularly gorgeous and magnificent woman with a new flower in her hair. Coverdale is typically more interested in the general effect of her person and presence than in the details of her clothes. However much these clothes may contribute to her gorgeousness, they are mentioned only in passing.[3] We are informed that she has a fan, a dress of "homely simplicity," but that is about all (*BR* 69). We are also duly informed by Coverdale that Zenobia is an extremely wealthy woman whose money, he suspects, is coveted by Hollingsworth. But few conclusions are derived by Coverdale from his voyeuristic bouts of observation. Yet clothing, as we know, is extremely informative. The social messages relayed by clothing and accessories, by the shape, length, or color of a dress, can involve social status, occupation, ethnic and religious affiliations, marital status, and sexual availability. Clothing and ornament declare membership in society, or proclaim dissent from cultural norms and mainstream beliefs. When they are articles of fashion, they also typify the wearer's belonging to a particular class in a period of history; they may also betray the wearer's personality.

In these capacities, however, clothes and fashion are conspicuously absent from Hawthorne's novels. As a proclaimed antirealist, Hawthorne showed little interested in what clothes might mean socially or in what kind of attraction his characters might feel for them and what attention they might devote to clothes. There are exceptions, always significant and complex, as in the episode just before the recovery of Zenobia's dead body in *The Blithedale Romance*. One of Zenobia's shoes, embedded in the mud of the river bank, is picked up by Silas Foster who identifies it with almost forensic precision: "There's a kid shoe that never was made on a Yankee last," he oberves. "I know enough of a shoemaker's craft to tell that. French manufacture and see what a high instep!—and how evenly she trod in it! There never was a woman that stept handsomer in her shoes than Zenobia did!" Foster then moves on to address Hollingsworth and offers the shoe for him to keep, but he demurs and Coverdale steps forward to claim it: "I dabbled it in the water to rinse off the mud, and have kept it ever since" (*BR* 207). As a rule, Zenobia's elegant clothes are never referred to at any great length though they are repeatedly said by Coverdale to enhance her charm and beauty, an opinion he expresses in characteristically negative terms: "The homely simplicity of her dress could not conceal, nor scarcely diminish, the queenliness of her presence" (*BR* 69). Coverdale, a recognizable, though not self-confessed, voyeur, has never focused on the specifics of Zenobia's vesture. His eagerness and embarassment in the surprising episode of the shoe, as Foster's detective-like reaction indicates, is that as a tell-tale article it reveals too much about Zenobia, makes her too real, belonging reductively to the material world as a wearer and bearer of clothes, and too much of an individual, with a unique character that inevitably has weaknesses and limitations. Keeping the shoe to himself, he preserves her aura in a fetishistic move.

This episode shows that there are many (and, in Coverdale's appreciation, certainly too many) connections between clothes and what they reveal about rank or character. Realist literature relies heavily on clothes. In works by Hawthorne's contemporary Charles Dickens, clothes (boots, dresses, and an impressive array of such articles) are ubiquitous. In *Great Expectations,* the lawyer Jaggers lives surrounded by his stock of boots, and Miss Havisham wears only one of two shoes from the pair that goes with her withered bridal dress, while the other lies unused on her dressing table; the bridal dress itself is compared to "grave-clothes," and "the long veil so like a shroud."[4] In 1851, Hawthorne was reading *David Copperfield* to his children during the long winter evenings at Lenox, and as Millicent Bell reminds us in *Hawthorne and the Real,* he had just finished *The House of the Seven Gables,* a work of Dickensian mingling of the grotesque with social fact though "without Dickens's plenitude of reference."[5] Clearly clothes are socially accepted bearers of meanings and objects of attention in the world of the Victorian novelists Hawthorne admired most, Dickens, William Thackeray, or even Anthony Trollope.

Hawthorne's neglect of the material presence and social/individual significance of clothes would thus be related to his constant claim that he aimed to escape the American insistence upon actuality and create a so-called "fairy precinct, where actualities are not terribly insisted upon as they are or must be in America."[6] I do not, however, take it for granted that Hawthorne was the hopeless idealist he would like to make himself out to be. His many self-descriptions as remote from common reality are misleading, if not plain disingenuous. Hawthorne had his own way of dealing with the actualities of the moment, their disfiguring and refiguring being a major concern for him as an artist. He deals with the transformative capacity of art ("reality" into art, one art into another, art into reality) including his own art of writing; the original title of *The Marble Faun* was "The Transformation." The discussion we are dealing with in *The Marble Faun* revolves around the question of how an emotion (Kenyon's, Miriam's) can be transformed into a statue, or vice versa, just as the clay from the Tiber had been changed into a woman or rather, as Hawthorne writes: "In a word, all Cleopatra . . . was kneaded into what, only a week or two before, had been a lump of wet clay from the Tiber" (*MF* 127).[7]

"Was kneaded into" and not, as might be expected, "was kneaded from." The relevant point here is not that the clay serves as the material out of which artifacts are made, but instead an idea comes into such material artifacts (sculptures) and operates as the shaping force, the ultimate reality they express beyond their physical nature and appearance. Does this imply that the idea is preexistent and therefore more real than its material embodiment? There is a degree of inconsistency, even incoherence, in the sentence; one might read the phrase as a deliberate anacoluthon. But why would the narrator emphasize the materiality of the artifact if he endorses an idealist conception of the work of art, which this highly unconventional turn of phrase seems to deny? The phrase seems to imply that the idea is constructed and shaped into/as clay, the form of which becomes the expression, however inadequate, of the idea. Here, however, notwithstanding the dialogism that makes it impossible to determine whether or to what extent Hawthorne endorses whatever his characters say, emphasis is clearly laid on the difference between idea as interpretation after the fact (the sculptor finishes a statue out of a block of marble and decides that it shows such and such a scene) and idea as preexisting concept or intention: "my statue is intended for Cleopatra," meaning that "Cleopatra," whoever or whatever she is, will take shape as this statue (*MF* 125). This might be related to, but should not be mistaken for, the ancient, idealist notion, rediscovered and developed in the Renaissance by Michaelangelo and others, that a statue exists beforehand within the block of marble and that the sculptor's work is to find and release it. Such a notion is clearly discussed and, simultaneously, undermined in the dialogue between Kenyon and Miriam and had already been criticized in Hawthorne's tale "Drowne's Wooden Image." The phrase "was kneaded into" is ambiguous in itself: it might refer to some preexisting or archetypal idea of Cleopatra, but it also draws attention to the contingency of the particular situation in which a given statue (which might as well be a nondescript effigy as the figure of any other character) comes to function as the enmarbled shape of a specific historical character, one that trails a heavy cloud of history behind her.

On several occasions in the course of the novel, Hawthorne mentions or alludes to the way in which a marble statue is finally "completed" after modeling a clay version of the statue as the first stage in a process (he refers to Bertel Thorwaldsen's dictum requiring this clay version). After the clay model comes the plaster cast, with the marble carving last. At this stage, the ideality of the idea "kneaded into" the statue must be balanced by the many references to the complicated process that started with the modeling by hand of a vile lump of clay, a clear indication that Hawthorne favors an expressive conception of art: once the process has been completed, the idea and its expression have necessarily become one but are clearly separate given how they came into being. The idea that consists in its expression in/as a work of art has by itself little or no tangible reality prior to its being actualized as a manu-factured (i.e., "hand-made") artifact; it becomes real when processed and materialized into the piece of artistic workmanship that provides its outward reality for the senses. The resulting artifact, or rather artwork, is

shaped initially by the hand of the sculptor, the outcome of a gradual fashioning that enables the idea to come home as it becomes indistinguishable from the material object it lets itself be shaped into or as. This process reasserts the (historical) contingency of the link between idea and (material) shape. The idea "in" the work will appear to have existed in and by itself prior to the work only after the work has been succesfully completed. Achieving the idea is thus heavily bound to the material completion of the work. The conception that the idea is preexistent to whatever material shape it happens to assume at a given time should be understood as the semiotic aftereffect of the existence of a work of art that itself is intended for the idea it is expected to accomodate. Intended, however, need not be construed as referring to the work as the result of an agent's deliberate action. Actually, the shape the idea is likely to receive is unpredictable, cannot be foreseen from examining the idea itself. The idea is an uncertain or indeterminate notion before the material form it receives shapes it into existence. It becomes intelligible when made fully historical and circumstantial, when the indefinite material substratum intended for it reaches the stage at which the process of its completion demands that it should acquire the meaning without which it could not be received as complete. Meanings come to objects socially or historically or both because there are objects that stand in need of meanings to function as artworks, that is, as possibilities of an experience that would not exist without them.

The existence of whatever qualifies as a work of art, in need of significance, is the precondition for the idea to emerge as something existing on its own in a different sphere beyond the work of art that is assumed somehow to originate in it. Thus the idea of Cleopatra as Queen of Ancient Egypt cannot possibly emerge as pure art in a history-conscious (con)text. She does not rise from the remote days of ancient Egypt. The Egyptian-ness of the statue is made manifest through her clothes, reconstructed in a thoroughly un-Egyptian way to appear Egyptian to a culturally alienated eye: "She was dressed from head to foot in a costume, minutely and scrupulously studied from that of ancient Egypt, as revealed by the strange sculpture of that country" (*MF* 125). These clothes have significance for the present, as indices of the character's historical remote-

FIGURE 6.1 William Wetmore Story (1819–95), *Cleopatra*, modeled 1858, carved 1860. Marble on polychrome wood platform. 55 × 24 × 48 in. (139.7 × 61 × 121.9 cm). Gift of Mr. and Mrs. Henry M. Bateman. Los Angeles County Museum of Art. Copyright 2012 Museum Associates/ LACMA. Licensed by Art Resource, NY.

ness. This embarasses the narrator who refrains from declaring his embarassment, though the mildly skeptical tone with which he refers to the statue's "costume" indicates its unconvincing presentation: a clutter of details does not make a genuine whole. He ascribes the (mostly historical) strangeness of the sculpture to the fact that it comes from "that country," thus hinting at the predominant orientalism, a modern bias that accompanies things Egyptian. Even "from head to foot" is a muted indication of the narrator's sense that the costume's presence is excessive, and not only signals it as overbearing but suggests that there are advantages to nudity, or nakedness, when women are supposed to be conveyors of meaning.

The display of period clothing helps signify the pastness of the past; the clothes serve to reconstruct a degree of pastness for the present eye, but their presence also expresses the impossibility of experiencing as truly present the historical past when flesh-and-blood Cleopatra lived. In this respect, Cleopatra is indeed an idea depending on the historical significance of her clothing, which authorizes the spectator to see her in historical/historicist terms but eliminates the necessity for actual reconstruction: "the special epoch of her history you must make out for yourself" (MF 125). Cleopatra, as she stands clothed in Egyptian garb, sufficiently (and literally!) suits the needs of the modern age that requires only a bit of the antique to make the statue appear not too modern. A modicum of archaism leaves room for imagining what ancient Egypt may have been like, as is known from other sources (excavations, monuments, remains, and texts). Clearly, whatever historical relevance the statue carries with it as an artifact relates equally if not more to its presence in the present moment before the spectator's eye than to its being a metonym for the context of ancient Egypt. An experiment in sartorial historicism enables the spectator to experience the past as reality, as bodied forth in clothes worn by a woman. Women have always worn the fashionable clothes of their times, even though the wearing of clothes is in itself timeless; they are thus not really a matter for history. For the illusion of a presence to be complete, for the statue to be legitimately referred to as "she" and not "it," the perception of the statue should reach a degree of specificity, of individuality, beyond the historical and the general: the text also purports to explain how the spectator comes to cancel out the imaginary aspect of his "making out," and the extent to which the reader can still share in the illusion of presence that is being deconstructed for him as the narrator tells the lengthy, entangled tale of how it came into existence. For this contorted purpose, and at this stage, the statue must, and does, become a woman, or a woman has become the statue.

Clothes play an ambiguous part not for living women with whom Hawthorne is barely concerned but for women as they stand for figures of the ideal and the sublime: clothes enable the spectator to historicize the figure that wears them. Such historicizing is not without its problems and limitations as it contradicts the idealization imposed upon women as a result of the process in which sculpture, and in particular neoclassical sculpture in the wake of Johannes Winckelmann (a major exponent of the theory), Antonio Canova, and Bertel Thorwaldsen, represents women in the nude as marble statues.[8] Hawthorne tends to do the opposite, reversing the direction of the Pygmalion myth in which inanimate matter is invested with the appearance of life. Hawthorne invokes what he calls "the Pygmalion problem": "namely that sculpture which successfully imitates flesh excites desire, and is therefore morally suspect."[9]

In the case of Kenyon's Cleopatra, clothes complicate the picture. The public idea of beauty prevailing at the time implies that, as a precondition for beauty to come alive in the sculpted image of a woman, this figure should not be recognizable as a particular woman or as belonging to a particular age, time, or period. Nude figures are at once exposed and dehistoricized. Hence the chaste nudity of the ideal woman in neoclassical sculpture, sublimated by or into the idealized whiteness of her marble image. However much she may look like a woman, her cold whiteness guarantees that she does not imitate the plump, pink softness of incarnate flesh, even when she stands nude. Through the contemplation of such discarnate beauty as statues, the spectator is led into the contemplation of the idea of beauty; these sculpted images of nude women thus retain their purity. Hawthorne's two characters, Miriam and Kenyon, sarcastically refer to this neoclassical ideal of purity, and that it was uncritically accepted by almost everyone at the time, in the course of their spirited, humorous discussion. The novelist reveals a cultural situation in which nudity is allowed for women provided such women are statues; exposed buttocks and breasts created or contemplated in the cold whiteness of Carrara marble exempt the artist and the spectator from the reprobation they would incur if they touched them or gazed at them in the flesh, especially in public.

Art historians generally trace the invention of what is called the "moral nude" in America (I borrow the phrase from Robert Hughes) to the exhibition of Hiram Powers's *Greek Slave* in 1844, "an adapted copy of The Uffizi's Medici Venus, with some chains on her wrists as a *cache-sexe*." This immensely popular statue of a demure young woman supposedly "divested of clothes by the impious and lustful Turks who put her on the auction block" (as Powers explained in a pamphlet that accompanied the exhibition) elicited no end of comments on how chaste and virtuous she stood though exposed to the gaze of crowds fully clothed and eminently Victorian, both male and female.[10] Innumerable poems appeared including one by Elizabeth Barrett Browning; many others, by less distinguished, anonymous scribblers, were also published in periodicals.

One of the major points raised by Hawthorne's two protagonists in the course of their sprightly conversation is that the decided approval of "moral nudity" vindicates a historical fallacy of the kind denounced by Charles Baudelaire in "The Painter of Modern Life": by suppressing clothes and references to clothing in the arts one ends up falsifying indications by which the art of one particular age coincides with itself, and it then fails to authenticate itself in representations of whatever is most elusive and transient, especially fashion.[11] One interesting paradox is underscored by Miriam when she says that "Now-a-days people are as good as born in their clothes, and there is practically not a nude human being in existence" (*MF* 123): whereas clothes materially hide nudity, or rather nakedness, with symbolic and social meanings attached, the nudity of statues serves not so much to suggest the Ideal of Beauty as to hide the inevitability of clothes as a social marker and a historical phenomenon. Joy Kasson remarks, apropos Powers's statue, about an engraving of the period, on the "striking contrast between the fussily overdressed Victorians gazing in fascination" and what she describes as "the uncluttered white marble nude."[12] Nakedness in statues eludes modernity, even as the making of modern nudes involves a venal, quasi-pornographic relationship between artist and model.

The Victorians extolled ideal nudity and invented the moral or holy nude. But they did not approve of fashion because of the necessary wearing of clothes for decency; comfort was only too often waylaid from such worthy purposes by frivolity. Hundreds of pamphlets, poems, and magazine and newspaper articles to say nothing of whole books inveighed against the profligacy of women who overspent on crinolines and bonnets. The crinoline itself was an object of derision because of its size and cost: fashion-conscious women were repeatedly accused, especially during the financial panic of 1857, of causing the ruin of their husbands and of the country because of their extravagant spending on crinolines (some of them imported at great cost) and other such superfluities.[13] Wearing crinolines had detrimental moral effects. In one poem, entitled "Nothing to wear" and originally published in *Harper's* in 1857, the incriminated belle persistently complains that she has "nothing to wear" and is sarcastically compared to the exemplary Powers statue to expose her hyperbolic pretensions and complaints.[14]

The echoes of these daily polemics are in general extremely muted in Hawthorne's texts, and in this one in particular where, like Baudelaire, Hawthorne's characters deride the jejune principles of neoclassical aesthetics while he says little on the moral or financial implications of clothing. Unlike Baudelaire, however, Hawthorne does not trust, preach, support, or in any way cultivate modernity. He will not endorse the chroniclers of the manners and fashions of his age. Whenever Hawthorne mentions period clothing, he seems to imply that clothes are not a reliable sign that any era ever really coincided with itself; in fact, any period of history, including the current one, creates for itself a whole array of spurious traditional or modern clothing.

Thus the way Cleopatra is dressed is a major indicator of where she comes from, to which period and historical context she is to be referred. Yet this indicator, though required to make a credible deidealized Cleopatra, is extremely misleading because it is not as an Egyptian Queen of long ago that she is appreciated and even appropriated by Miriam and Kenyon: "so that Cleopatra sat attired in a garb proper to her historic and queenly state, as a Daughter of the Ptolemies, and yet such as the beautiful woman would have put on, as best adapted to heighten the magnificence of her charms" (*MF* 126). The term "garb" is not used innocently here. It suggests the display of period clothing of a distinctive style worn for a particular occasion. Hawthorne, however, uses the same word on several other occasions in the novel to suggest that clothes worn by someone are always, or seem to be, naturally suited to the occasion yet are the result of calculation or a deliberate imposition. Such is the case with the model when he first appears: "The stranger was of exceedingly picturesque and even melodramatic aspect. He was clad in a voluminous cloak . . . still commonly worn by the peasants of the Roman Campagna. In this garb, they look like antique Satyrs" (*MF* 30). Penitents in public ceremonies wear a so-called "penitential garb" (*MF* 392), and even the apparently innocent contadinas are "costume[d]" in their peasant clothes as they dance with Donatello and the rest (*MF* 87). The word "clothes," more plain and neutral, is used in the novel almost exclusively as a metaphor in connection with Hilda's impossibly remote purity, for instance in the phrase "that white wisdom which clothes you as a celestial garment" to indicate not so much an uncompromising virtue as a fairly general freedom from the taint of original sin (*MF* 460–61). "Garb," by contrast, seems to be used almost systematically whenever clothes indicate rank or office, or more generally the outward or external appearance of the person concerned.[15]

Cleopatra's "garb," however, is not incompatible with the passion and fire that Miriam (who would rather not have discovered herself as, potentially, Cleopatra's fleshly counterpart) detects in the statue and that lies beyond the sculptor's intention and power to control, as he himself acknowledges: "But I know not how it came about at last" (*MF* 127). In other words, it is not as a reenactment of the past, or of what used to be present in the past, that the clay statue addresses Miriam and the reader/spectator. The statue draws its *energeia,* its lifelikeness, from a source beyond its displayed historicism. Imitating clothing typical of a given period or portraying individual features, what they may have been like at the time or may be like at the present moment, contributes little to lifelikeness, which originates not in material similarity or fleshly resemblance but in the fire of passion it simultaneously creates and expresses for the sculptor ("I kindled a great fire," *MF* 127) and for the spectator past and present, real or imaginary: "kindle a tropic fire in the cold eyes of Octavius" (*MF* 126). This "tropic fire" turns the not yet enmarbled clay statue into a trope of *energeia;* hence the ubiquitous fire metaphor, which, being both metaphoric and commonplace, simultaneously expresses and represses the consuming eroticism it seeks to communicate.

The statue, however, becomes the vehicle not just of meaning but for some radical significance it was not intended or simply expected to bear and that does communicate itself, but only to those (characters or readers) who are in a position to feel and experience it. The effect of the "tropic fire" is a matter of pragmatic experience and not of understanding or contemplation, a matter not of aesthetic detachment and confrontation but of passionate involvement with the object concerned. It is irrelevant to determine whether Miriam refers to Kenyon's statue as object or to a living woman when she cries out "What a woman is this?" (*MF* 127). The tropic energy asserts itself as the motive force that precipitates the transformation of the statue into something that as an object is lifeless and as a trope is lifelike, but object and trope cannot be disentangled, only distinguished. The statue's clothes seem to locate her in and confine her to a particular era, as the partly imaginary portrait of a Queen of Ancient Egypt, but her tropic energy will not be contained by the tentative historicizing that her archaeologically reconstructed costume places on her.

The statue's clothes tend to contextualize it and re-create the distance that the trope strives to abolish. For this reason, as always in Hawthorne's texts, there is minimal description: the existence of clothes is always asserted as an indicator of some degree of reality (no Ideal Woman here), yet no actual description of these clothes or specification of what they consisted in is ever provided: the reader is simply referred by the text to what he knows or what one knows in general from archaeological evidence, or what one may have heard or read about the way an Egyptian Queen is or should be dressed to appear as an Egyptian Queen, who is duty bound to sit dignified in flowing draperies. Because allusion perpetually displaces description, readers are inevitably tempted to compare Kenyon's Cleopatra to a known object, namely William Wetmore Story's statue of Cleopatra. Hawthorne's preface vindicates this reading; let me insist on this: the text itself refrains not only from describing the clothes in any detail but also from validating any correspondence between what it refers to, or would seem to refer to, and such a known object. Description implies that one relies on the capacity of language to give the reader the impression of reality he would have if and when confronted with an object. Hawthorne's readers are positioned at one remove, are not supposed to be confronted with an object, but with a character's experience of an object. Any reference to the materiality of this object has thus already been displaced and relocated in language and as a substitute for language. Yet this substitution and relocation needs accounting, and only through language can this occur.

In *The Marble Faun,* language thus functions as both a tool and a hindrance. The relevant notion here is that of the statue as object, the artifact, as the dominant trope. Therefore, the mode in which such a trope operates is not purely inscribed in linguistically performed operations: language in its capacity as an instrument of reference and communication is regarded here, by Miriam, as a most inadequate form of expression, with little power to give shape to what, nonetheless, would otherwise remain shapeless and ineffable. Miriam visits Kenyon to bridge what she calls a "voiceless gulf" and, quite logically, will not trust Kenyon when he invites her to speak. She will not trust words. In this context, the statue/woman is not a mere provider of historical meaning; it functions for her as an expression of passion that purely verbal confession would destroy along with that tropic force ("fire") that animates the statue for her. During the conversation, the clay lump turned Cleopatra thus undergoes a further transformation: the verbal account of the encounter between characters is mediated by the statue and conveys the ineffability of a "tropic" experience different than, but building itself into, the verbal transactions that the existence of the statue has occasioned. This Cleopatra can be referred to both as an inanimate object and as an intimate force (the "tropic" power) beyond the powers of language to express and owes part of its lifelikeness to the linguistic exchanges about it, conveying feelings and affects that are fortunately unexpressed through "troping" in the impossible task of fully expressing them. Miriam, who distrusts mere words, still calls upon words in their "tropic" capacity, little realizing her expectations are too high and the unreliablity of words unhinges her troping: for all purposes beyond well-defined, referential communication, language is both the doing and undoing of her meaning.

Hawthorne, speaking in his own voice, seems to give priority to the referential power of language: we could justifiably conclude from his belated and oblique confession in his "Preface" to *The Marble Faun* that he took his idea of Kenyon's Cleopatra from a statue by the American sculptor William Wetmore Story, the son of a U.S. Supreme Court justice. He originally befriended Story in Salem and met him again while staying in Rome. Julian Hawthorne, in his account of one encounter between his father and Story, describes what the statue or at least one of its versions possibly owes to Hawthorne's discussion of "deep matters" with the sculptor.[16] What Julian Hawthorne barely alludes to, however, is the fact that Hawthorne might also owe something to Story: *Cleopatra* was originally a poem by Story who is remembered today only, if at all, as a sculptor.[17] His scribed "Cleopatra" is lascivious, decadent, depraved, a classic figure of Orientalism—exotic, highly seductive, highly animalistic (here Hawthorne may have found his conception of Cleopatra as a tigress), an altogether dangerous woman.

Hawthorne did not simply plagiarize Story's poem, quite the opposite. He makes Miriam experience what the poem merely reconstructs by staging Cleopatra as a speaker (Story's poem is in fact a dramatic monologue, overly theatricalized and awkwardly modeled on the formula of Robert Browning's poems). In Hawthorne's novel, Miriam, not the reader, is confronted with the statue, and the reader is thereby made to share indirectly in whatever he can construe of her experience (fictional but not fictive) of this object. The reader thus sees Miriam confronting the full force of the same "tropic fire" that Mark Antony felt, latent in the still moist clay of the statue. In Hawthorne's quite sophisticated narrative formula, no attempt is made to let the reader see or hear Cleopatra directly; she does not speak in the overdone though conventional diction of Story's poem, which constructs a venomously erotic but artificial and unconvincing figure of

Cleopatra. Moreover, Hawthorne has chosen to focus on the moment when the statue is not yet marble but is no longer the vile, formless lump of clay from the river. It has not yet become the marble woman; it has not yet withdrawn into the solid whiteness of the marble, to become one of those rather commonplace neoclassical statues. With patronizing amusement, and characteristic insight, Henry James astutely referred to those brought to fastidious completion by too many sculptors, in his 1903 book about William Wetmore Story, as a "white marmorean flock" running around over the seven hills of Rome.[18]

Kenyon's Cleopatra is clearly not one of the flock because she is not yet the marble queen in flowing draperies that took definite shape under Story's chisel and today stands in the halls of the Los Angeles County Museum of Art. But this is the finished piece, and in *The Marble Faun* Cleopatra is not yet hardened into that marble effigy. Kenyon's woman-statue is kept moist and available under a veil: "My new statue! . . . Here it is under this veil!" (*MR* 123, 125). Yet another veiled lady, then, who unlike Priscilla in *The Blithedale Romance* is, fortunately, not flesh and blood though far more erotically charged. Kenyon's and Miriam's Cleopatra turns out to be neither a definite object nor a definite person nor does she ultimately refer to any definite historical period despite clothing indications to the contrary. Neither does she, for this reason, originate in contemporary American culture and its Egyptomania: she is designed by Hawthorne to be ideally readable as something more or other than a cultural construction because she is both abstract object and almost palpable trope, not quite finished, a still uncompleted artifact not trailing a history of its own and the whole history of its age behind it (as Story's *Cleopatra* had).

When it signifies a return to reality, such a (critical) gesture as lifting the veil generally disappoints; what or whom you find under the veil is inevitably a letdown. In *The Blithedale Romance*, Priscilla is a spurious clairvoyant exhibited to audiences eager for entertainment and public performance.[19] In *The Marble Faun*, things are different; the lifted veil is demystified but not the object underneath it: "He drew away the cloth, that had served to keep the moisture of the clay model from being exhaled" (*MF* 126). The veil, become plain "cloth" with a very practical use, is disenchanted and loses its power of fascination when drawn away. Kenyon's gesture is undramatic indicating that the not yet enmarbled queen under it should, if only briefly, retain for Miriam and for us the fullness of its tropic power.

1. Page references are to Nathaniel Hawthorne, *The Marble Faun,* with an introduction and notes by Richard Brodhead (New York: Penguin, 1990). Cited as *MF* followed by page number.

2. Charles Paul de Kock, *La Jolie Fille du Faubourg,* in *Oeuvres Complètes,* vol. 4 (Paris: Gand, 1841), 42.

3. Page references are to Nathaniel Hawthorne, *The Blithedale Romance,* ed. William E. Cain (Boston: Bedford Books/St. Martin's Press, 1996). Cited as *BR* followed by page number.

4. Charles Dickens, *Great Expectations* (London: Wordsworth Classics, 2000), 332, 79, 51.

5. Millicent Bell, *Hawthorne and the Real* (Columbus: Ohio State University Press, 2005), 2.

6. Hawthorne, "Preface," *MF,* 3.

7. This discussion between the protagonists is obviously related to a passage in Nathaniel Hawthorne, *The French and Italian Notebooks,* ed. Thomas Woodson, Centenary Edition 14 (Columbus: Ohio State University Press, 1980). Cited as *FIN* followed by page number. On February 14, 1858, Hawthorne was in Rome visiting the studio of the American sculptor William Wetmore Story and saw a statue of Cleopatra in its early stages: "The statue of Cleopatra, now only fourteen days advanced in the clay . . . is a grand subject, and he appears to be conceiving it with depth and power, and working it out with adequate skill. He certainly is sensible of something deeper in his art than merely to make beautiful nudities and baptize them by classic names. By the by, he told us several queer stories about American visitors to his studio; one of them, after long inspecting Cleopatra (into which he has put all possible characteristics of her time and nation and her own individuality) asked 'Have you baptized your statue yet?' as if the sculptor were waiting till his statue were finished before he chose the subject of it; as, indeed, I should think many sculptors do" (*FIN* 73). A similar anecdote about a statue of the sculptor's father is mentioned later on. The discussion of this point in the fictive context of *MF* complicates the sculptor's sense of a self-evident identity for

"Cleopatra," and explores barely apparent misgivings that crop up in Hawthorne's account of his visit to Story's studio.

8. About this, see the relevant passage in *FIN*. Following a conversation with the British sculptor John Gibson, on March 14, 1858, Hawthorne dismisses most of the other sculptors he met in Rome because, as it appears, Gibson has been particularly eloquent about his own art, whereas the others were virtually mute; the passage is worth quoting at length: "The sculptors especially, I suspect, are of the stone-mason and figure-head carver fraternity. They appear to be a jovial set of people but without education, refinement, poetic feeling. . . . Possibly they can only express themselves in their own art, and what poets say in words they must say in marble. If so, I will try to know them better in their sculptures, of which I have as yet seen nothing. I heard nothing worth remembering or repeating from anybody's lips, except the following which is attributed to Thorwaldsen —'The Clay is the Life; the Plaster is the Death; and the Marble is the Resurrection.' The perfect truth of these analogies can only be estimated by observing a piece of sculpture in its three stages" (*FIN* 132–33). Even before he has seen any of their works, Hawthorne is disappointed by a host of (mostly American) sculptors unable to discuss their art. To him, artistic expression is incomplete if it does not incorporate (meta-artistic) verbal transactions at some stage in the process of conception. Hawthorne turns out to be mildly ironic toward Gibson's self-assertive disquisitions but measures Gibson's merit and intellectual sophistication against the American sculptors' incapacity to comment even wrongly on their art; this is consonant with his point in *MF*, which seems to be that the ultimate ineffability of the art experience in sculpture is precisely what needs to be verbalized if sculptures are to cross the border from mere objecthood into the realm of human significance. This passage throws retrospective light on some of the more cryptic aspects of "Drowne's Wooden Image" and prospective light on Hawthorne's lifelong interest in the pattern of the Pygmalion myth, in which a statue assumes life.

9. Gabrielle Gopinath, "Harriet Hosmer and the Feminine Sublime," *Oxford Art Journal* 28, no. 1 (2005): 61. Discussing the "Pygmalion problem" in Hawthorne's texts would involve reexamining the notions of literary and artistic creation developed by Hawthorne in his handling (declared and undeclared) of the myth and narrative (originally by Ovid) and in a variety of texts. The sheer quantity of critical literature on the subject of Pygmalion should probably serve as an index of the complexity of the issues involved in the continued presence of the myth in nineteenth-century art and literature, where it is ubiquitous; among major studies are Andreas Blühm, *Pygmalion: Die Ikono-*

graphie eines Künstlermythos zwischen 1500 und 1900 (Frankfurt am Main: Peter Lang, 1988); Essaka Joshua, *Pygmalion and Galatea: The History of a Narrative in English Literature* (Aldershot: Ashgate, 2001); Kenneth Gross, *The Dream of the Moving Statue* (Ithaca, N.Y.: Cornell University Press, 1992); J. Hillis Miller, *Versions of Pygmalion* (Cambridge, Mass.: Harvard University Press, 1990); Gerhard Neumann and Mathias Mayer, eds., *Pygmalion: Die Geschichte eines Mythos in der abendländisches Kultur* (Freiburg im Breisgau: Rombach, 1997); Victor Stoichita, *The Pygmalion Effect: From Ovid to Hitchcock*, trans. Alison Anderson (Chicago: University of Chicago Press, 2008). More specific studies are limited to aspects of the myth and its aftermath: Douglas F. Bauer, "The Function of Pygmalion in the *Metamorphoses* of Ovid," *Transactions of the American Philological Association* 93 (1962): 1–21; Sally R. Davis, "Bringing Ovid into the AP Latin Classroom: Pygmalion," *Classical Journal* 90, no. 3 (1995): 273–78; John Elsner and Alison R. Sharrock, "Re-viewing Pygmalion," *Ramus* 20 (1991): 149–53 (text and translation of *Metamorphoses* 10.243–97, a major classic source); John Elsner, "Visual Mimesis and the Myth of the Real: Ovid's Pygmalion as Viewer," *Ramus* 20 (1991): 154–69; Rosemary Lloyd, "Lire la pierre: Pouvoir politique et sexuel dans la sculpture littéraire du XIXè siècle," *Nineteenth Century French Studies* 35, no. 1 (Fall 2006): 151–65; Alison R. Sharrock, "Womanufacture," *Journal of Roman Studies* 81 (1991): 36–49. For an anthology of texts with an entire section devoted to Pygmalion, see Geoffrey Miles, *Classical Mythology in English Literature* (London: Routledge, 1999).

10. Robert Hughes, *American Visions: The Epic History of Art in America* (New York: Knopf; London: Harvill, 1997), 217–18. Despite Hughes's insistence on the statue's exhibition of spurious modesty to titillate lustful propensities in ogling crowds of Victorian (male) viewers, it may be worth remarking that the nudity of the statue was supposed to be subservient to its idea or "moral message," a fact duly recorded in Elizabeth Barrett Browning's poem on the subject:

> They say Ideal Beauty cannot enter
> The house of anguish. On the threshold stands
> An alien Image with the shackled hands,
> Called the Greek Slave: as if the sculptor meant her,
> (That passionless perfection which he lent her,
> Shadowed, not darkened, where the sill expands)
> To, so, confront men's crimes in different lands,

With man's ideal sense. Pierce to the centre,

Art's fiery finger! — and break up erelong

The serfdom of this world! Appeal, fair stone,

From God's pure heights of beauty, against man's wrong!

Catch up in thy divine face, not alone

East griefs but west, — and strike and shame the strong,

By thunders of white silence, overthrown!

> (*Poetical Works*, 14th ed. (London: Smith, Elder, 1886), 2:302)

Not the figure's nakedness but the impassive acquiescence of the girl as she stands in shackles requires explanation; the (female) poet refuses to endorse both the latent impurity of exhibited flesh and the theory of the pure ideality of art; to her, the statue embodies the condemnation of slavery everywhere. What the poem establishes is that the statue's naked weakness (and weak it is in more ways than one!) is to be rehistoricized for a full appreciation of its effect. The very existence of the poem, and its assertive tone as well, would seem to indicate that it was indeed necessary to write such a poem to fully reveal the "thunders of white silence" in Powers's statue. Browning's text functions as a corrective to contrary leanings in the viewers' minds: the ocular charm inherent in the spectacle of a naked woman may interact with the lure of female clarity and exhibited simplicity to lift the moral problem into the realm of ideality. The whiteness of the statue masks the reality that most slaves were black. The reactionary aesthetics of the statue deny the actuality of the problem it is designed to expose, paradoxically raising, as it leaves untouched, the problem of the compatibility between idea and vehicle.

11. See Charles Baudelaire, "Le peintre de la vie moderne," in *The Painter of Modern Life and Other Essays*, ed. and trans. Jonathan Mayne (London: Phaidon, 1964), 1–40. The essay originally appeared in *Le Figaro* on November 23 and 26 and December 3, 1863.

12. Joy Kasson, *Marble Queens and Captives: Women in Nineteenth Century American Sculpture* (New Haven, Conn.: Yale University Press, 1990), 46–72. The question of flesh-colored nude sculpture, as opposed to the ideally (i.e., safely deerotized) white stone bodies of the "marble queens," was much debated in the middle of the nineteenth century, with many discussions revolving around Royal Academician John Gibson's lifesize (in one of its versions) *Tinted Venus:* made of polychromed marble, it was called by one reviewer "a naked, impudent English woman." The

statue was exhibited along with other tinted statues at the International Exhibition of 1862 at South Kensington, London, in a specially designed "Greek" temple. Something of a Pygmalion himself, Gibson had become enamored of some of the statues, had kept them in his studio for several years before showing them, and would not part with them. See Alison Smith, *The Victorian Nude* (Manchester: Manchester University Press, 1996) and Smith, *Exposed: The Victorian Nude* (London: Tate Gallery; New York: Watson-Guptill, 2002). Conversely, actresses on the stage were not infrequently assimilated to sculptural images: looking like living statues increased their popularity; see Gail Marshall, *Actresses on the Victorian Stage: Feminine Performance and the Galatea Myth* (Cambridge: Cambridge University Press, 1998). For a broader context on the subject of nineteenth-century colored sculpture, see Andreas Blühm, ed., *The Colour of Sculpture, 1840–1910* (Amsterdam: Van Gogh Museum; Leeds: Henry Moore Institute; Zwolle: B. V. Waanders Uitgeverij, 1996). Well before the tinted statues were exhibited to the public, Hawthorne had seen some of them. He met Gibson several times while in Rome; on one occasion in 1858, when he was accompanied by his wife and his daughter Rose on their way to Harriet Hosmer's studio, some of Gibson's tinted statues caught his eye; the experience is recorded in *FIN* under "April 3rd. Saturday. Rome": "we had the opportunity of glancing at some of his beautiful work. We saw a Venus and a Cupid, both of them tinted, and side by side with them, other statues identical with these, except that the marble was left in its pure whiteness. The tint of the Venus seemed to be a very delicate, almost imperceptible, shade of yellow, I think, or buff . . . and the eyes and hair of both, especially the Cupid, were colored so as to indicate life rather than imitate it. . . . I must say there was something fascinating and delectable in the warm, yet delicate tint of the beautiful nude Venus, although I would have preferred to dispense with the colouring of the eyes and hair; nor am I at all certain that I should not, in the end, like the snowy whiteness better for the whole statue. Indeed, I am almost sure I should; for this lascivious warmth of hue quite demoralizes the chastity of the marble, and makes one feel ashamed to look at the naked limbs in the company of women" (*FIN* 157). Hawthorne's hesitation before his own response to the tinted statues refers back to the difference he mentions between indication and imitation of life, the latter being too much of an embarassment because it breaks the proprieties of art as a socially acceptable activity by reinstating nudity as overreminiscent of the nakedness of female flesh. The whiteness of the marble is what is admirable in marble nudes: it seemingly dissipates the gendered voyeurism of the male gaze at the cost of denying women the recognition of the specifics of the female body and the extent to which they may be fantasized, but not for art's sake. The situation is further complicated by the fact that the intention behind the tinting of the statues may have originated in a concern by Gibson for archaeological correctness, thus reverently imitating the Greek past with no lewd connections to present life. As Hawthorne is prompt to point out, however, this laudable aim resulted in the (re)construction of "a vast progeny of marble dream-work" (*FIN* 132) and a series of titillating artifacts: far from granting the past a new life in the imagination of the present, whatever there was of the past in the experiment was appropriated by the present for its own "realistic" purposes in the name of "imitation," where a more limited "indication" might have done the trick. The problem again is that of the "entanglement" (the word frequently appears in the course of the novel) of cultural and social values surrounding whatever the work of the artist results in; in *MF*, the statue of the Laocoön is to some extent the material correlate that gives a degree of visibility to this situation, in which past and present, history and art, materiality and ideality constantly interact and change places. The "Marble Queens," however nude, are far from "uncluttered." For Hawthorne's oblique engagement with art in America, see Deanna Fernie, *Hawthorne, Sculpture, and the Question of American Art* (Farnham: Ashgate Publishing, 2011).

13. This point has been convincingly documented by the "U.S. Women's History Workshop" on their website at http://www.assumption.edu/whw/; popular middle-class magazines such as *Frank Leslie's Illustrated* contained endless jests about crinolines, their properties, and the nefarious effects that resulted from their wearing.

14. The satirical poem by William Allen Butler, telling the story of frivolous Miss Flora M'Flimsey, her three separate journeys to Paris, and six consecutive weeks of shopping on each occasion, was first published in *Harper's Weekly* in the issue dated Febuary 7, 1857. As it proved immensely popular, it was reprinted in Harper's other magazine, *Harper's Illustrated Monthly,* where it appeared nine months later.

15. The word is used similarly in *The Scarlet Letter.* The most obvious example is located in chapter 21, "The New-England Holiday": "The fathers and founders of the commonwealth . . . deemed it a duty then to assume the outward state and majesty, which, . . . was looked upon as the proper garb of public or social eminence." Nathaniel Hawthorne, *The Scarlet Letter,* ed. Leland S. Person (New York: Norton, 2005), 147. Cited as *SL* followed by page number. Another instance is in chapter 7, "The Governor's Hall": "Her Mother, in contriving the child's garb, had allowed the gorgeous tendencies of her imagination their full play" (*SL* 69). The garb then is the outward shell of an abstract or imaginative principle or idea, and there is little that is genuine about it. On the contrary,

it is worth noting that, in chapter 5, "Hester at Her Needle," the narrator describes Hester's needle-work as much in demand among the Puritan worthies. Even "our stern progenitors," or at least the men of note among them, indulged in these vain fashions, while sumptuary laws forbade such extravagance to the plebeian orders. But then the narrator half-humorously concludes on a paradox: "Vanity, it may be, chose to mortify itself by putting on, for ceremonials and pomp and state, the garments that had been wrought by her sinful hands" (*SL* 58). The word "garment" is rarely used by Hawthorne and, when it is, denotes a degree of authenticity in clothing that is rarely attained; it is used here with comic/ironic effect to point to the Puritan's unwitting sincerity in donning sumptuous clothes embroidered by a sinful outcast. The fashionable "garments" exhibited in a potentially legitimate show of legally instituted authority have been ornamented in the hands of one who defies authority but obeys her own instincts in being that talented seamstress whose wares are in high demand among those magistrates who have sentenced her to the indignities of her condition.

16. The information in this paragraph derives from Julian Hawthorne, *Nathaniel Hawthorne and His Circle* (New York: Harper & Brothers, 1903; repr. Hamden, Conn.: Archon Books, 1968), ch. 15.

17. Story's poem consists of 152 lines and is hard to come by. I have not been able to read the full text of it except on a semicommercial website (www.bartleby.com). Substantial portions are available in Mary E. Phillips, *Reminiscences of William Wetmore Story, the American Sculptor and Author, Being Incidents and Anecdotes Chronologically Arranged Together with an Account of His Associations with Famous People and His Principal Works in Literature and Sculpture* (Chicago: Rand McNally, 1897), on which I had to rely as a printed source.

18. Henry James, *William Wetmore Story and His Friends; from Letters, Diaries, and Recollections,* 2 vols. (Edinburgh: Blackwood & Sons; Boston: Houghton, Mifflin, 1903; repr. as one volume, New York: Kennedy Galleries, 1969).

19. Richard Brodhead, "Veiled Ladies: Toward a History of Antebellum Entertainment," *American Literary History* 1, no. 2 (Summer 1989): 273–94.

7

FLORENCE

Beryl Korot

Video threads cut from footage of waterfalls, snow storms, boiling water.

I look and listen to the result in front of me, this weaving of moving time, and think of Florence Nightingale. Who was she?

I go to Amazon and have books of her writings sent to the house. I fall in love with her words and select phrases spread over hundreds of pages to make a poem. We collaborate. Since childhood I've written poetry. Now it is with someone else's words.

Florence, born in 1820, intensely rejects her upper-class English destiny and seeks a life of meaning and purpose. At thirty-four, she sets off with a ragtag group of women to save men outside of Istanbul during the brutal Crimean War and transforms what had been complete neglect on the battlefield into a system of caring for the wounded. The year is 1854.

In 1974, I find myself working in three media simultaneously: in print (as coeditor of *Radical Software*), in video, and in weaving. I am drawn to the ancient technology of the handloom as the first computer on earth in that it programs pattern according to a numerical structure. I am drawn to the loom after being involved in print and video because I am interested in creating works on multiple channels of video—get people out of the house, into public spaces, expand the image, play with time, experiment with for-

FIGURE 7.1 Beryl Korot, *Florence* (2008).

mats for presenting information—the loom is the sine qua non of technologies based on multiples. But what really fascinates me is that the information in all three of these media is encrypted in lines: in video the electronic camera reads an image at thirty frames a second, line by line; we read printed material line by line; pattern on the loom is built up line by line, or thread by thread. Time is an important component of this linear structuring in terms of how quickly and effectively information is received and stored. Instant storage and retrieval systems characterize modern technology while tactility and human memory remain earmarks of more ancient tools.

Texere in Latin refers to web, texture, structure, or translates as weave. Throughout the years, different ways of visualizing thought have been manifest in my work. The loom has remained a potent metaphor for organizing information. Here the thoughts are manifest in falling words to create a new sense of reading and time as each word has its own position, speed, and transparency as it moves down the canvas. Unlike my earlier works, where the structure or information in the work was analagous to the organization of threads on a loom *(Dachau 1974, Text and Commentary),* here the moving threads form the background or web to the falling words.

FLORENCE

God has something
for me
to do
for him,
Or he would have let me
die
some time ago.

Women dream,
Dreams which are their life,
Without which they
could not live,
Those dreams go
at last.

Did not God speak to you
during this retreat,
Did he not ask you
anything,

He asked me to surrender my will,

And to whom,

To all that is upon the earth.

But

Oh

You

GENTLEMEN

We are steeped to
our necks in blood,
The wounded left lying
up to our very door.

Occasionally,
the roof is torn off,
the windows blown in,
And we are flooded
under water
for the night.

IMAGINE
all December,
in the trenches,
lying down or half lying down,
without food,
only raw salt pork
sprinkled
with sugar,
rum and biscuits.

When we came
there was not a
sponge, nor a
rag of linen.

Everything is gone
to make slings
stump pillows and shirts.

Oh my poor men who
died so patiently.

As for me,
I have no plans,

If I live
I should like to go
to some foreign hospital
where my name has
never been heard,

Free myself of all
responsibility,
anxiety,
writing,
administration,
and work
as a nurse
for a year . . .

If not for the
story I have to tell,
I would never enter
the world
again.

8

ACCESSORIES TO THE CRIME
IN WHAT MAISIE KNEW

Clair Hughes

The costume of a period unfailingly reflects its aims . . . the fin de siècle *woman . . . insists . . . upon sex in the* chapeau.

WILLETT CUNNINGTON, *The Perfect Lady*

The close connexion of bliss and bale, of the things that help with the things that hurt.

HENRY JAMES, *What Maisie Knew*

Henry James was quite sparing with his descriptions of dress in his novels. He does, however, often give his readers a generalized image of the dress-effect of a character, usually an image with a symbolic function that places that character within the novel's dramatic conflicts in a vivid and convincing fashion. James's economic use of dress is very far from indicating that he was uninterested in clothes. Rather the opposite. He was extremely interested, but he wanted every touch to count, to be an integral and essential "brick" in the structure of what he referred to, in one of his prefaces, as his "house of fiction."

In *What Maisie Knew* (1897), we have a fascinating example of James at work, but this time using an even more economical version of his highly economical technique. In this novel, dress, for reasons connected to narrative strategies, becomes largely a question of accessories. With the exception of one character, what counts are not the images of the dressed person as a whole, but bits and pieces: jewels, gloves, sticks, shoes—things that perhaps mean something, but for the reader do not logically cohere. They are seen in this way because they are seen by a child, and by a child whose world is criminally broken into incoherence.

The novel opens in a courtroom, where a custody battle rages over Maisie, the young daughter of a pair of sordid divorcés, Ida and Beale Farange. "They had wanted her not for any good they could do her, but for the harm they could . . . do each other."[1] Custody is given to the husband, Beale, but like "a little feathered shuttlecock," Maisie is tossed between them, first a bearer of insults and then an unwanted burden. We are told how the gentlemen at Beale's "handle" her, pull her hither and thither, and pinch her "till she shrieked." When Ida abandons Maisie, Sir Claude, Ida's second husband, calls it "a hideous crime. . . . She [Ida] has chucked our friend here overboard . . . out of the window and down two floors to the paving stones." Sir Claude's violent metaphor replays—if he but knew it—an earlier episode when, to punish her silence to questions about Beale, Maisie is "dashed by Mrs. Farange almost to the bottom [of the stairs]."[2] Today her parents would find themselves in court for child abuse.

In his study of the realist novel, *Realist Vision*, Peter Brooks notes how "law and criminology respond, in the nineteenth century, to the same phenomena and problems as the novel does."[3] Much of James's fiction was concerned with the corruption of the contemporary marriage relation—its manipulations, exploitations, and terrors more than its injustices, perhaps. He felt Anglo-American novelists, unlike their French *confrères*, treated relations between the sexes cravenly, with "floods of tepid soap and water."[4] In works such as *The Awkward Age* and "The Pupil," however, he was as much concerned with the damage done to the innocent in the wake of the sexual freedoms to which his society now treated itself: "the mind of Mayfair when it aspires to show what it can really do," he wrote, "lives in the hope of a new divorce case."[5] James's secretary, Theodora Bosanquet, described how "when he walked out of the refuge of his study and looked about him, he saw a place of torment, where creatures of prey perpetually thrust their claws into the quivering flesh of the doomed, defenceless children of light."[6]

How can Maisie—one of those "children"—survive, survival being a child's central instinct? In his preface to the novel, James addresses the question of what Maisie could have understood of her situation: "I should have to stretch the matter to what my wondering witness materially and inevitably saw."[7] Maisie *sees*. And often she sees *things*, trinkets and accessories. Visual objects rather than abstract issues interest her. As Adrian Poole says, she takes in "all the rich surface of things . . . she has an eagle eye for salient accessories, from her father's shoes and her mother's jewellery, to gloves and coins and hat-pins and sticks."[8] We cannot at the end, Peter Brooks says, "exactly say how far [her knowledge] extends"; to ask "would rob her of whatever innocence remains to her."[9] But we know what she witnesses, and it is by what she makes of this evidence that she will survive—if she does. For if she is defenseless, she is also—in James's view—doomed.

HEADGEAR, GLOVES, JEWELS, AND EYES

At first there is a certain thrill to Maisie's "shuttlecock" life—the noisy games in Beale's house and the glamour of Ida's social round, where Maisie sits up "ever so late" to see her mother go out "in silks and velvets and diamonds and pearls." But as the two camps conduct their bewildering battles across and through her, she learns to scan appearances for clues to her situation. Her first governess at Beale's keeps a bonnet on during lessons, which Maisie justifiably but mistakenly takes to indicate a brief stay—ladies at this period in England retained their hats indoors when simply calling or taking tea. The governess proves not only socially but educationally impossible and is replaced by pretty Miss Overmore, her governess at Ida's, who has now, however, broken with Ida and "gone over" to Beale.

Ida then employs Mrs. Wix who strikes Maisie as "terrible" after Miss Overmore. Her greasy gray hair is done in "a glossy braid, like a large diadem on top of her head, and behind, at the nape of her neck, a dingy rosette, like a large button . . . her ugly snuff-coloured dress trimmed with satin bands in the form of scallops [was] glazed with antiquity"; with "the added suggestion of her goggles"—her "straighteners" as she calls them—she reminds Maisie "of a horrid beetle."[10] But Maisie is learning to read beyond surfaces, and neither Mrs. Wix's goggles nor her "old odd headgear" get in the way of the "tucked-in and kissed-for-good-night feeling" she gives Maisie. Mrs. Wix is the exception in the novel: the character whose appearance is described in such a way as to give a full, coherent image. No one else is so soothingly safe, not parents, nor lovely Miss Overmore, nor the smart ladies in her mother's salon, whose beautiful white gloves have "thick black stitching like ruled lines for musical notes."[11] Hands—and by extension gloves—are to the fore in Maisie's vision. Partly, no doubt, it is simply because these objects are at her eye level, but gloves, like hats, were also essential at the period to the respectable female of any age. Pansy Osmond in James's *Portrait of a Lady*, for example, is given a dozen pairs by Mme. Merle when she leaves her convent. "During most of the century," Willett Cunnington notes, "gloves were almost as much an indoor accessory to the toilet as an outdoor . . . the etiquette was extremely strict."[12] Gloves conceal hands, and hands, as we have seen, "handle," pinch, and push; they reach to possess or to reject. Maisie never knows which it is to be—so she watches gloves warily.[13]

If gloves take on animate life, in a metamorphosis that is an aspect of what James called the "phantasmagoric" nature of Maisie's vision, physical attributes of characters may turn into accessories—like Mrs. Wix's hair, or Ida's eyes. Maisie scrutinizes Ida's appearance for clues to her "terrifying strangeness": Ida's eyes, Maisie notes, have "the stare of some gorgeous idol described in a story-book."[14] Glittering, beautiful, and false, Ida's eyes are identified with her jewels, a conventional image that suddenly turns ugly. Maisie and Sir Claude (now Ida's husband) meet Ida in the park with her latest lover, the Captain, and Maisie feels the glare of Ida's "huge painted eyes" like swinging "Japanese lanterns." After angry words with Sir Claude, Ida grabs Maisie to her breast, "where amid a wilderness of trinkets, she felt as if she had suddenly been thrust, with a smash of glass into a jeweller's shop-front, but only to be as suddenly ejected with a push."[15] All associations of a mother's breast are nullified: the shards of icy ornament where a heart should be evoke Hans Andersen's dark story of *The Snow Queen*. Ida's perverse fury to possess and reject fuses cruelty with criminality in a smash-and-grab raid on Maisie.

BEARDS AND TEETH

The identification of costume accessory with the physical body is particularly striking in Maisie's father. Beale has "natural decorations, a kind of costume in his vast fair beard . . . and in the eternal glitter of his teeth." In a replay of the scene in the park with Sir Claude, Maisie is with Miss Overmore (now Mrs. Beale) at an exhibition when they come across Beale, accompanied by an exotic "brown lady." (It is not clear whether "brown" refers to her dress or her complexion.[16] She appears briefly, but always to Maisie's intense dislike.) Abruptly Maisie finds herself at the center of a fight between her father and his new wife. Beale throws Maisie into a cab and drives off to the brown lady's apartment, where he stands smiling down at her, "his wonderful lustrous beard completely concealing the expanse of his shirt-front."[17] At a time when men were mustachioed or clean-shaven, so much beard would have seemed outré, even grotesque.

He paces about, abusing Mrs. Beale, but is sure Maisie will like the "Countess"—the brown lady, evidently. Maisie, having learned the wisdom of keeping counsel, says blandly, "Oh I'm sure I shall!" He puts her on his knee and, "while he showed his shining fangs," lets her "inhale the fragrance of his cherished beard"—shades of Red Riding Hood. Retrospectively, Maisie perceives "a hundred things." She sees he had been "in a good deal of a flutter, yet wished not to show it . . . in this attempt he was able to encourage her to regard him as kind." She spots the wolf in the beard but she lets him "pretend he knew enough about her life . . . to give a natural domestic tone."[18] In fact, he wants rid of her, but he wants it to seem that it is she who rejects him. His beard, a villain's disguise, is, in effect if not reality, as fake as his caresses. Maisie is now sharp enough to see through both, canny enough to keep her perceptions to herself, adult enough to use them.

SHOD FOR DEPARTURE

Maisie sees Beale's beard and his teeth, and also—importantly—his shoes. He tells her he is going to America—but not with his wife—and asks if she wants to come along. She hesitates, terrified at the prospect of losing those she now loves—Mrs. Wix, Sir Claude, and Mrs. Beale—but heroically makes the right answer: "Dear Papa, I'll go with you anywhere." This is not what he wants. He fidgets, rubs her face in his beard, and then announces that her declaration is really a refusal. "It rolled over her that this was their parting . . . he had brought her there for so many caresses only because it was important such an occasion should look better for him than any other." Beale, unable to meet Maisie's gaze, looks down at his shoes. "Maisie also for a minute looked at his shoes though they were not the pair she most admired, the laced yellow 'uppers' and patent leather complement. At last, with a question, she raised her eyes. 'Aren't you coming back?'" When he admits he is not, Maisie sobs that she will never give him up, at which he grimaces in a "perfect parade of his teeth."[19] Beale tells the Countess that Maisie has refused his offer and bundles her back into a cab, paid for by the Countess.

In contrast to her vulnerability with Ida, Maisie, aware of Beale's "fangs," manipulates the situation to allow him the pretence, even the chance, of normal fatherliness. But fatherliness is not on the agenda, and Maisie realizes that Beale intends to abandon her. Maisie's seemingly random attention to shoes is a detail that is worth examining. The pathos of her persistent admiration of her parents' looks is evident in her familiarity with Beale's wardrobe. Shoes, after all, loom large in a child's angle of vision, and she recalls a favorite pair. Maisie's interest in shoes seems part of her general wonder at aspects of the visual world that float into her line of vision; this pair brings to mind another pair, shiny patent leather ones, familiar to her in the past. Maisie likes them; readers, however, might imagine them as rather too flashy. But after all, if accessories seem to have meaning in our social exchanges, they are bound to have different meanings and associations for children. The fact that children's meanings do not coincide with those of adults is a fundamental and frequent problem. Maisie does not place Beale socially or morally by his shoes; she simply remembers the shinier pair she prefers.

According to Christopher Breward, a belief in the moral character of a man's shoes has lasted across two centuries, "offering a model for aesthetic discernment . . . that embraces broader issues of taste, modernity, and gender."[20] Beale's garish two-tone footwear is not only in questionable taste but gives us an example of what came to be known as "co-respondent shoes," racy items, Sarah Levitt notes, "associated with the type of person who might be an accessory to a divorce case"—a louche touch of modernity.[21] It has become apparent that Beale, reversing gender roles, is "kept" by the Countess—he can't even pay Maisie's cab. He is revealed as at best a vulgar dandy, at worst, a swindling gigolo. Maisie, unaware of the moral character of shoes, might wonder why, when home life is so pinched, her father's shoes are so smart. One could add that, as Beale is about to flee his country, his child (for whom he is legally responsible), two wives, and—the text hints—even the Countess, he needs to be fleet of foot.

What Beale is up to with the Countess, or Ida with the Captain, does not concern Maisie: "Everything had something behind it: life was a long, long corridor with rows of closed doors. She had learned that at these doors it was wise not to knock." To survive, be educated, and forge her adult identity she needs safety and loving-kindness—St. Augustine's prayer for childhood—and she examines anxiously the various configurations of parenthood that emerge from those doors for signs that these primary needs will be met. She recognizes that her real parents wish her gone—"Mama doesn't care for me, not really"—but their rapid turnover of partners simply produces inexplicable rows, not new families.[22]

If people in the novel, like Ida, are at first unreadable to Maisie, surely there is something to be learned from the things they carry. From the canes men swagger with, or the umbrellas women treasure, or the jewelry they display. Every little thing might mean something, if only one could fathom it. Mr. Perriam, who is Sir Claude's successor with Ida, impresses Maisie with his diamond ring, "of dazzling lustre," a match for Ida's bosomful of trinkets, but he seems a storybook figure, not a father: "if he had only a turban he would have been quite her idea of a heathen Turk." His successor, the Captain, is first seen walking in the park with one arm in her mother's, while the other "behind him, made jerky movements with the stick that it grasped."[23]

Sticks and umbrellas play key roles in the novel, and the nervousness of this one suggests tension in the relationship. Maisie, however, likes the Captain and wistfully hopes he will be fond of her mother. Responding to her plea, he "raised her hand to his lips with a benevolence that made her wish her glove had been nicer." When Peter Brooks speaks of James's effort "to make the surface yield something that is not purely of surface," it is details such as this that make his point.[24] Maisie is not only starved of affection, education, and home comforts, she is "overgrown and underdressed"; no one pays for her upkeep.[25] She is sufficiently socially aware, as we have seen, to know the importance of gloves, and feminine enough to want to please the Captain: her grubby glove is poignant evidence of general neglect.

So when she realizes that kind Sir Claude and pretty Mrs. Beale like each other, Maisie feels "entrancingly the extension of the field of happiness." Sir Claude is not only fun to be with, he is also generous. While he is still with Ida, Maisie and Mrs. Wix lead a life of "great prosperity." He disappears for days at a time but brings treats on his return—"an umbrella with a malachite knob" for Mrs. Wix, chocolate creams, storybooks, and "a lovely greatcoat" for Maisie. His consideration for Mrs. Wix particularly touches Maisie. But when he brings Mrs. Wix a second and even more elegant umbrella from Paris, Maisie is puzzled by his forgetfulness, for she knows how Mrs. Wix treasures the

FIGURE 8.1 Augustus Edwin John (1878–1961), *Sir William Nicholson*, oil on canvas, 190.2 × 143.8 cm, 1909. Copyright Fitzwilliam Museum, Cambridge/Art Resource, NY.

first—"buried in as many wrappers as a mummy of the Pharaohs, she wouldn't have done anything so profane as to use it." Umbrellas evidently signify: but what? Much mystifies Maisie at this point. Mr. Perriam is Ida's attentive visitor, while Sir Claude and the new Mrs. Beale become friends, and as a puzzling consequence of this, Mrs. Wix's disapproval "was now an attitude as public as a posted placard."[26]

With Ida busy elsewhere, Maisie and Sir Claude ramble around London together, ride on buses, walk in parks, try the best places for tea, and companionably "pull off their gloves for refreshment." Umbrellas become friendly objects, and "when the streets are all splash" she and Sir Claude share one. This is the happiest period in Maisie's life. Then, abruptly, she is sent to her father's, but Sir Claude seems to come too. He has quarreled with Ida, Mrs. Beale explains—as she has with Beale. Maisie, making the best of things, declares enthusiastically to her stepparents that "it's beautiful to see you side by side" and assumes that their pleasant routines will be resumed. Taking up his hat and stick, Sir Claude promises to come next day, but it is many weeks before he returns, telling her not to make a scene but "to clap on something smart and come out with me."[27]

Because Maisie loves Sir Claude and is happy to be treated to another ramble, she forgives him despite "her sense of being duped." "She clung to his hand, which was encased in a pearl-grey glove ornamented with thick black lines that, at her mother's, always used to strike her as connected with the way the bestitched fists of the long ladies carried their umbrellas upside down."[28] The gloves seem to connect gentlemen to ladies and connect ladies to their umbrellas, and they remind her of the stitching on the gloves of Ida's smart lady-friends. The blissful companionship of Maisie's earlier excursions with Sir Claude is now gone; an ambiguous tension has entered the relationship. Maisie clings to his hand, desperate not to lose him. Maisie's association of the ornamental stitching with Ida's friends feminizes and destabilizes our impression of Sir Claude. If we sometimes see more knowingly, more darkly than Maisie, she sees intuitively, more than she can understand or formulate. Sir Claude's image is diminished on both accounts.

Mrs. Beale and Sir Claude, discarded by their respective spouses, now become a couple, to Maisie's delight and to Mrs. Wix's dismay. It is Maisie, they declare, who makes them "all right." Nonetheless, their position is socially untenable, and Sir Claude decides to take the time-honored route of the morally compromised Englishman and cross the Channel; how both Mrs. Beale and Mrs. Wix figure in his plan is unclear. Ida, meanwhile, has gathered up some remnants of motherhood and turns up in Folkestone, overdressed. Maisie feels "she had never been so irrevocably parted with as in the pressure of possession now supremely exerted by Ida's long-gloved, many-bangled arm." Like

Beale, Ida wishes to be rid of Maisie but also to save face. They sit together uneasily, while Ida's "gloved hand sometimes rested sociably on the child's and sometimes gave a coercive pull to a ribbon too meagre or a tress too thick." The narrator cuts through the muddle of Ida's self-serving lies: "she draped herself in the tatters of her impudence . . . she quite did think her wretched offspring better placed with Sir Claude than in her own soiled hands," be her gloves never so long.[29]

Ida's gloved hand frees Maisie and fumbles "in some backward depth of drapery" reappearing "with a small article in its grasp. . . . The act had significance for a little person trained . . . to keep an eye on manual motions." It is a reticule, and Maisie wonders if a sovereign or a shilling is to be extracted. On impulse Maisie alludes to the kind Captain's affection for Ida, but "never in a career of unsuccessful experiments had Maisie had to take such a stare . . . 'What Captain?'" Ida demands. The hand stiffens, "the whites of her eyes were huge," and as Maisie listens bewildered to a torrent of abuse, she sees what lies ahead for Ida—"madness and desolation . . . ruin and darkness and death."[30] This time Maisie's "trained" eye reads through appearance and behavior; she doesn't need to understand the mechanics of Ida's interminable couplings to discern their consequences. The purse clicks shut, and in a final volley of insults, Ida exits. Sir Claude calls Ida's desertion "a hideous crime"; Maisie's prevision of Ida as one of the damned hurtling toward a Last Judgment is, however, a more compassionate and more "knowing" verdict.

HATS AND BAGS

We have seen gloves, soiled or unsoiled, covering hands that may also be soiled. Hats, caps, and bags now come into focus.[31] Maisie and Sir Claude cross to Boulogne with Mrs. Wix, in a new outfit supplied by Sir Claude. Events take on "a new tone—as new as Mrs. Wix's cap." With Ida and Beale gone, Mrs. Wix declares that for Maisie "there must at last be a *decent* person," and Mrs. Beale, she says, is not that person. Sir Claude, evading the issue of Mrs. Beale's decency, makes as if to leave and "glanced about for

FIGURE 8.2 Patterns from "Women's & Child's Costume" from the *Young Ladies Journal*, February 1897. Reprinted in *Paris Fashions of the 1890s*, ed. Stella Blum (New York: Dover, 1984).

his hat." Maisie sees the hat and holds it out to him. He takes it, "and then something moved her still to hold the other side of the brim; so that united by their grasp of this object, they stood some seconds looking many things at each other. . . . 'You *are* going back?'" Mrs. Wix challenges. "To Mrs. Beale?" Maisie asks, and then surrenders the hat, sensing the pull of a power of which she is jealous but unclear. "We'll see about it," he says, sidling out.[32] If a child's central instinct is survival, its central fear is abandonment. Gloves and hats are accessories of respect, but they also signal departure. Sir Claude's intentions are not respectable, and without quite knowing why, Maisie retains his hat to keep him from leaving, to "save" him, as Mrs. Wix says.

But Sir Claude leaves, bribing them with the means to amuse themselves in Boulogne. Maisie feels that luxury is "in the air," and in preparation for an outing with Mrs. Wix she looks in the glass, "pulling on her gloves and with a motion of her head, shaking a feather into place," imitating—who knows—her mother, the Countess, Mrs.

Beale? At all events, appalled by Maisie's easy adaptability to what she sees as the gross immorality of Mrs. Beale and Sir Claude, Mrs. Wix exclaims "Haven't you really and truly *any* moral sense?" "Is it a crime?" Maisie asks.[33] The question of what Maisie intends by "it" hangs in the air—"it" could be as much a question of hats as of Sir Claude's relation to Mrs. Beale.

Hats, according to Fred Robinson's history of the bowler hat, "are stressed words in the history of costume."[34] Maisie's coquettish adjustment of hers brings home to Mrs. Wix (the drably dressed but comforting Mrs. Wix) the awfulness of Maisie's role models. She fears that Maisie understands and accepts the "crime" and will herself one day take part in some sexual shenanigans. A few years later, at the start of *Wings of the Dove,* James places one of his heroines, Kate Croy, before a glass, adjusting her feathered hat, as she waits for her deplorable father. The novel traces her descent into corruption as she sets up the seduction of Milly Theale. It ends with Kate again adjusting her hat, a last shred of self-respect in the face of moral, financial, and sexual catastrophe.

Hats, as I have noted elsewhere, are a relatively cheap, quick way of keeping up with fashion, of advertising or concealing status and identity. Fictional hats are "transitory or ambiguous . . . hats can be performances or deceptions."[35] Maisie's hat might simply represent a child's instinctive aping of grown-up manners, or just pleasure in something pretty. But as she is possessively in love with Sir Claude, and as we do not know what she knows, an element of ambiguity, of coquetry creeps in. The reader of *What Maisie Knew,* Victoria Coulson observes, "becomes involved in a distasteful pursuit of knowledge . . . definitively sexual."[36] Maisie could after all become Kate.

Mrs. Beale arrives in Boulogne, "in her hat and her jacket, amid bags and shawls." Disconcerted, Maisie makes "a quick survey of the objects surrounding Mrs. Beale," establishing that "there was no appurtenance of Sir Claude's. She knew his dressing-bag now—oh with the fondest knowledge!" This lack strikes her to the heart—"a foretaste of the experience of death": the passion that she has invested in Sir Claude, transferred to his accessories, makes this absence a harbinger of loss, abandonment, even of death.[37] Where is he?

Mrs. Beale launches into a exaggerated monologue on hats for Maisie and Mrs. Wix. Millinery, we might recall at this point, was dramatically large at the turn of the century, expanding upward and outward in elaborate arrangements of flora and fauna. Such confections required anchorage, and rather than greeting Mrs. Wix and Maisie—as good manners and affection dictate—Mrs. Beale raises her hand "with a pretty gesture . . . to a long black pin that played a part in her back hair. 'Are hats worn at luncheon?' . . . 'I wear mine,'" Mrs. Wix replies. Glancing at Mrs. Wix's new headgear, Mrs. Beale exclaims, "Oh but I've not such a beauty!"—conveying at once her guess at its provenance and its absurdity on Mrs. Wix. Having put Mrs. Wix in her place as employee, she turns to play mother to Maisie. "'I've got a beauty for *you*, my dear.' 'A beauty?' 'A love of a hat—in my luggage. I remembered *that*'—she nodded at the object on her stepdaughter's head—'and I've bought one with a peacock's breast. It's the most gorgeous blue!'" Maisie, sensing her stepmother's mockery of Mrs. Wix, is not sure about this "beauty" of a hat, and Mrs. Beale has quickly substituted the more affectionate "love of a hat," adding color and feathers. At the same time, she has dismissed Maisie's own hat, an object that earlier gave Maisie pleasure. "It was too strange, this talking with her . . . not about Sir Claude but about peacocks—too strange for the child to have the presence of mind to thank her . . . she had a vague sense of its being abysmal . . . such a want of breath and welcome."[38] Maisie is not only frightened by Mrs. Beale's unaffectionate and solo arrival, but also unnerved by a seemingly irrelevant fuss with hats. We sense her mistrustful reluctance to be bought by Mrs. Beale.

Mrs. Wix declares it is a game that Mrs. Beale has won. She will use Sir Claude's sense of duty to Maisie to draw him to herself; furthermore Beale's custody of Maisie makes Mrs. Beale Maisie's legal guardian, and whoever is Maisie's guardian has the income that goes with her. If Sir Claude and Mrs. Beale are in the "shoes" of their defunct partners, as James puts it, Mrs. Beale's shoes were "the very pair to which . . . the divorce court had given priority"—and we might remember just how nasty Beale's shoes were.[39]

Next morning Maisie picks up a hat—but which one? James says it is her "judgement-cap." Hats are for outings, and Maisie is determined this one will be with Sir Claude. She finds him in the salon, ready for "the grandest of grand tours" in "a straw hat with a bright ribbon," but when he does not embrace her and she sees he has been ready to leave for some time, "in a flash she saw he was different." Looking at a closed door, she asks if he has seen Mrs Beale: "'Not the tip of her nose' . . . there settled on her, in the light of his beautiful smiling eyes, the faintest purest coldest conviction that he wasn't telling the truth." He quickly improvises: "'I say—we'll go out!' 'That was just what I hoped. I've brought my hat.' . . . he glanced round the room. 'A moment—my stick.' But there appeared to be no stick. 'No matter; I left it—oh!'" They leave and Maisie helpfully suggests he left it in London. "Yes—in London: fancy!"[40] She does not need to reach for phallic symbols to understand the betrayal implicit in the stick left in Mrs. Beale's bedroom.

In the hall of the hotel, Maisie sees "a battered old box that she recognized, an ancient receptacle with dangling labels that she knew and a big painted W . . . that seemed to stare at her with a recognition and even with some suspicion of its own." As with Sir Claude's earlier absent bags, Maisie invests these boxes with her feelings about their owner: battered and old, but evidence, above all, of familiarity and enduring concern. Mrs. Wix enters, thundering "I *don't* leave the child." She is "armed with a small fat rusty reticule which, almost in the manner of a battle-axe, she brandished in support of her words."[41]

There follows, as James says, "a tough passage." Maisie, between the three, makes clear her position—she will go with the one who, forsaking all others, places her first. Mrs. Beale grabs Maisie, but Sir Claude insists she be allowed to choose freely. "Will you be so good," Sir Claude pleads, "as to allow these horrors to terminate?"[42] And they do: the novel ends with Maisie and Mrs. Wix on the way to England, leaving who knows what fresh hell for Sir Claude to face.

FIGURE 8.3 Patterns from "Women's & Child's Costume" from the *Young Ladies Journal*, February 1897. Reprinted in *Paris Fashions of the 1890s*, ed. Stella Blum (New York: Dover, 1984).

The novel's spirit "of savage, unbuttoned hilarity" can lead us to overlook what are in fact appalling events, as Sir Claude finally recognizes.[43] The procession of lovers, the repeated revelations of sexual misdemeanor are as ridiculous as the clichés of a French theatrical farce. The difference in *What Maisie Knew* is that these things are transmitted through the eyes of a child. That her eyes should come to accept any number and condition of strangers who might tumble in and out of her home is an indefensible assault on innocence. But we cannot know how far this has gone without violating that innocence. As Victoria Coulson observes, "we have to read [Maisie] as if she were a realist text, in order to make out the relationships between signifiers (Maisie's perceptions) and signified (the ugly events of the adult world)," and so we subject those perceptions to a "remorseless interpretative scrutiny," a prurience that uncomfortably puts us in Mrs. Wix's shoes.[44]

Reading this novel is then a game of hide-and-seek, where hats, gloves, shoes, bags, and sticks figure as clues. Maisie needs to use her eyes: "they are all," as Tony Tanner says, "she has."[45] The objects Maisie sees are important to her and to others, but they do not cohere into full images of characters or into meaningful codes. We do not know for certain the meaning Maisie gives to them, for she defends with silence her cache of knowledge and her sense of self. She knows nice gloves are vital to the conventions, but experience suggests they might cover violence. Shoes, usually signifiers of social status, can be reminders of family life for Maisie but, more crudely, could be pointers to a quick getaway. Umbrellas mean not only bad weather, but rambles arm in arm, a pair united under a "roof." As James himself wrote in his preface to the novel, there is a close connection "of the things that help with the things that hurt."[46] Sticks, unexpectedly, have no violent associations in this otherwise violent story, but they are decidedly male. Maisie knows where Sir Claude left his, and this prompts her ultimatum to him. He can redeem his betrayal, retrieve his stick, as it were, by electing to stay with her.

Hats from the start are anxious objects for Maisie. Because we have largely ceased to wear them, we have lost the key to their implications, but until the mid-twentieth century hats were a mandatory part of outerwear. James himself had a hat (and stick) for every occasion. For women, hats were the crowning flourish to sexual display and a byword for frivolity and extravagance: it is when Maisie plays the coquette in hers that Mrs. Wix asks if she has a moral sense. Unsaid things pass between Maisie and Sir Claude as they hold his hat between them. With her love of pretty things, does Maisie succumb to Mrs. Beale's "love of a hat"? To do so would be treachery to Mrs. Wix and acknowledgment of Maisie's submission to her stepparents' values.

Mrs. Wix's "reticule," the final accessory, is small and rusty—ugly, in fact, like Mrs. Wix and her heap of battered boxes. But it gives Maisie that "kissed-for-goodnight feeling" that, in fairy-tale fashion, turns ugliness to beauty. In contrast, Ida's reticule snaps meanly and conclusively shut. The absence of Sir Claude's dressing case is critical—another empty promise; but worse, it warns of his disappearance from Maisie's life, for he is, for all his weakness, the best thing in it. The "process of vision," by which the material world is read, is, as James said in the preface to *The Ambassadors,* "the precious moral of everything."[47] At the end, Maisie views her future with "foreboding," not with the happy ignorance of an innocent lamb. Sir Claude spoke of "sacrificing" Mrs. Wix; Maisie counters by asking him to sacrifice Mrs. Beale. But it is Maisie who is sacrificed.

Why in this novel has James focused almost exclusively on accessories? Elsewhere in his fiction dresses are vividly represented; here, only Mrs. Wix is fully clad for us. Mrs. Wix, however, is the one character with nothing to hide, the one who is comfortably "known" to Maisie. We see her whole; others, including Maisie, we have seen only darkly. If we have guessed at the implications of jewels, hats, gloves, shoes, and bags, their significance is uncertain.

Discussing Honoré de Balzac's passion for detail, James noted that "things" in Balzac's novels are described *"only in so far as they bear upon the action . . .* which are accessory to action."[48] The point of James's plot, his "action," is that for all our reading of her, we can't know what Maisie knew. She may interpret hats, gloves, and sticks in recognizable, adult ways, but just as often she does not. We must guess the unseen from the seen, James said. What we see are aspects of the surface. Surfaces speak; they communicate with the depths, like doors to a cellar. If what lies below remains forever unspoken, however, or unspeakable, we are driven to question ceaselessly but not unproductively. We see what Maisie saw: we do not know—or we do not know fully—what Maisie knew.

NOTES

1. Henry James, preface to *What Maisie Knew* [1897] (Oxford: Oxford University Press, 1996), xv.

2. James, *What Maisie Knew*, 22, 18, 19, 190, 127.

3. Peter Brooks, *Realist Vision* (New Haven, Conn.: Yale University Press, 2005), 225.

4. Letter to William Dean Howells, quoted in Philip Glover, *Henry James and the French Novel* (London: Elek, 1972), 207.

5. Henry James, *Essays in London and Elsewhere* (New York: Harper, 1893), 8–9.

6. Theodora Bosanquet, *Henry James at Work* (London: Hogarth, 1924), 32.

7. James, preface to *What Maisie Knew*, vii.

8. Adrian Poole, introduction to James, *What Maisie Knew*, xvi.

9. Peter Brooks, *Henry James Goes to Paris* (Princeton, N.J.: Princeton University Press, 2007), 146.

10. James, *What Maisie Knew*, 30.

11. Ibid., 20, 42, 31.

12. C. Willett Cunnington, *English Women's Clothing in the Nineteenth Century* (London: Faber & Faber, 1937), 22.

13. When the horror-film actor Vincent Price was asked how he achieved his sinister effects, he said the answer lay in perfectly fitting black leather gloves.

14. James, *What Maisie Knew*, 63.

15. Ibid., 117, 118.

16. For a discussion of this point, see Kendall Johnson, "The Scarlet Feather: Racial Phantasmagoria in *What Maisie Knew*," *Henry James Review* 22, no. 2 (2001): 128–46.

17. James, *What Maisie Knew*, 18, 141.

18. Ibid., 141, 143.

19. Ibid., 146, 148, 152.

20. Christopher Breward, "The Fashioning of Masculinity," in *Shoes,* ed. Giorgio Riello and Peter McNeil (Oxford: Berg, 2006), 207.

21. Sarah Levitt, *Fashion in Photographs, 1880–1900* (London: Batsford, 1991), 87.

22. James, *What Maisie Knew,* 36, 73.

23. Ibid., 79, 114.

24. Brooks, *Henry James Goes to Paris,* 149.

25. James, *What Maisie Knew,* 122, 40.

26. Ibid., 56, 64, 82.

27. Ibid., 92, 108, 112.

28. Ibid., 112, 113.

29. Ibid., 164, 170, 171.

30. Ibid., 173, 175.

31. For a comprehensive discussion of the meanings and uses of hats in literature, particularly in the American novel, see Cristina Giorcelli's essay, "Tra Costume e Letteratura: I capelli femminili negli Stati Uniti," in *Abito e Identità: Ricerche di storia letteraria e culturale,* ed. Cristina Giorcelli, vol. 5 (Rome: Ila Palma, 2004), 105–64.

32. James, *What Maisie Knew,* 188, 193.

33. Ibid., 193, 219.

34. Fred Robinson, *The Man in the Bowler Hat* (Chapel Hill: University of North Carolina Press, 1993), 16.

35. Clair Hughes, *Henry James and the Art of Dress* (Houndmills: Palgrave, 2001), 93.

36. Victoria Coulson, *Henry James, Women and Realism* (Cambridge: Cambridge University Press, 2000), 93–94.

37. James, *What Maisie Knew,* 222, 223.

38. Ibid., 225, 226.

39. Ibid., 231.

40. Ibid., 242, 243, 244, 245.

41. Ibid., 263, 265.

42. Ibid., 273.

43. Poole, introduction to James, *What Maisie Knew,* ix.

44. Coulson, *Henry James, Women and Realism,* 93.

45. Tony Tanner, *Henry James: The Writer and His Works* (Amherst: University of Massachusetts Press, 1985), 88.

46. James, preface to *What Maisie Knew,* v.

47. Henry James, *The Ambassadors* [1903], ed. S. P. Rosenbaum (New York: Norton, 1994), 2.

48. Henry James, *Literary Criticism: English and American Writers* (New York: Library of America, 1984), 608.

9

COSTUME AND FORM
D'ANNUNZIO AND MUTABLE APPEARANCES

Marta Savini

As one would expect, attitudes toward clothes vary significantly from one historical period to another, often in close relation to painting, art, and culture in general.[1] But the
ephemeral world of clothing is less apparent in the Italian literary tradition, because
writers do not seem "attracted to clothes, as much as to the physical and spiritual beauty
of the person wearing them."[2] From this perspective, Gabriele D'Annunzio represents
an exception, given his passionate interest in fashion, his careful and detailed descriptions of dress and accessories, and his cult of the image shaped by clothes,[3] even more
so when compared to the taste of his contemporaries, who, unlike artists during the two
previous centuries, tended, for a number of reasons, not least social ones, to downplay
the importance of clothes. Almost no attention was paid to clothes by Giacomo Leopardi
or Alessandro Manzoni, except for a few details indicative of characters' social condition.[4] Even in the second half of the century, starting with Giòsuè Carducci–inspired
classicism, detailed descriptions are uncommon. When, for example, Carducci describes Queen Margherita, he provides only a quick reference to her dress: "dove grey, I
would think, loosely cascading."[5] In Giovanni Pascoli, too, detailed references to outer
apparel is unlikely, except in the case of Greek or Roman mythological figures.

A full development in the representation of garments, without precedent in Italian literature, occurs with the passionate and sophisticated, though at times provincial, effervescence of D'Annunzio, especially in his initial Roman phase. For example, in 1884, D'Annunzio, working as a journalist under the pseudonym of "Vere de Vere," celebrated the blond beauty of the queen in the royal box of the Apollo Theater in Rome for the premiere of *Lohengrin:*

> Her majesty the Queen had a real triumph of beauty, last night. She was wearing a white brocade dress, closed around the neck, of the utmost simplicity; and in her hair a few tea-roses. With this plainness her royal graces shone even more brightly. Next to the Queen, blond and bright, sat Duchess Sforza Cesarini, in a black dress studded with diamond patterns, looking extremely noble as she held her iridescent mother-of-pearl fan against the light.[6]

Rosita Levi Pisetzky notes the care with which D'Annunzio in his newspaper column Cronache mondane (Mundane Chronicles) describes the appearance of new textiles and trends, such wearing special accessories

> to go for walks, the so-called *footing*, a great discovery for the health of ladies used to letting themselves be gently transported in their carriages. And here is D'Annunzio describing Countess Lara, an extremely unfortunate woman and now forgotten writer, while walking on the Corso in Rome, accompanied by a serpent-like "Caucasian" greyhound, wearing a tight-fitting dress of "venatory velvet" [i.e., corduroy], with a bodice closed by large buckles of chiseled and oxidized silver and a belt of Russian leather.[7]

Pisetzky follows this citation from D'Annunzio by an author one would not expect in this context, Emilio De Marchi,[8] who spends many words on a "nice brilliant pearl-colored dress of *surah*" worn by the beautiful wife of a middle-class clerk: "Beatrice, preceded by the swishing rustle of her train, came in, as splendid as a princess, in her beautiful new dress which embraced her waist, the root of her firm arms and her ample bosom with the soft and tense precision of a glove . . . bare shoulders of a soft milky

whiteness," a bust "open to the point where decency agrees with beauty . . . arms bare from shoulder to elbow where the long Swedish gloves arrived."[9] One sees a difference between the two, not solely in terms of stylistic quality, but also between De Marchi's easy, almost banal, sensualism and D'Annunzio's seductive attention to the dress as such, an element that recurs repeatedly in his newspaper columns Cronache Romane, demonstrating his perceptive attention to that high society to which he aspired.

After 1884, along with his various Cronache, D'Annunzio published in the journals

Cronaca Bizantina and *La Tribuna* a number of short stories collected as *Favole mondane*. These evidence the evolution of D'Annunzio's narrative technique and his transition from the naturalism of his early novellas to the decadentism of *Il piacere (The Child of Pleasure)*. D'Annunzio gives full vent to "his inventive and expressive potential" shining especially in the description of outdoor settings and fashionable events. Special attention, however, is also paid to clothes.[10] In "Per un vaso" (For a vase), for example "donna Laura" shows off "a beautiful smile, manifesting in all her other attitudes a sort of languidness, of natural indolence mixed with grace":

> She was dressed in vicuna wool of dry-leaf green, and the shape of her head, favored by her hairdo with her hair curving upward and pinned high, was purely outlined on the splendid damask of the armchair. The gay traits of her face reminded one of certain womanly outlines in the drawings of Moreau the Younger, of Gravelot's vignettes.[11]

As in his Cronache, the dress often complements the complexion of the character's face: "The color of the epidermis, that hue which seemed made with the inner leaves of a white rose, was enriched by these almost fugitive transparencies."[12] However, in another tale, "Una donna metodica" (A methodical woman),

> She had a dress of black lace, pleated at the back and open in front, surrounded by a bit of lace that went up from the two sides of the *tablier* forming a spiral over a *jupe di satin* of which the front was embroidered from neck to toe. At the *encolure*, which was cut very low, very large lace *à tuyaux* went straight up to the chin, round the neck, and cascaded down to the middle of her back, ending in a large lace knot that fell back on *la jupe*. . . . Yesterday, between a languid laugh of sunshine and a tear of rain, we saw her on the Corso. She had a *toilette en étamine vert mousse*, with a *visite Kanguroo*. The straw hat of brown and white *chinée*, with a large brim, covered her face; a scarf *d'étamine* created some folds on the front and a velvet bunch of borage and poppies rose daringly on the left. The brim of the hat was lined with an *étamine lamée* whose countless golden threads shone as the rays of a sacred nimbus.[13]

The description is like a portrait painting, of which, in the same decadent context, the foremost representative was an Italian painter in Paris, Giovanni Boldini. D'Annunzio creates his characters using the same sophisticated strategy adopted by the Marquisa Aurora Canale who desired to become "the incarnation of the Mongolian feminine type," and so was nicknamed the "Mandarine" by her friends:

> She affected this curious tendency towards *Japanism* in her clothes, in her attitudes, even in her voice.[14] . . . She spent her time looking for ideal clothes or in the solitary contemplation and adoration of her beauty. . . . Thus she carefully arranged her person as a number of elegant figures which had at times perhaps the defect of being some- what theatrical, somewhat scenic. She made sure the screen agreed with her dress; and moderated the shadows and the sunrays. She loved "false" hues, those spent and bro- ken colors, those indefinable gradations that one finds at times in certain flowers, in certain virgin minerals, in certain vapors of the air; and she loved the richness of the folds, the flowing softness of the crepe, that almost evanescent *je ne sais quoi* under which one perceives a supple body. One day, she appeared in a seagreen robe covered with cherry flowers; and, in sitting, she artfully had in the background a screen on which over a soft wheat-gold hue two great cranes flew, two of those fair celestial mes- sengers with fiery crests and black throat. Another day she showed up in a tragic dress resembling a gloomy sky.[15]

Like the "Mandarine," written in 1884, D'Annunzio became his own director, shaping an image of himself suited to the public whose admiration he craved. When he acquired a greater self-awareness—after his private school years in Prato, later narratively reelab- orated to cast himself as exceptional protagonist, and after his first contact with Rome— D'Annunzio dedicated himself to fashioning, through clothes, his image as an elegant intellectual destined to gain his rightful place among the fashionable crowd of the cap- ital. Even old friends were surprised by his gradual transformation, having originally met him as the seductive but unsophisticated, almost rustic, provincial social-climber. Edoardo Scarfoglio, who came from the same region as D'Annunzio and was undoubt-

Figure 9.2. Alberto Martini,
Marquisa Casati-Martini (1912).

edly a perceptive observer as well as a close friend, wrote in 1884: "I shall never forget my painful surprise in seeing for the first time Gabriele all dressed up and perfumed at a party."[16] When the country youth opened his imagination to the allure of the great city, something was unleashed in him. After what we can imagine were his stops in front of the attractive shop windows of via del Babuino, via Condotti, and Piazza di Spagna, his imagination became populated with objects that appealed to his pent-up aspirations. In 1890, at twenty-seven, D'Annunzio confessed: "I have, for temperament, for instinct, a need for the superfluous. . . . The education of my spirit irresistibly pushes me toward acquiring beautiful things." This voracity spurred the inevitable, almost fatalistic instinct that outlined D'Annunzio's existence: the love of excess, the expensive apparatus beyond his means, at the price of any daring initiative, and, in intimate connection, the elaboration, *ad personam,* of his external image. If, on the one hand, this was the beginning of his never-ending story of luxury and ruinous debt, on the other, we are far from a "Stendahlian heroism."[17] But it is not solely Julien Sorel–like social aspirations that animated D'Annunzio. His search for absolute, undeniable social preeminence occurs in the context of a tactile delight in luxury: "We love with great ardor the vibrations of the *pierreries,* the luminosity of *pailletés* textiles, and the daring décolletage and the splendid hairdos with heraldic jewels and all the feminine magnificence that turn the stalls of a theater into a congress of beauty delightful to the eyes of mortals."[18] Yet it goes beyond this. The important thing for D'Annunzio is to turn his sumptuous, fascinating congeries into the very identity of the man, even at the cost of creating bric-a-brac, a devastating heap of junk.

D'Annunzio was determined to acquire a starring role in that milieu, in that world, but not merely through literature and art: "I am not and do not wish to be a mere poet."[19] His aspiration was not the circulation of his work as much as the connection with those who read him: "the true reader is he who loves me."[20] In this way, D'Annunzio took "the inevitable path toward stardom."[21] He wanted to give his public an idol, a persona capable of captivating at first glance its more or less repressed instincts, based not on eccentricity as much as on being a perfect gentleman. Beyond this, in expanding his aestheticism and turning it into an exhaustingly sophisticated love for his entire world both social and domestic, D'Annunzio inevitably set at its center the autobiographical character that his Nietzscheanism would turn into a European icon and ultimately a national war hero. When D'Annunzio immersed himself in the analysis of himself, the result was never a psychological, moral, or spiritual insight. The only connotations that suit him are a sort of epic of costumes, an impressive coterie of masks that make us hesitant to look beyond, to reach for the inner reality of the persona we have in front of us: after the gentleman, the sportsman, and the soldier; after the writer and beyond the writer, the man of action, the warrior, the leader; and, in each episode of his life he adopted a different script, each almost contradicting the former. When thinking of D'Annunzio, unlike any other great author, it is impossible to avoid taking into account the external persona, the costumes he chose to wear, presenting himself alternatively as man of the world, crowd rouser (starting with his speeches in favor of Italy's intervention in World War I), the sailor of Buccari, aviator, footsoldier, then commander, or finally the solitary and bitter old man wandering in the gardens of his "Vittoriale," stopping to ponder the tombs of his dogs. In every phase, in every moment, from his polished youth to the slovenly and lonely decadence of his last years, D'Annunzio remained a figure obsessively determined by his external appearance.

During his phase of self-scrutiny, from his nocturnal prose to his last, desperate diaries, D'Annunzio continued to drag after himself the irresolvable shadow of his outer self, of his costume. Even his desperate passion for his beloved ephemera, which had been his dominant overtone and which one would have expected to fade away in his later diaries, remains attached to the very physiognomy of the artist, of the writer. It is a sort of devastating, yet fascinating, damnation that accompanies the last phase of his life, associating him with figures like Dorian Gray while depriving him of the gory suicidal redemption of Oscar Wilde's hero. In the history of nineteenth-century symbolism, only the life of Ludwig II of Bavaria, made famous by Luchino Visconti, provides a similar sensation of a subjectivity entirely transfused into the circumambient manners and fashions.

D'Annunzio's wardrobe becomes "serial and exhaustive like the vocabulary [of the artist], made up of items chosen in rigorous adherence to a code, where any infraction is always minimal." Beyond the long and detailed catalog of clothes and accessories, we have few clues to D'Annunzio's authentic self. We are not surprised in the least by the truly disarming lists of "dresses and coats, shirts and waistcoats, ties and bow ties, pajamas and dressing gowns, shoes and boots and hats and socks and handkerchiefs and gloves" that in other cases would seem incredible, absurd, or trivial frivolities without significance.[22] If it is not difficult to metaphorically pluck away the white gardenia that Oscar Wilde flaunted in his fortunate days and think of his disastrous decadence, and if, in the case of other nineteenth-century writers, like Giovanni Pascoli and Giovanni Verga or, in France, like Honoré de Balzac and later Gustave Flaubert, Guy de

Maupassant, and Marcel Proust, the ideal image of these authors is divorced of any outer apparel, in the case of D'Annunzio there is not a single item of clothing that can be ignored in his incredible wardrobe. His figure, like his language, is intrinsically determined by the costumes he wears at any given moment. Even when he adopted the ideal persona of the writer, he could not help translating himself into something more garish, into a sequence of gestures and movements and, finally, into a sort of unnatural or hypernatural metamorphosis. Here, for example, is D'Annunzio reminiscing about the writing of the poem "La morte del cervo":

> Now I become furious. . . . I'm in front of the bookstand, with my high poetic forehead, but against my strong ribs I feel the urgency of a force I can no longer control nor measure. . . . It is the fight of the centaur against the deer. A sort of mimetic demon seizes me. His vehemence pushes me away from my sheets, it seizes me, it holds me. It presses at the back of my neck, it bends my back, pulls down my arms, places my open hands on the brick floor, turns my hands and feet into four hooves, envelops my tongue between the word that growls and the neighing that speaks.[23]

The neophyte from the Abruzzi region, as well as the later urbanite for that matter, cared little for the sentimental, psychological, moral identity of the feminine subject. Indeed, this remains a permanent characteristic of his literary production; there is little divergence between the more or less precious objects that the esthete and collector examined and the personified identity of a woman, one of his incalculable partners. In *Fuoco*, for example, the first image of she who was to become a *unicum* in D'Annunzio's sentimental journey, the actress Eleonora Duse, takes its rhythm from the color of her hair, the tone of her skin, the intensity of her gaze, and so on.[24] D'Annunzio, here and later, is an unquenchable recorder of outer appearance, in the same way as he loves the more fluctuating and iridescent aspects of nature and life. Thus, in D'Annunzio's work, the costume, the dress, is not an instrument, a means to approach the reality of the character, but is one with the character: the iridescent nuances, the colors, the folds of a gown or a shawl express the substance, in D'Annunzio's notion of the word, of a given female character, in the same way as the outline of his greyhounds or the nostrils of his galloping horse, which he masterfully noted.

D'Annunzio loves the shape of things, that which normally and simply can be called the outer shell, the exterior manifestation, the mutable world of appearances. This, however (and herein lies his originality) is not due to an innate superficiality as much as to his firm belief that there is nothing worth observing beyond external appearances—what can be touched and visually examined. The very soul of things, as well as of humans, is one with their chromatic essence, with the beauty of the dress in which the shape of a woman is cast, with the refined nobility of a gesture; a fan, the reflection of a diamond, pertain, in D'Annunzio's view of life, to human essence, just as much as the laughing or crying of the person who is loved or unloved.

For D'Annunzio, color is the means through which one signifies the impulses of the self, the soul. In the luminous hue of a dress or a hand stretching out on a velvet background, D'Annunzio strives to pick out the strands of the intrinsic identity of a character. From here, the frequent insistence—incomparable to that of any other author, whether past or contemporary—on artistic comparison. Looking at a dress or a human figure, whether feminine or masculine, D'Annunzio instantaneously transfers it to a pictorial dimension, of which he has an uncommonly acute and extensive knowledge. To validate his capacity for observation, he does not refer only to actual works of art but also to imaginary paintings and sculptures. From the creatures he loves, he strives to extract a characteristic through chromatic, plastic, or luminous details. Beyond this fascinating figurative repertoire, there is nothing other than the nullification, not only of any image, but also of the very living essence of the image. The writer is not interested in the woman or the man per se; he is interested in them as images, as a counterpart of an imaginary pictorial ideal. For this reason, clothes receive more attention than in the writings of any other author. It is not, however, a naturalist or *verista* attention. While Verga needed only one glance to provide a sense of the social status and destiny of a character, minor *veristi* often offered more extensive descriptions.[25] But D'Annunzio—who at the beginning had shared the features of the Italian naturalist tradition, and who had been a careful reader of French naturalism, echoing its themes and motifs in his own work—gradually transcended Verga, Federico De Roberto, or Luigi Capuana's anxiously scrutinizing gaze on objects and the environment, to focus on the atmosphere with a highly sensitive ear.

D'Annunzio's highly personal way of giving new emphasis—through linguistic innovations or careful catalogs of colors—to features of *verista* flavor occurs in notations on the poor, the ugly, the waifs in *Il trionfo della morte (The Triumph of Death)*, written between 1889 and 1894, far from Rome, between San Vito Chietino, where Francesco Michetti had arranged a refuge for the writer and Barbara Leoni (Ippolita in the novel), and the "Convent" of Francavilla a Mare. These characters impress because of their strident contrast with the sophisticated elegance of the lady from Rome. For example a shepherd girl "in rags" begs for money, "poorly covered in her bluish rags," and, after having kissed the coins and let go of the ropes that held her sheep, "removed from her head a rag which no longer had either form or color, stooped to the ground, and slowly, with greatest care, tied up the pieces of money in a multiplicity of knots."[26] But the body of a drowned boy "appeared, inert, stretched on the hard beach. It was the body of a child of eight or nine, a thin and frail blond. For a pillow, they had put beneath his head his poor rags rolled up in a bundle: his shirt, blue breeches, red belt, soft felt hat."[27] This exasperated, curious, precise description at times shatters the enchantment of a situation and atmosphere. Again in *The Triumph of Death*, for example, the secret correspondence between the emergence of evening and the aspect of his beloved, enjoyed by the protagonist during the famous walk in the Pincio, is given unnecessary detail: "From beneath the pallor of her dark face a light, violet-colored effusion shone through; and the narrow ribbon, of an exquisite shade of yellow, which she wore about her throat disclosed the brown marks of two beauty spots."[28] Perhaps the memory of Ippolita's narrow yellow ribbon dictated, years later, the elegant though admittedly bizarre gesture mentioned by D'Annunzio in his *Libro segreto:* "When leading my caravan in the Arabian Desert, I had with me precious oriental cloths. I placed the most beautiful around the neck of my dromedary."[29]

Like Rainer Maria Rilke and Hugo von Hofmannsthal, D'Annunzio believed, not in

PLATE 1 Engraved title page, Gerhard Mercator,
Atlas/Historia Mundi (1628). James Ford Bell Library,
University of Minnesota, Minneapolis, Minnesota.

PLATE 2 [ABOVE] William Wetmore Story (1819–95), *Cleopatra*,
modeled 1858, carved 1860. Marble on polychrome wood platform.
55 × 24 × 48 in. (139.7 × 61 × 121.9 cm). Gift of Mr. and Mrs.
Henry M. Bateman. Los Angeles County Museum of Art. Copyright
2012 Museum Associates/LACMA. Licensed by Art Resource, NY.

PLATE 3 [FACING] Giovanni Boldini, *Madame Michelham*, 1913.
Oil on canvas, 166 × 112.5 cm.

PLATE 4 Titian (Tiziano Vecellio, ca. 1488–1576). *Young Man with the Glove.* Photograph: Le Mage. Louvre, Paris, France. Réunion des Musées Nationaux/Art Resource, NY.

things, but in their capacity to lend themselves to a dimension that transmutes them. And in the dominant climate, halfway between Pre-Raphaelitism and the symbolism-decadentism to which he belonged, he arrived at peaks of linguistic effrontery, of hallucinated self-complacency. We are dealing apparently with a precision of naturalist origin; but the obvious pleasure with which D'Annunzio peppered his description of clothes with refined details, like a couturier, goes beyond convention.

In his role as *arbiter elegantiarum*, D'Annunzio adhered to current fashion and was up-to-date with its latest prescriptions and its most sophisticated and expensive inventions. He experimented with his own sartorial abilities, styling some high-fashion models and even designing personalized clothes and foulards as special presents. Even in fashion—especially that reserved for women of the aristocracy and upper bourgeoisie—D'Annunzio chose the best, always aiming for sophistication and for that which best suited the enigmatic femme fatale he favored.[30] For this reason, he paid less attention to the *tailleur,* the masculine type of dress that gained favor toward the end of the 1880s, supported by the idea of a more active and simple life. He also neglected heavy cloth and the severe line typical of the male tailor—the *tailleur,* opposed to the *couturière*—in favor of "sumptuous cloths such as velvet, brocade and satin, with the ornament of lace, embroidery, and sequins," in line with the floral Liberty style.[31]

He took instead, from late nineteenth-century fashion, a rarity—the "long visible furs," not a more traditional winter coat, lined with otter, marten, or mink[32]—and gave ample scope to hats and hat-veils, which, toward the end of the century, added mystery and fascination to the faces of women, as more than one writer noted. A fashion echoed in theater and painting.[33] He also paid attention to the ornaments that highlighted "the luxury of night dresses: sequins, lacework, real flowers or artificial ones made of velvet or silk"; nor did he neglect any of the accessories necessary to achieve an elegant *mise:* gloves, umbrellas, stockings, shoes, busts, jewels, glasses, always in line with the fashion plates circulated by Italian and foreign newspapers.[34]

When, however, D'Annunzio was not bound to a visual description tied to contemporary life or a specific fashionable invention, he was capable of imparting an evanescent quality to the costume and the person. Here, for example, is the first glimpse that Andrea Sperelli, the protagonist of *The Child of Pleasure,* has of Elena Muti:

> She ascended in front of him with a slow and rhythmic movement; her cloak, lined with fur as white as swan's-down, was unclasped at the throat, and slipping back, revealed her shoulders, pale as polished ivory, the shoulder-blade disappearing into the lace of the corsage with an indescribably soft and fleeting curve as of wings. The neck rose slender and round, and the hair, twisted into a great knot on the crown of her head, was held in place by jewelled pins. (4)

In the same novel, the protagonist, Maria Ferres,

> wore a dress of a curious indefinable dull rusty red, one of those so-called aesthetic colors one meets with in the pictures of the Early Masters or of Dante Gabriel Rossetti. It was arranged in a multitude of straight regular folds beginning immediately under the arms, and was confined at the waist by a wide blue-green ribbon, of the pale tinge of a fedel turquoise, that fell in a great knot at her side. . . . Another ribbon of the same shade, but much narrower, encircled her neck and was tied at the left side in a small bow, and a similar ribbon fastened the end of the prodigious plait which fell from under her straw hat, round which was twined a wreath of hyacinths like that of Alma Tadema's Pandora. (126)

Even in the fantasies and dreams of Andrea, Maria, the pure lover, is symbolically associated with dress; she appears as a revelation, a mystical-erotic transfiguration: "And behold, she comes! *Incedit per lilia et super nivem.* She comes, robed in ermine; her tresses bound about with a fillet; her steps lighter than a shadow; the moon and the snow are less pale than she. *Ave!* A shadow, azure as the light that tints the sapphire, accompanies her" (261).

Elsewhere, as in *The Triumph of Death,* an item of clothing crystallizes emotion into memory.[35] One could go on reading countless descriptions of clothes from all his novels, in a sort of literary fashion show. But below D'Annunzio's indubitable pleasure in the polished word or the fantastic description runs an undercurrent of detachment from the character by which he is apparently absorbed. Those who accused him of an attitude of provincial admiration toward the great aristocratic and urban society were right after all. But that acquisitive attitude typical of a social climber transforms him into something different. There are ironic nuances when, for example, Andrea Sperelli abandons himself to a reverie in which he imagines the phantom of love: "But he could not make up his mind which of the two women he would prefer as the center of this fantastic scenario: Elena Heatfield robed in imperial purple, or Maria Ferres robed in ermine" (*Child of Pleasure*, 260). Reflecting on the "night of moonlight and snow," Sperelli seems to incline toward "the dominance of Maria Ferres, as under some invincible astral influence," and continues with a truly surprising conclusion despite the inventive capacity of fantasy, denouncing, in the end, the inner evolution of the writer who meditates over his page: "The image of the pure creature grew symbolically out of the sovereign purity of the surrounding aspect of things. The symbol re-acted forcibly on the spirit of the poet" (261).

D'Annunzio moved with ease, literally, within symbolism. Images that, when caught in the flurry of a past fashionable life, jump out of the page bright and distinct, with time tend to lose their colors, to blur, through a sort of Leonardo-like technique. So in *Notturno:*

> Renata returns from her visit to the tombs. She enters my room and sighs with fatigue. Lets herself fall on the chair; stretching her arms she takes off her hat which has a Thessalian form, adorned with two small round roses. She is tired. She has walked through alleys and canal banks and squares large and little, from church to church. The room is full of a crimson twilight. Her bare face is very white, almost phosphorescent. On her brown dress I seem to perceive the smell of candles, the smell of certain pallid herbs.[36]

This change from sight to scent might have been determined by the situation of the author, forced by a wound to one eye to renounce visual sensations as his primary input.

But certainly here the dissolution of form is complete; the woman's physiognomy is wrapped up in perfume, in memory, in echoes, in references both to the environment and to faraway lands and nuances.

Shortly thereafter, the image of Renata (the "Sirenetta," the daughter who is devotedly nursing him) will be further defined by the sound of her voice: "—I'm so tired!—says the Sirenetta. And her childish voice drunk with salty air and broken by the effort of swimming, her voice of the mouth of the Arno touched my heart of yore." Moreover, "A human face is made up of flesh and bones, perforated by the vigilance of the senses. The hair is a living mass that fills your hands and weighs. But this face is nothing other than the airy figment of my soul, and these locks resemble one of those extraordinary feelings in which the soul remains suspended and frees itself from the error of time" (227). In other words, almost as if re-creating the autobiographical process of his literary evolution, D'Annunzio conceived of dress as a uniform, armor, to hide his vulnerable sensibility. Miss Macy in *Il Venturiero senza ventura* (The adventurer without adventures), the "Clarisse from overseas," the American artist who makes plaster replicas of the most famous buildings of Venice, "is dressed up in a long bluish cloak, like a pioneer soldier. She is blond, with her hair raised above her forehead and pulled back, with a few gray strands. She has blue eyes, splendid, pure, childish, where her sympathetic emotions seem to flow continuously like running water. She has the strong and rough hand of a working woman."[37] Even the nurse Nerissa of *Cento e cento e cento e cento pagine del libro segreto di Gabriele D'Annunzio tentato di morire* seems lost in her Red Cross nurse uniform: "Nerissa is as chaste as a Clarisse, I know her story of conjugal martyrdom, I know her harsh everyday struggle, she is perpetually vigilant, her eyes of 'new iron' keep guard over her seditious flesh. Her 'Red Cross nurse' dress has somewhat of a monastic smell, a smell of enclosure."[38]

With *Notturno*, D'Annunzio attains a spiritual dimension, detaching himself from the *verista*-symbolist tradition to which he historically belongs; in this phase, his descriptions of characters (like the creatures of Rilke or Proust), whether inventions, memories, or direct impressions, seem to lack corporeality, favoring instead an impalpable form of evocation, like a melody. Yet this remains a parenthesis. As his eye healed, D'Annunzio regained the full range of sensations and began once again enjoying every visual perception. And immediately he resumed contemplating himself, watching himself from the outside, watching his clothes:

> For the first time I'm allowed to go down to the garden. An illusory vigor seizes me. With childish glee I abandon the senile accoutrements of the invalid. I become once again a white Lancer. My horseman trousers, so finely caught at the knee, now show a few folds. With a fluttering of hope I see once again on the sleeves of my jacket the badge of the aviator, the golden wings reddened by the salt of the Adriatic sea. I seem to perceive the smell of altitude. These gray clothes have known the blue beyond the clouds, have been suspended four thousand meters above the desert of air. . . . I smile hearing the clinking of the stirrups rubbed one against the other by the person who is kneeling at my feet to put them on. I prevent him from doing so.[39]

Even in *Notturno,* when he remembers the past, the details of clothes are not neglected as in his reminiscence of the exotic atmosphere of a musical soiree, "at Ilse's house, on a chimerical winter night in Paris": "Around a wooden unicorn, which came from that Burmese emperor who is the friend of mysticism, Alastair, dressed in a sky-blue tunic . . . had danced his Gothic dances. . . . The singer was sitting calmly, as if the smoke came from the bonfires of his father river and could not offend his voice. He was wearing a pinkish yellow tunic and a long ambergris necklace."[40] At times this descriptive excess breaks the rhythm of an emotion that might have been truly profound. Consider, for example, the passage in which the patient evokes a dramatic, emotional night of battle above the ship *Impavido:*

> Nothing escapes the relentless careful eyes that nature has given me, and everything nourishes and augments me. This thirst for living resembles the need to die and become eternal. For death is as present as life, as warm as life, as beautiful as life, inebriating, promising, transfiguring. I stand straight, on my two feet wearing light shoes that can be easily untied, I stand straight on the bridge of this small battle-ship, where there is room for nothing other than the weapon and the warrior.[41]

After so much talk of clothes, uniforms, wardrobes, masks, atmospheres evoked by memory based on a single detail of a dress, there is still D'Annunzio's evocative ability to fix the purity of a female nude whose flesh is "wet as if caught in the transparency of liquid ambergris, irrigated with warm and fluid gold like a lamp of Olympic blood."[42] So let us finish with a scene from "Svestizione" ("Undressing"), fluid and precise as an ancient rite of seduction:

> The Diambra began undressing, with slow and languid, and at times hesitant, gestures, pausing every now and then to listen. She takes off her fine silk stockings, of such a rare color that it has no name among known colors; and casts them away like wilted flowers, languidly. Her naked legs come to light, polished like sea marble of Parios, and her small and slender feet, and her malleoluses as fragile as those of a boy, and her delicate knees, which hide with such beauty the weaving of the muscles and the knot of the bones. Then she undoes the ribbon on her shoulder that holds the last hostage, the most thin and precious undershirt of yellow cloth that in ancient times was brought over by the merchants of Bactria.[43] That snow flows on her breast, follows the arch of her back, pauses for a moment on her hips; falls suddenly to her feet, like flakes of foam. And Diambra rises all pure in her divinity. . . . But, as her eyes fall on her ringed hands, with graceful gestures she takes her rings off, which are many and fiery. Then she disseminates them on the carpet. Having remained thus, in her simple perfection, she turns toward her bed. The silence is very intense; the lamps burn softly; and she is free of all desire.[44]

Ultimately he concludes with the touch of self-complacent narcissism with which the woman, alone, without desires or fears, contemplates her own essential beauty, "secretly" whispering to herself "words of praise."

1. Attention to clothes is related to social and economic aspirations, as well as being a response to an aesthetic ideal, to a desire to mark one's identity, and, especially in younger people, to seduce. Every new fashion is "a refusal to inherit, a subversion against the oppression of the preceding fashion." Roland Barthes, *The Fashion System* [1967], trans. Matthew Ward and Richard Howard (Berkeley: University of California Press, 1983), 273.

2. An overview of the role of clothes in Italian literature is found in Rosita Levi Pisetzky, *Il costume e la moda nella società italiana* (Turin: Einaudi, 1978), 14–16. Unless otherwise noted, all translations from Italian are mine.

3. Gabriele D'Annunzio is one of the foremost representatives of Italian decadentism. He was born in Pescara in 1863 and studied at the prestigious Cicognini high school of Prato. His first published works were series of poems (*Primo vere* and *Canto novo*) and stories (*Terra vergine* and *San Pantaleone*) inspired by everyday life in the Abruzzo region where he was born. In 1881, he began studying at the Faculty of Letters of the University of Rome. Though he never got his degree, he acquired an exceptional literary, musical, and artistic education. While in Rome, he contributed to many major newspapers and magazines, writing critical essays on literature and art and a series of journalistic pieces on the life of the city. In 1888, he ceased writing for *La Tribuna* and retired for six months in a house at Francavilla a Mare, owned by his friend Michetti. Here he wrote his first novel, *Il piacere,* published in 1889. This was followed by other successful novels *(Giovanni Episcopo, L'Innocente, Il trionfo della morte, Le vergini delle rocce, Il fuoco)* and collections of poetry *(Poema paradisiaco, Odi navali).* His love affair with the actress Eleonora Duse spurred his interest in the theater, for which he wrote a number of plays *(La città morta, La Gioconda, Sogno di un mattino di primavera).* In the years in which he lived in Tuscany, in the villa he nicknamed "la Capponcina," he wrote many short poems collected under the title of *Laudi del cielo, del mare, della terra e degli eroi,* but also the novel *Forse che sì, forse che no* and the tragedies *Francesca da Rimini* and *La figlia di Jorio.* Forced by creditors to leave Italy in a hurry, he took refuge in Paris, where he frequented the symbolist and Parnassian circles. Here he wrote the fourth book of his *Laudi* and a few works in French such as *Le martyre de Saint Sebastien.* During the First World War, he distinguished himself as a soldier and pilot; he participated in the "Buccari hoax," an attack by Italian "MAS" torpedo speedboats on Austrian ships anchored in the bay of Buccari, eighty kilometers behind enemy lines, and directed a famous propaganda flight over Vienna. He was wounded in one

eye and, during his difficult recovery, wrote *Notturno*, a beautifully styled autobiographical work. Dissatisfied with the peace treaty, he organized a march on the city of Fiume, which both Italy and Croatia claimed, and for three years, from 1919 to 1921, occupied the city as regent. Forced to leave Fiume by Italian troops, he retired to a villa on Lake Garda, which he called "Il Vittoriale degli italiani" (the monument to victory of the Italians), where he died in 1938. In the last years of his life, D'Annunzio wrote various autobiographical works, in which he casts himself as a Nietzschean superman endowed with exceptional qualities *(Il venturiero senza ventura, Il compagno dagli occhi senza cigli, Cento e cento e cento e cento pagine del libro segreto di Gabriele D'Annunzio tentato di morire).*

4. At the beginning of the nineteenth century, Ugo Foscolo produced an unforgettable series of descriptions of neoclassical dresses. In his case, however, clothes directly refer to the personality of the character, as an additional element of the character's native grace and divine beauty.

5. Giosuè Carducci, "Eterno femminino regale," *Cronaca Bizantina*, January 1, 1882.

6. "Un vero trionfo di bellezza l'ebbe, iersera, S.M. la Regina. Aveva un abito di broccato candido, chiuso intorno al collo, semplice molto; e su i capelli alcune rose thee. In quella semplicità le regali grazie luminavano più vive. A canto alla Regina, bionda e chiara, sedeva la duchessa Sforza Cesarini, vestita d'un abito nero tutto tempestato di rabeschi, di brillanti, nobilissima nell'atto con cui teneva contro la luce un ventaglio di madreperla iridescente": Gabriele D'Annunzio, *Scritti giornalistici,* ed. Annamaria Andreoli (Milan: Mondadori, 1995), 1:470. All translations mine except *The Child of Pleasure,* trans. Georgina Harding (Boston: Page, 1898) (page references in text), and *The Triumph of Death,* trans. Arthur Hornblow (Boston: Page, 1896).

7. Levi Pisetzky, *Il costume e la moda nella società italiana,* 16.

8. Emilio De Marchi (Milan, 1851–1901) is known for his novels offering a middle-class version of naturalism: *Il cappello del prete, Demetrio Pianelli, Arabella, Giacomo l'idealista.*

9. Levi Pisetzky, *Il costume e la moda nella società italiana,* 16.

10. Gabriele D'Annunzio, *Favole mondane,* introduction and notes by Federico Roncoroni (Milan: Garzanti, 1981), 6.

11. "bellissimo sorriso, in tutte le altre attitudini manifestando une specie di mollezza e d'indolenza naturale e mista di grazie. . . . Vestiva una lana di vigogna d'un color verde di foglia secca, e la forma del capo, secondata dalla pettinatura dei capelli pieganti su la nuca verso l'alto ed in alto raccolti, svolgevasi puramente sul damasco splendido della poltrona. I tratti gai del volto rammentavano certi profili muliebri dei disegni di Moreau il Giovine, delle vignette di Gravelot." Both cita-

tions from Gabriele D'Annunzio, "Per un vaso," in *Tutte le novelle*, ed. Annamaria Andreoli and Marina De Marco (Milan: Mondadori, 1992) [hereafter cited as *TN*], 526.

12. "La colorazione dell'epidermide, quella tinta che pareva fatta con le interne foglie d'una rosa bianca, si arricchiva di certe quasi fuggitive trasparenze": "Per un vaso," in *TN*, 527.

13. "Aveva una veste di merletti neri pieghettata posteriormente e d'avanti aperta e circondata d'un piccolo merletto che risaliva dalle due parti del *tablier* formando spirale sopra una *jupe di satin* di cui la parte anteriore era tutta ricamata dal collo ai piedi. All'*encolure*, tagliata molto bassa, un merletto larghissimo *à tuyaux* saliva diritto sino al mento, girava il collo e discendeva in cascata nel mezzo della schiena, terminando in un gran nodo di merletto che ricadeva su *la jupe*. . . . Ieri poi, tra un riso languido di sole e una lacrima di pioggia, la vedemmo pel Corso. Aveva una *toilette en étamine vert mousse*, con una *visite Kanguroo*. Il cappello di paglia *chinée* bruna e bianca, a larghe falde, le circondava la faccia; una sciarpa *d'étamine* metteva delle pieghe sul davanti e un mazzo di borragine di papaveri di velluto si levava audacemente a sinistra. Le falde del cappello erano foderate d'una *étamine lamée* di cui gli innumerevoli fili aurei scintillavano come i raggi d'un nimbo sacro": "Una donna metodica," in *TN*, 538.

14. Roncoroni notes how this story is the first example of D'Annunzio's interest in Japanese exoticism that began in Italy in the 1880s, under the influence of French taste. *Favole mondane*, 193–94.

15. "Ella aveva questa curiosa affettazione di giapponesismo nelle vesti, nelle pose, perfino nella voce. . . . Passava il tempo nella ricerca di abbigliamenti ideali o nella contemplazione e nell'adorazione solitaria della propria bellezza. . . . Ed ella così componeva studiosamente la sua persona in una quantità di figurazioni eleganti che certe volte avevano forse il difetto d'essere un po' teatrali, un po' sceniche, Armonizzava il paravento e la veste; e moderava le ombre e i raggi. Amava i toni falsi, quelle tinte smorte e rotte, quei digradamenti indefinibili che si trovano talvolta in certi fiori, in certi minerali vergini, in certi vapori dell'aria; ed amava anche la ricchezza delle pieghe, la mollezza fluente del crespo, quel non so che di quasi evanescente dentro cui il corpo flessibile s'indovina. Un giorno, si mostrò in una roba verdemare tutta cosparsa dei fiori del ciliegio; e, nel sedersi, ad arte ebbe per fondo un paravento dove su una mite tinta aurea di frumento volavano due grandi gru, due di quelle candide messaggere celesti dalla cresta di fuoco e dalla gola nera. Un altro giorno si mostrò in una tragica veste simulante un ciel fosco": "Mandarine," in *TN*, 518–19.

16. "Non dimenticherò mai lo stupore che mi ferì vedendo per la prima volta Gabriele

addobbato e azzimato e profumato per una festa": Edoardo Scarfoglio, *Il libro di don Chisciotte* (Rome: Sommaruga, 1885), 201.

17. See Annamaria Andreoli, *Conformismo e trasgressione: Il guardaroba di Gabriele D'Annunzio, una mostra di Pitti Uomo Italia* (Florence: La Nuova Italia, 1988), 13.

18. "Noi amiamo con molto ardore le vibrazioni delle *pierreries*, la luminosità dei tessuti *pailletés*, e le scollature audaci e le acconciature splendenti di monili araldici e tutte quelle magnificenze femminili che mutano la sala di un teatro in un convento di bellezza dilettoso alla vista dei mortali": "Cronaca Romana," *Cronaca bizantina*, January 16, 1885.

19. "Io non sono e non voglio essere un poeta mero." *Favole Mondane*, 14, "All manifestations of the intellect equally attract me" ("Tutte le manifestazioni dell'intelligenza mi attraggono ugualmente").

20. "Il lettor vero è quegli che m'ama": Ibid., 14.

21. Andreoli, *Conformismo e trasgressione*, 14.

22. Ibid., 19, 20.

23. "Ora m'imbestio. . . . Sono in piedi davanti al leggio, con alta la mia fronte di poeta, ma contro le mie coste forti sento l'urgenza di una forza che non so più dominare né misurare. . . . È la lotta del Centauro con il cervo. Una specie di dèmone mimetico mi possiede. La sua veemenza mi respinge dalle mie carte, mi prende, mi tiene. Mi preme la nuca, mi piega la schiena, m'atterra le braccia, mi porta le mani aperte su l'impiantito di mattoni, mi cangia le mani e i piedi in quattro zoccoli, m'avviluppa la lingua tra parola che rigna e nitrito che parla": Gabriele D'Annunzio, *Prose*, vol. 1 (Milan: Mondadori, 2005), 1222. About this passage Andreoli correctly notes: "Does not this passage already predict the sailor of Buccari, the aviator of Cattaro, the foot-soldier of Veliki?" (*Conformismo e trasgressione*, 20). In other words, even in his heroic transformations, D'Annunzio exclusively sees, feels, suffers for, and takes pleasure in his image, his "mask," as it appears to the eyes of others.

24. The writer arrives at this metaphor: "She was there, dressed up in her secret gentle soul, so easily destroyed, sacrificed, without blood" ("Era là, vestita di quella sua segreta anima tenera, così facile a essere distrutta, immolata, senza sangue"). Gabriele D'Annunzio, *Il Fuoco*, ed. Gianni Oliva (Rome: Newton Compton, 1995), 100.

25. See Carmela Covato's observations on the desire of Maria, the protagonist of Verga's *Storia di una capinera*, to wear something different and more practical than the black dress of the convent girl, in this volume, chapter 12.

26. D'Annunzio, *Triumph of Death,* 205. A curiosity about *The Triumph of Death:* the attention to accessories intrudes even in the passionate love letter that Giorgio writes to Ippolita, while impatiently waiting for her arrival for their holiday at a solitary hermitage, in which he offers some practical advice on what to wear: "You must be careful to come provided with heavy shoes, and gigantic parasols. As to dresses, it is useless to bring many; a few gay and durable costumes for our morning walks will suffice. Do not forget your bathing suit" (168).

27. Ibid., 345.

28. Ibid., 10. The yellow ribbon could be echoing the "ray of light, yellow as sulphur, straight as a sword" that "lightly touched Monte Mario behind the pointed tops of the cypress-trees" (ibid., 9).

29. "Quando conducevo la mia carovana nel Deserto d'Arabia, avevo meco preziosissime stoffe d'Oriente. Misi la più bella al collo del mio dromedario": Gabriele D'Annunzio, *Cento e cento e cento e cento pagine del libro segreto di Gabriele D'Annunzio tentato di morire,* in *Prose scelte,* ed. Gianni Oliva (Rome: Newton Compton, 1995) [hereafter *PS*], 540. Anyone who visits the "Vittoriale" will notice the extent of D'Annunzio's interest in clothes: the statues, plaster replicas of ancient and Renaissance masterworks, were dressed up, made up with special colors, and adorned with jewels and rare cloths, shawls, Turkish silk, brocades, all products of Fortuny fabrics.

30. See Dario Cecchi, *Corè: Vita e dannazione della Marchesa Casati* (Bologna: L'inchiostro blu / Ritz Saddler, 1986) on one of D'Annunzio's characters—the protagonist of *Forse che sì, forse che no,* in real life Marquise Luisa Casati—lover of eccentric and outrageous luxury, and so a perfect companion for D'Annunzio.

31. Levi Pisetzky, *Il costume e la moda nella società italiana,* 333.

32. Ibid., 338. About furs, Levi Pisetzky notes that, toward the end of the 1880s, the "boa" and the muff came back into fashion "adorned by the little head of the animal and at the sides the little paws that hang low swinging back and forth . . . ; a graceful artifice is to attach to the muff a bunch of freshly-cut flowers. During gentler winters a caprice of fashion is the so-called fantasy muff, in velvet or lined silk, adorned with embroidery" (310).

33. "Winter hats, of velvet, plush or felt, straw during the summer," comments Levi Pisetzky, "have luxury ornaments; feathers, almost always placed vertically, velvet knots, *aigrettes,* often fixed with clasps that shine as the head moves, little birds or even just tiny hummingbirds, with little feathers shining with reflections of emerald and ruby, but also others described by fashion magazines that seem to our current taste much less suited, such as a seagull with spread wings or even

an owl" (ibid., 340). As for the veil, "attached to the brim and hanging down so as to completely cover the face down to the neck, attached behind the neck with small knot or pin," Pisetzky notes that "the vibrant art of sculptor Medardo Rosso fixes this fashion in a torso where with magic skill the face of a lady is precisely represented under the hat-veil. Even D'Annunzio, reporting under the pen name of Vere de Vere, mentions this fashion, which must have been still worn in 1885, as, of the many married and unmarried ladies watching a concert at the Doria Pamphili palace in Rome, only one is described wearing 'a pearl-colored veil on her ruby face'" (ibid.).

34. Ibid., 334. Among fashion magazines, the most up-to-date and detailed was *Margherita*, which drew its name and its inspiration from the queen, a leader in fashion. .

35. "—Do you remember the first anniversary, asked George, that of last year?—Yes, I remember.—It was a Sunday, Easter Sunday. And I came to your rooms at ten o' clock, in the morning. And you wore that little English jacket that pleased me so. You had brought your prayer book" (D'Annunzio, *Triumph of Death*, 21).

36. "Renata ritorna dalla visita dei sepolcri. Entra nella mia stanza con un sospiro di stanchezza Si lascia cadere sopra la sedia: Inarcando le braccia si toglie il cappello che ha la forma tessalica, ornata di due piccole rose rotonde. E' stanca. Ha camminato per calle fondamenta campi e campielli, di chiesa in chiesa. La stanza è piena di crepuscolo violaceo. Il suo viso nudo è bianchissimo, quasi fosforescente. Su la sua veste bruna mi sembra di fiutare un odore di ceri, un odore di erbe scolorate": Gabriele D'Annunzio, *Notturno*, in *PS*, 227.

37. "È vestita d'una lunga casacca azzurrognola, come un artiere. È bionda, con i capelli rilevati su la fronte, rigettati indietro, sparsi di qualche filo grigio. Ha gli occhi cerulei, splendidi, puri, infantili, ove la commozione sembra passare di continuo come un'acqua corrente, Ha la mano robusta e rude della lavoratrice": Gabriele D'Annunzio, *Il Venturiero senza ventura*, in *PS*, 281. Note how the observation of the details of the dress precedes other acute psychophysical observations.

38. "Nerissa è casta come una clarissa, conosco la sua storia di martire coniugale, conosco la sua lotta severa di ogni giorno, è in perpetua vigilanza, i suoi occhi di 'ferro nuovo' custodiscono la sua carne sediziosa. Nell'abito di 'crocerossina' ha non so che odore monacale, non so che profumo di clausura": Gabriele D'Annunzio, *Cento e cento e cento e cento pagine del libro segreto di Gabriele D'Annunzio tentato di morire*, in *PS*, 503.

39. "Per la prima volta m'è concesso di scendere in giardino. Un vigore fittizio mi solleva. Con un'allegrezza fanciullesca abbandono i vestimenti senili dell'invalido. Ridivento un Lanciere

bianco. Le mie brache di cavaliere, così bene aggiustate al ginocchio, ora fanno qualche piega. Con un palpito di speranza rivedo su le maniche della giubba le insegne del volatore, le ali d'oro arrossate dalla salsedine dell'Adriatico. Mi sembra di fiutare l'odore dell'altezza. Questi panni grigi conobbero l'azzurro di là dalle nuvole, rimasero sospesi a quattromila metri nel deserto dell'aria. . . . Sorrido udendo tintinnire gli speroni sfregati l'un contro l'altro da chi si curva ai miei piedi per affibbiarmeli. Non me li lascio mettere." And, on the same page, note the sophisticated considerations of the bandages on the head: "My hand goes to the bandage. It is *more severe* than usual. It is not *white, but dark*. It is not *linen, but silk*. My eye is *dressed for mourning, it is wearing a pall.*" D'Annunzio, *Notturno*, in *PS*, 233 (emphases mine).

40. "Intorno a un liocorno di legno, proveniente da quell'impero birmano che è amico della mistica, Alastair vestito d'una tunica azzurra broccata d'oro aveva danzato le sue danze gotiche. . . . Il cantore era seduto con pacatezza, come se quel fumo gli venisse dai roghi del fiume padre e non gli potesse offendere la voce. Portava una tunica d'un color giallo rosato e una gran collana d'ambra": D'Annunzio, *Notturno*, in *PS*, 162.

41. "Nulla sfugge agli occhi senza tregua attentissimi che la natura mi ha dati, e tutto m'è alimento e aumento. Una tal sete di vivere è simile al bisogno di morire e di eternarsi. La morte è infatti presente come la vita, è calda come la vita, è bella come la vita, inebriante, promettitrice, trasfiguratrice. Sto dritto sopra ai miei due piedi calzati di scarpe leggère che facilmente si slacciano, sto dritto sopra il ponte di questa piccola nave da battaglia, dove non c'è posto che per l'arme e per il combattente": D'Annunzio, *Notturno*, in *PS*, 172.

42. A description of Giorgione's *Festa campestre*, from "Note su Giorgione e la critica" [1895], in Gabriele D'Annunzio, *Pagine sull'arte*, ed. Stefano Fugazza (Milan: Electa, 1986), 71.

43. D'Annunzio had already dedicated an untitled article to this item of clothing, preceded by an editorial abstract: "the luxury of the clothes one does not see—the simple undershirt—the spinal undershirt—the Medioeval undershirt etc" ("Cronaca della moda," *La Tribuna*, January 21, 1887; the piece was signed "Lila Biscuit"). "The most exquisite elegance and the more provoking sophistication [was the journalist's comment] are found in those light clothes of cambric or fine linen, which through their transparency take the smell and the gentle pink hue of the female skin" (D'Annunzio, *Favole mondane*, 123).

44. "Diambra incomincia a svestirsi, con gesti lenti e languidi, talora esitanti, soffermandosi ad ogni poco quasi per tender l'orecchio. Si toglie le fini calze di seta, d'una tinta così rara che non

ha nome fra le tinte conosciute; e le gitta lunghi come fiori appassiti, mollemente, Appaiono le sue gambe ignude, polite come di marino pario, e i piedi piccoli e snelli, e i malleoli fragili come quelli d'un fanciullo, e i ginocchi delicati che con tanta venustà nascondono l'intreccio dei muscoli e il nodo delle ossa. Quindi scioglie di su la spalla il nastro che trattiene l'ultima spoglia, la camicia più sottile e preziosa della tela gialla che nel tempo antico riportavano i mercanti della Battriana. Quella neve fluisce lungo il petto, segue l'arco delle reni, si ferma un attimo ai fianchi; cade poi d'un tratto ai piedi, come un fiocco di spuma. E la Diambra sorge tutta pura nella sua divinità. . . . Ma, come li occhi le corrono alle mani inanellate, con un gesto di grazia si toglie gli anelli, che son molti e fiammeggianti. Quindi li semina sul tappeto. Rimasta così, nella sua semplice perfezione, si volge al letto. Il silenzio è altissimo; le lampade ardono dolcemente; ed ella è senza alcun desio." "Svestizione" was a reelaboration of the first chapter of a story published in *La Tribuna* on March 7, 1887, and signed as "Il Duca Minimo" in the column Favole mondane. It was published again in *La Tribuna* on October 22, 1887, with the same signature; almost without change, the passage was used again by the author for a "magic novella" signed "Gabriele D'Annunzio," with the title "La tiranna di Policoro" (*Vita Italiana*, Rome, January 10, 1888). See D'Annunzio, *TN*, 740.

10

REDEFINING AMERICAN WOMANHOOD
SHAWLS IN NINETEENTH-CENTURY LITERATURE

Anna Scacchi

> *There are people who will sympathize with a girl starving for bread, but*
> *only an artist . . . can sympathize with a girl starving for beautiful clothes.*
> ANZIA YEZIERSKA, *Salome of the Tenements*

During the last decades of the nineteenth century, shawls underwent a radical change in the United States: they disappeared from middle-class women's wardrobes to become an ethnic badge, an item of clothing worn by immigrant women. They later returned to vogue as exotic accessories for the well-off. Until the early 1870s, shawls had been a recurring presence in women's magazines, literature, and the visual arts, where they were presented as a comfortable and practical protection against the cold and apparently lacked strong class, racial, or ethnic connotations. In short, they democratically cloaked all the women of the Republic without raising anxieties in middle-class wearers about their social position, which could be reinscribed in these garments by means of material, embroidery, and other decorations, such as fringes and ribbons. Yet, according to an editorial column in the December 1850 issue of *Harper's New Monthly,* many Anglo-American women apparently did not feel at ease with shawls, since their flowing lines and simplicity left to the wearer the task of imbuing it with elegance:

We scarcely know a truer test of a gentlewoman's taste in dress than her selection of a shawl, and her manner of wearing it. . . . Generally speaking, the shawl is not [Anglo-American women's] forte, in fact they are rather afraid of it. They acknowledge its comfort and convenience for the open carriage, or the sea-side promenade, but rarely recognize it for what it is, a garment capable of appearing the most feminine and graceful in the world. They are too often oppressed by a heap of false notions on the subject; have somehow an idea that a shawl is "old" or "dowdy"; and yet have a dim comprehension that the costly shawls which they more frequently hear of than see, must have some unimagined merits to prove an excuse for their price.

The Frenchwoman, on the contrary, . . . played at dressing her doll with one, you may be sure; chronicled as an epoch in her life, her first possession of the real thing; holds it as precious as a diamond, and as something to which appartains the same sort of intrinsic value. . . . Truly the taste for the shawl is a little inherent, and a great deal acquired and cultivated; as appreciation for the highest attributes of every department of art ever must be.[1]

The adjectives "old" and "dowdy" point to reasons behind the shawl's imminent disappearance from middle-class women's wardrobes. As a remnant of old times lacking refinement, associated with America's rural past and women's restricted access to the public sphere, it would soon be discarded in favor of garments symbolizing modernity and women's freedom. Ethnic and immigrant women eagerly joined in the rejection of the shawl and adopted the modern urban fashion that had become a symbol of the New Woman.

"TRUE WOMEN" AND SHAWLS

Immediately before and well after the American Revolution, dressing was a social practice invested with a highly ideological and symbolic value for both men and women. Homespun clothes had played a fundamental role in galvanizing the rebel colonists' pride in their identity as plain, unrefined yeomen. Clothes were a badge of the political and cultural novelty of the United States, and of its self-appointed mission of regeneration for humankind. When, in 1776, Benjamin Franklin arrived in Paris in search of support for the colonists' struggle for independence, he was obviously exploiting the French people's love for the rugged *homo naturalis* of the New World. Wearing a sober, dark Quaker coat and fur cap, he turned himself, a learned author, world-recognized scientist, and astute politician with a taste for the good life, into an icon of American republican virtues and democratic restraint.

Dress, in other words, could be a signifier for American democracy, and shawls were ideal outerwear items equitably shielding all the women of the American Republic regardless of class from the wintry weather. Race and ethnicity did not play a significant role in the semiotics of shawls: when free and enslaved African Americans dared to wear stylish outfits, they were often censured for this "uppity" behavior or ridiculed as clumsily aping white women, which was considered a form of social trespassing,[2] but the wearing of shawls by black women was not regarded by whites as an inappropriate breach of the racial hierarchy. As nondescript garments, shawls lack a significant symbolic function in early and mid-nineteenth-century women's literature, even though they are recurring fixtures of the heroine's wardrobe. In *Uncle Tom's Cabin* (1852), for example, Eliza leaves behind her shawl and bonnet in her hasty flight from the tavern where she has stopped to rest with her son, when the slavetrader Haley arrives. But the notion that panic and love for her child make her forget the rules of proper womanly behavior is carried across the text less by the lack of protection against the cold than by her bare head. Eliza's desperate flight across the Ohio holding little Harry in her arms became a staple of *Uncle Tom's Cabin*'s iconography in the second half of the nineteenth century and into the first decades of the twentieth century. The image of her escape on the ice was constantly reproduced in illustrated editions of the novel and advertising posters for its onstage versions. Revealingly, many of these images show Eliza wearing a shawl loosely wrapped around her shoulders, but only a few restore a bonnet, though partly tied, while all invariably signal her distress through her disheveled hair.[3]

Shawls also appear in Mrs. Bird's episode, where the Yankee woman—who deliberately defies the Fugitive Slave Act that her husband, a senator, has just helped to pass—manages to convince Mr. Bird to become active in the Underground Railroad and help Eliza reach the Quaker settlement. The passage has a very important didactic function in the novel, because its pathos directly involves white women readers in Eliza's plight and leads them to identify with a black woman. It works, in other words, as an exemplum, teaching American women to act according to their principles, even when they go against the law, and to perceive gender similarities beneath racial difference. Mrs. Bird gives Eliza some old clothes and a shawl, but the real pivot in the scene, the action on which solidarity among women as mothers is built, is her gift of her dead son's clothes to little Harry.

The shawl is such a neutral signifier in *Uncle Tom's Cabin* that it does not bestow any connotations on its wearer as a symbol of true womanhood. Indeed, both Ophelia and Marie, characters occupying the opposite ends of the spectrum of femininity, wear one as their appearance is contrasted in moral terms:

[Marie St. Clare] stood, gorgeously dressed, on the verandah, on Sunday morning, clasping a diamond bracelet on her slender wrist. . . . Marie patronized good things, and she was going now, in full force,—diamonds, silk, and lace, and jewels, and all,—to a fashionable church, to be very religious. Marie always made a point to be very pious on Sundays. There she stood, so slender, so elegant, so airy and undulating in all her motions, her lace scarf enveloping her like a mist. She looked a graceful creature, and she felt very good and very elegant indeed. Miss Ophelia stood at her side, a perfect contrast. It was not that she had not as handsome a silk dress and shawl, and as fine a pocket-handkerchief; but stiffness and squareness, and bolt-uprightness, enveloped her with as indefinite yet appreciable a presence as did grace her elegant neighbor; not the grace of God, however,—that is quite another thing![4]

The shawl, then, was an appropriate garment as much for the stern Yankee spinster as for the self-indulgent Southern belle. But in a few years it would lose its neutrality and acquire the semantic ambivalence of a contested sign to become a hot issue in the national discussion on the new American woman.

After the Civil War, the republican ideology that had sustained the colonists' struggle during the Revolution had to compete with discourses that attacked its ethos and increasingly emphasized a new role for women as intelligent, expert purchasers and—to use Thorstein Veblen's phrase—as conspicuous consumers who displayed the taste and economic possibilities of the leisure class. In writing dealing with the transition to modernity, shawls often acquire nostalgic connotations; they represent a type of female subjectivity under siege: the thrifty frugal housewife celebrated in the domestic fiction of Lydia Maria Child, Catherine Beecher, and other antebellum authors. The virtues of the "true woman" appeared threatened by the extravagant behavior of modern American girls, who were responding to the economic needs of a capitalist nation by becoming compulsive shoppers addicted to Parisian couture.

Rich American girls like Daisy Miller, who shocked Europeans and old-fashioned Americans alike with their exuberance and outrageous outfits, seemed to have nothing in common with their sensible, sober mothers. Yet the troubling continuity linking the pure, innocent America of the past with the new urban, decadent nation that will be uncovered by twentieth-century writers such as Edith Wharton and Francis Scott Fitzgerald is already visible in Louisa May Alcott's novels, where the heroine's modest, plain clothing symbolizes republican values on the verge of extinction. In Alcott's novels the "old-fashioned" girl triumphs over the spoiled "girl of the period," whose unfortunate fate is meant as a cautionary tale teaching American girls to beware of consumerism. Her triumph will be short-lived—she too is attracted to luxurious trifles.

The shawl indexes Alcott's ambivalence in *Little Women* (1868), where the four March sisters' relationship with female fashion is an important key to their characters. While Meg is fascinated by beautiful clothes and envies rich girls who can afford to be elegant, and Amy's taste is offended by hand-me-downs that do not fit her, Jo does not care about the way she looks. She loves dressing up as a man when performing in her tragedies but finds women's clothes uncomfortable and unreasonably complicated. When Amy forces her to go visiting and dress up for the occasion, her body and her spirit alike rebel against the constrictions of fashion and society:

> While Amy dressed, she issued her orders, and Jo obeyed them, not without entering her protest, however, for she sighed as she rustled into her new organdie, frowned darkly at herself as she tied her bonnet strings in an irreproachable bow, wrestled viciously with pins as she put on her collar, wrinkled up her features generally as she shook out the handkerchief, whose embroidery was as irritating to her nose as the present mission was to her feelings, and when she had squeezed her hands into tight gloves with three buttons and a tassel, as the last touch of elegance, she turned to Amy with an imbecile expression of countenance.[5]

Jo's reluctant acceptance of proper feminine appearance emphasizes femininity as masquerade. For Jo March, paying calls on neighbors whom she does not like and wearing female fashion are similar acts, which make hypocrisy and falsity pass for politeness. She rejects both social conventions and women's clothes, whose main purpose is to underline delicacy and fragility, qualities she neither possesses nor desires. Yet she, not Meg or Amy, is the one who knows how to wear a shawl. Despite being a tomboy who cannot keep her clothes clean and spills lemonade on her white gloves, she appears as the most elegant March sister when she dons a shawl. "There's one thing you can do well, Jo, that is, wear a shawl. I can't, but it's very nice to see you, and I'm so glad Aunt March gave you that lovely one. It's simple, but handsome, and those folds over the arm are really artistic," says Amy, the aesthete and *arbiter elegantiarum* in *Little Women*.[6]

Alcott bestows on Jo an innate vocation to shawl-wearing that appears rather unlikely, revealing that the author is not completely comfortable with her heroine's disregard for conventions. At the end of the March sisters' process of transformation from "little women" into "good wives," Jo will embody the model American mother because, having been a rebellious child and adolescent, she is able to understand other wild souls and persuade them, through the exercise of moral suasion, to comply with the demands of society. In *Little Women*, the shawl refutes conventional, artificial femininity prescribed in late Victorian America and signals womanhood sharing in manly virtues unnatural to women. Yet it is also, paradoxically, what tells us that those manly virtues must recede and be left behind in order for the heroine to exert her benign influence over the Plumfield children. Jo's elegance when wearing a shawl in part reveals that inside the tomboy who will never become "Josephine" hides a truer woman than even ultrafeminine Meg. The shawl acts as a textual index to Jo's progress toward self-control and sacrifice of her desires for the benefit of others, while the plot in which she is the true American hero—ready to stage a new Bunker Hill against Laurie's aristocratic and deceitful English friends—is destined to abort.

NO LADY WEARS ONE TODAY

At the end of the nineteenth century, the fashion scene in the United States had radically changed. Even from afar, or at dusk, the sharp, neatly defined silhouette of a middle-class woman returning home from shopping could not be mistaken for the shapeless form of an immigrant woman clad in her checked shawl. In turn-of-the-century literature, the shawl vanished from the heroine's wardrobe and only appeared as a symbol of lower-class status or outdated taste. In Henry James's *Tragic Muse* (1890), for example, its fall from vogue is made clear by Mrs. Rooth's whimsical fondness for her shawl:

> One of them was an old lady with a shawl; that was the most salient way in which she presented herself. The shawl was an ancient, much-used fabric of embroidered cashmere, *such as many ladies wore forty years ago in their walks abroad, and such as no lady wears to-day.* It had fallen half off the back of the wearer, but at the moment Biddy permitted herself to consider her she gave it a violent jerk and brought it up to her shoulders again, where she continued to arrange and settle it, with a good deal of jauntiness and elegance, while she listened to the talk of the gentleman. Biddy guessed that this

little transaction took place very frequently, and was not unaware of its giving the old lady a droll, factitious, faded appearance, as if she were singularly out of step with the age.[7]

The shawl indeed became old and dowdy, obsolete and annoying, worn by extravagant old ladies who used it to put up a pretense of self-assurance and social prestige. It links Mrs. Rooth to her aristocratic past and at the same time serves as a token, together with other accessories in her daughter's and her own outfits, of their membership in a select circle of artists:

> Both these ladies were clad in light, thin, scant gowns, giving an impression of flowered figures and odd transparencies, and in low shoes, which showed a great deal of stocking and were ornamented with large rosettes. Biddy's slightly agitated perception travelled directly to their shoes: they suggested to her vaguely that the wearers were dancers— connected possibly with the old-fashioned exhibition of the shawl-dance.[8]

In *The House of Mirth* (1905), Edith Wharton depicts the swift rise and fall of fortunes that rearranged the New York social hierarchy. The only shawl is the one that covers the shoulders of Mrs. Haffen—the char-woman who wants to extort money from Lily in exchange for letters she found in Selden's fireplace—and immediately connotes her as low class and vulgar. In this early twentieth-century novel, genteel ladies have a considerable freedom of movement in the city, which provides new spaces where they can go unescorted. Yet, as Lily's fate shows, their recently acquired mobility on the urban scene is still socially risky and dangerously exposes them to gossip and loss of reputation. Their anxiety about roaming the streets in close contact with prostitutes and other female villains, and possibly being mistaken for one of them, may have been one of the reasons behind the swift disappearance of the shawl as outerwear.

In many turn-of-the-century novels, the constricted shoulders of the women of the past—which Edith Wharton in *Madame de Treymes* (1906) referred to as "the sloping shoulders of a generation of shawl-wearers"—were opposed to the athletic busts of modern girls as symbols of their former dependence on men.[9] In other words, shawls were not simply associated with the nation's rural past. They had also become the icon of a passive, acquiescent femininity. The tailored suit, with its neat, uncluttered cut and padded shoulders, was a visible reminder to men of modern women's determination to find their place in the public sphere.

As Anne Hollander notes, while the male costume has been the visible sign of the male subject's rationality and inscription in the discourse of modernity since the Enlightenment, until the end of the nineteenth century female fashion followed a different script:

> [The male costume] reflects the modern esthetic principles that were conceived out of Neo-classic aspirations in the late eighteenth century, just like modern democratic impulses. Also like them (as embodied in the United States Constitution, for example), it proposes an ideal of self-perpetuating order, flexible and almost infinitely variable. By contrast, women's fashion after 1800 consistently suggested quite different ideas, none of them modern at all, most of them following quite ancient and general sartorial custom.[10]

When they entered the all-male public spheres of work, politics, and higher education, women adopted the tailored suit, which mimicked the sobriety and functionality of the male costume and appeared more convenient to their newly acquired mobility.

> There was nothing modern about modern women's clothes until the female imitation of the modern male scheme was gradually accomplished during the course of this century. Emancipated women seeking to modernize their clothes found no better way than to imitate what men had done a century earlier, copying the idea of a loosely fitting envelope that would reveal its own clear tailored shape while suggesting that of the body under it, and allow concerted movement of invented dress and living body together.[11]

The hourglass shape emphasizing bust and hips was abandoned in favor of garments that followed the female body without constricting it into artificial forms. Yet function-

FIGURE 10.1 Mrs. Skeffington and other ladies. Courtesy of the George Grantham Bain Collection, Library of Congress, LC-B2-3962-9.

ality was not the only reason, nor the most important one, behind the transformation of female fashion at the end of the nineteenth century. A more central role was played by the fact that women's clothes, manufactured by the highest craftsmanship like those of men, became a product of technology, thereby acquiring the allure of the modern. Women, however, joined men only to a certain extent in the "great masculine renunciation." They allowed their clothes to shed some of those excessively decorative traits that, according to Thorstein Veblen and Charlotte Perkins Gilman, were only there to underline middle-class women's financial and cultural dependence on their husbands and their inability to perform any other social function than "conspicuous consumption."

But women's attraction to the extravagant and impractical—in shoes and hats, for instance, for that irrational, antiutilitarian force governing fashion that neither Veblen nor Gilman understood—survived in details and accessories that punctuated the discourse of modern female fashion, undermining its apparent subjection to the male code of functionality.

Bourgeois women were not the only ones to embrace the new fashion, which promised to transform them into modern, urban, self-assertive subjects. Shopgirls, secretaries, even sweatshop workers in the Lower East Side or others pursuing careers in the professions recently opened to their sex also disdained the loose, enveloping outlines drawn by the shawl and eagerly adopted the tailored suit. Many of them were among recently arrived immigrants and ethnic groups and had probably worn shawls when they had disembarked onto American shores, but their fascination with their new home suggests they will soon discard it. As a New York journalist noted, "I have seen young Italian peasants walking about the city, evidently just landed, and clad in their Sunday best— Giovanni in his broad hat, dark blue jacket, and leggings, and Lisa with her massive braids and gay shawl, open-eyed and wide-mouthed in the face of the wonderful civilization they are to belong to in the future."[12]

The shawl was a badge marking its wearer as outside the process of modernization. The protagonist of Anzia Yezierska's short story "America and I" (1923) exclaims, "In my imagination I already walked in my new American clothes. How beautiful I looked as I saw myself like a picture before my eyes! I saw how I would throw away my immigrant rags tied up in my immigrant shawl. With money to buy—free money in my hands—I'd show them that I could look like an American in a day."[13]

Early in the twentieth century, the shawl actually came back into vogue in women's fashion, but its function had radically changed. It was now no longer practical, comfortable outerwear but a costly accessory that complemented the dress and imparted an exotic touch to the more elegant ladies' outfits. With the emergence of an orientalism in women's clothing, made fashionable by Paul Poiret's elegant kimonos and sari-inspired evening gowns, shawls became exclusive, luxurious details that evoked the alterity of a mysterious Far East. They lost their connection with the necessary and the practical and entered the realm of the superfluous, sharing nothing with the uncut, shapeless wraps enveloping ethnic women in American slums.

MODERNITY, AMERICAN-STYLE

The transformation of the shawl from an item of clothing into an accessory graphically illustrates Georg Simmel's social theory of fashion. According to Simmel, fashion serves a very important social function as it works to incorporate individuals in a community

FIGURE 10.2 Discussing East Side rent strike, January 1908. Courtesy of the George Grantham Bain Collection, Library of Congress, LOT 10872-5.

while at the same time making class distinctions. Fashion is one of the strategies through which membership in the bourgeoisie is granted and defended from outsiders. It works, in other words, not only to signal status but also to construct and reproduce it:

> Fashion is the imitation of a given pattern and thus satisfies the need for social adaptation; it leads the individual onto the path that everyone travels, it furnishes a general condition that resolves the conduct of every individual into a mere example. At the same time, and to no less a degree, it satisfies the need for distinction, the tendency towards differentiation, change and individual contrast. It accomplishes the latter, on the one hand, by the change in contents—which gives to the fashions of today an individual stamp compared with those of yesterday and of tomorrow—and even more energetically, on the other hand, by the fact that fashions are always class fashions, by the fact that the fashions of the higher strata of society distinguish themselves from those of the lower strata, and are abandoned by the former at the moment when the latter begin to appropriate them.[14]

The disappearance of the shawl from Anglo-American middle-class women's wardrobe implies much more than a simple change in fashion: it was meant to distinguish and control access to the dominant group and, in particular, to safeguard the group's status as trendsetter and arbiter of social customs. It set middle-class women—who were accessing urban spaces as ladies of leisure and/or modern subjects vindicating their right to the city—apart from their ethnic others, whose passage in the city was marked by economic need and by their estrangement from the culture of consumption.

Yet reading turn-of-the-century literary texts written by ethnic writers—almost invariably containing references to the symbolics of clothing in the immigrants' acculturation process—one distinctly perceives that this is only part of the story, one that leaves out the newcomers' role in the making of American modernity as it turns them into passive matter to be processed in the American melting pot. Simmel's theory of fashion offers a unidirectional movement of cultural practices; that is, it imagines fashion as a system of styles that originate in the mainstream elite with exclusionary purposes and trickle down to the lower classes, only to be abandoned as fashion once they are no longer distinctive. The lower classes are envisioned as empty vessels, passively waiting to be filled from above, with no culture of their own devising. Yet, as contemporary revisions of trickle-down theories have shown, this is a rather simplistic way to understand cultural exchanges, which does not take into account the possibility that an active role can be played by the subaltern and is blind to "bubble up" phenomena, that is, street culture styles that travel up the social ladder.[15]

The decline of the shawl cannot be fully explained by Simmel's theory of fashion. While it is certainly a striking coincidence that the rejection of the shawl took place during the peak of immigration in the second half of the nineteenth century, when thousands of women from Eastern and Southern Europe invaded the streets of New York and other Northern American cities with their colorful shawls, it is also to be noted that these women readily rejected traditional costumes and claimed almost immediately a modern style. Jewish and Italian immigrants, who brought with them their sartorial skills, helped create modern fashion. Ready-made wear is an American invention, but it was produced by the eclectic fusion of New World technology and Old World sartorial craftsmanship and was made possible by Lower East Side sweatshops. Clothing as identity is, not surprisingly, at the core of Jewish American fiction written at the threshold of the new century, often involving the difficult passage from a society where clothing is a transparent, stable marker of status and character to one where individuals can create themselves anew simply by wearing the right outfit. Learning how to fashion new identities and pliable selves in order to survive in the New World, the protagonists do not merely go through a process of Americanization and modernization but also become active agents in the transformation of genteel America into a modern, mass society. The rejection of the shawl by immigrant women might appear simply as a step in their process of assimilation of American ways, yet the "democracy of beauty" to which they aspired—as the story of Sonya Vrunsky, the protagonist of Anzia Yezierska's *Salome of the Tenements* (1923) and a veritable avatar of the sartorial utopia of ethnic women, demonstrates—was as much a product of their labor and creativity as it was an outcome of American capitalism.[16]

"The average American woman is the best-dressed average woman in the world, and the Russian Jew has had a good deal to do with making her one," proudly declares the rich clothing businessman who is the narrator and protagonist of *The Rise of David Levinsky*, the novel Abraham Cahan published in 1917.[17] David Levinsky's life story is the ethnic and fictional version of one of the most popular genres of American literature, the self-made man's autobiographical story of success. Like Benjamin Franklin's narrated self, the representative American on whose life story these autobiographies are modeled, David is a champion of individualism and pragmatism, and his message to the mainstream is patent: Jewish immigrants fully participate in the spirit of America and are contributing to making it the vanguard of nations. Interestingly, he devotes several pages to the description of how the Jews—whom the mainstream press persistently described as an archaic, patriarchal group—were making American women modern by helping them discard their old-fashioned shawls in favor of well-manufactured cloaks:

> The time I speak of, the late '80's and the early '90's, is connected with an important and interesting chapter in the history of the American cloak business. Hitherto in the control of German Jews, it was now beginning to pass into the hands of their Russian co-religionists, the change being effected under peculiar conditions that were destined to lead to a stupendous development of the industry. If the average American woman is to-day dressed infinitely better than she was a quarter of a century ago, and if she is now easily the best-dressed average woman in the world, the fact is due, in a large measure, to the change I refer to.
>
> The transition was inevitable. . . . German manufacturers were the pioneers of the industry in America. It was a new industry, in fact, scarcely twenty years old. Formerly, and as late as the '70's, women's cloaks and jackets were little known in the United States. Shawls were worn by the masses. What few cloaks were seen on women of means and fashion were imported from Germany. But the demand grew.
>
> So, gradually, some German-American merchants and an American shawl firm bethought themselves of manufacturing these garments at home. The industry

progressed, the new-born great Russian immigration—a child of the massacres of 1881 and 1882—bringing the needed army of tailors for it. There was big money in the cloak business, and it would have been unnatural if some of these tailors had not, sooner or later, begun to think of going into business on their own hook.[18]

The simple story of Americanization becomes a complex narrative of exchanges and mutual transformation in David's account, which ends with a statement that, in fact, complete assimilation is unachievable: "I cannot escape from my old self. My past and my present do not comport well."[19] All his life, David oscillates between his proud vindication of American, that is, modern, fashion's Jewish genealogy and the desire to appropriate the look of the elite, but he can only put it on as a masquerade.

I sought to dress like a genteel American, my favorite color for clothes and hats being (and still is) dark brown. It became my dark hair well, I thought. The difference between taste and vulgar ostentation was coming slowly, but surely, I hope. I remember the passionate efforts I made to learn to tie a four-in-hand cravat, then a recent invention. I was forever watching and striving to imitate the dress and the ways of the well-bred American merchants with whom I was, or trying to be, thrown. All this, I felt, was an essential element in achieving business success; but the ambition to act and look like a gentleman grew in me quite apart from these motives.[20]

On him, clothes do not fit naturally; instead, like his tentative, heavily accented English, dress signals one of the numberless splits in his personality, that between his ethnic body and his "American" spirit. Yet it is precisely his fragmented self, his voice saturated with Freudian awareness of the contradictory nature of the psyche, that makes him a modern subject, in fact, a more modern subject than genteel Americans, who still naively believe that they have a natural right to the country. Toward the end of the novel, David, now a successful tycoon in the garment industry, once again muses over the "spectacle" of Jewish achievement in the garment district. This time he credits Jewish immigrants with the most American virtue of all: they have made fashion, once elitist, democratic.

Foreigners ourselves, and mostly unable to speak English, we had Americanized the system of providing clothes for the American woman of moderate or humble means. . . . This—added to a vastly increased division of labor, the invention, at our instance, of all sorts of machinery for the manufacture of trimmings, and the enormous scale upon which production was carried on by us—had the effect of cheapening the better class of garments prodigiously. . . . Indeed, the Russian Jew had made the average American girl a "tailor-made" girl.

When I learned the trade a cloak made of the cheapest satinette cost eighteen dollars. To-day nobody would wear it. One can now buy a whole suit made of all-wool material and silk-lined for fifteen dollars. . . .

It was the Russian Jew who had introduced the factory-made gown, constantly perfecting it and reducing the cost of its production. The ready-made silk dress which the American woman of small means now buys for a few dollars is of the very latest style and as tasteful in its lines, color scheme, and trimming as a high-class designer can make it. A ten-dollar gown is copied from a hundred-dollar model. . . . Nor is it mere apish copying. We make it our business to know how the American woman wants to look, what sort of lines she would like her figure to have. Many a time when I saw a well-dressed American woman in the street I followed her for blocks, scanning the make-up of her cloak, jacket, or suit. I never wearied of studying the trend of the American woman's taste.[21]

At the dawn of the twentieth century, the American woman was an icon—though an ambivalent one—of the country's modernity. It is not surprising, then, that Abraham Cahan's narrator insists on the fact that she, or rather her aggressive, masculine style, is the product of those same immigrants often perceived as utterly alien and constitutionally unable to became modern, democratic citizens.

In the nineteenth century, clothes became badges indicating their wearers' commitment to American democracy. Like language, customs, or dwellings, American dress differed from the Old World's sartorial practice, avoiding extravagance as well as shabbiness; it created an iconography of the United States patterned on simplicity and democratic uniformity. The change of clothes that immigrants went through was part of their Americanization process, which implied the shedding of Old World garb, ideas, and customs in order to become modern subjects. In 1870, Maximilian Schele de Vere, professor of modern languages at the University of Virginia and a keen social commentator, described the immigrants' change of clothes as a natural response to their change of country:

> The overwhelming power of absorption, which characterizes the ruling race, speedily transformed the newcomers in this aspect also, and the latter laid aside their hereditary costume with their hereditary language, habits, and convictions. They felt naturally disposed to avoid exciting public attention as foreigners; they preferred naturally to comply with the prevailing fashion and—to economize; for under the circumstances it would have been as expensive as troublesome to import tailors of their own, and to have their clothes made of the peculiar cut and the old-fashioned material to which they were accustomed in their native land.[22]

Using words that connote assimilation as an irresistible force to which the newcomer willfully surrenders and as a consequence makes the desire to maintain one's heritage unnatural and irrational—such as "overwhelming," "naturally," "disposed," "preferred," "comply," "expensive," "troublesome," "peculiar," and "old-fashioned"—Maximilian Schele de Vere, himself a Swedish immigrant who had arrived in the United States in his twenties, narrates the immigrants' traumatic experience of cultural adjustment as a story with a happy ending, where the protagonist acquires a better, more rational identity, along with more functional clothes, without any feelings of loss and displacement.

Schele de Vere's functionalist language, however, did not stand the test of mass migrations from Eastern and Southern Europe and Asia in the following decades or the anxiety they produced in the native stock. His confidence in the "overwhelming power of absorption" of the Anglo-American elites appeared naive and mistaken in the face of throngs of immigrants who seemed too different to ever become Americanized. The nativist movement contributed to the diffusion of a very different discourse on immigration, which portrayed the arrival of foreigners as a calamity introducing contagious diseases and moral pollution into the United States. Aliens seemed to threaten the American way of life, so inclusivists, who believed in the transforming power of the American melting pot, could no longer rely on metaphors depicting assimilation as a natural, unavoidable process. Emphasis shifted to the aliens' willingness to become American citizens, and their change of clothes, like their adoption of English, indexed their determination to shed the past and fully enter their new community. As New York missionary Helen F. Clark argued in 1896, Chinese immigrants' abandonment of traditional costume for American dress was not a choice dictated by pragmatic considerations such as its superior comfort and lower cost but, on the contrary, only a symbolic gesture. Immigrants' change of clothes sent a message to the mainstream that stressed a will to forget the past and assimilate the new culture:

> Other people who come here gradually adopt the American dress and way of living. Their children, if not themselves, learn to speak English, are taken into American business houses, become naturalized, and in time they are an integral part of the great whole, and no one asks, "Did you come from Italy, or Sweden, or Germany, or Turkey, or Austria, or Scotland, or France, or Ireland, or Spain?" They are thenceforward, to all intents and purposes, Americans. Their nationality is not continually thrust upon us by their dress. Unquestionably a Chinaman in American dress is better treated, more respected, than a Chinaman in Chinese dress; *and while in points of comfort the Chinese dress is probably to be preferred to the closer-fitting American suit, yet many Chinamen recognize this fact, and surrender their own clothes to don ours.*[23]

Ethnic literature also presented the adoption of American dress as an index of belonging. Where the narrator serves as a cultural mediator—partly cultural vanguard self-invested with the task of uplifting the ethnic masses, partly analyst of the psychological cost of acculturation—changing clothes often becomes a central textual knot in the construction of ethnic American identity. This American "make-up" arouses contradictory feelings and proves a less simple transformation than the mainstream culture would suggest. When David Levinsky arrives in New York from Russia and is given new clothes and a haircut by a sympathetic man he meets at the synagogue, he experiences the change of appearances as a new birth, a magic transformation turning him into a modern man:

> When I took a look at the mirror I was bewildered. I scarcely recognized myself. I was mentally parading my "modern" make-up before Matilda. A pang of yearning clutched my heart. It was a momentary feeling. For the rest, I was all in a flutter with embarassment and a novel relish of existence. It was as though the hair-cut and the American clothes had changed my identity.[24]

Yet the novel opens and closes with a declaration that the metamorphosis from poor Russian greenhorn to rich American businessman is only a surface matter, after all. Or better, that different selves coexist in him and his identity changes according to his current moods. Responding to the nativists' claim that Eastern European Jews were too different to be assimilated, Mary Antin, in her autobiography *The Promised Land* (1912), narrates the immigrant's contact with the new culture as a story destined to have a happy ending and relatively devoid of pathos. "Mashke" changes her name to "Mary" and puts on a "calico frock" for her first school day in America, beginning the miraculous journey that will make of her, "the granddaughter of Raphael the Russian, born to a humble destiny," a new being, "at home in the American metropolis," "free to fashion [her] own life."[25] Her change of clothes, from "costumes" to "garments," unlike David's, is a work of enchantment where, instead of a magic rod, her "fairy godmother" makes use of the American department store, the temple of consumer society where goods are democratically available to anyone with money:

A fairy godmother to us children was she who led us to a wonderful country called "up-town," where, in a dazzling beautiful palace called a "department store," we exchanged our hateful homemade European costumes, which pointed us out as "greenhorns" to the children on the street, for real American machine-made garments, and issued forth glorified in each other's eyes.[26]

Anzia Yezierska's works describe an even more dramatic change of clothes than either Antin's or Cahan's. Her heroines experience uprooting as traumatic, marking them as in-between subjects who do not belong to the Old World any longer and yet cannot find the place they aspire to in the new. Realizing their American dream proves a false hope, and when they discover that the United States has room for them only as domestic workers and is not interested in their spiritual aspirations, they are bitterly disillusioned and passionately denounce the betrayal of the American promise. Yezierska's heroines know that they have to discard the past in order to have access to the opportunities offered by their new homeland, and they are eager to cast off their Old World shawls. In "Wings" (1920)—a short story that, like much of Yezierska's fiction, revolves around an interethnic romance between a cold Anglo-American intellectual and a passionate Jewish woman—Shenah Pessah becomes painfully aware of her greenhorn looks during a date with John Barnes, a professor of sociology who has moved to the Lower East Side to study immigrant culture:

> For the first time she realized how shabby and impossible her clothes were. "Oi weh!" she wrung her hands. "I'd give away everything in the world only to have something pretty to wear for him. My whole life hangs on how I'll look in his eyes. I got to have a hat and a new dress. I can't no more wear my 'greenhorn' shawl going out with an American."[27]

Lacking money, she is ready to pawn the feather bed her dead mother left her, her only link to her family, thus making the cut with her roots much deeper than it may seem. Once they have grasped the new dress they yearn for, however, Yezierska's heroines often discover that it is not enough to ensure their inclusion in American society and realize their hopes. At times, changing clothes proves only a superficial crust hiding a deep cultural difference that refuses to disappear. In "My Own People" (1920), Sophie Sapinsky leaves her family and friends for a room of her own where she can write, only to discover that solitude chokes the words in her throat and that she needs her people and the ghetto just as much as they need her to become their voice to America. In other works, such as "The Fat of the Land" (1920), their ethnic difference takes the form of a mother whose doggedness not to become an American lady threatens to disclose her daughter's passing:

> [Mother] will spill the beans that we come from Delancey Street the minute we introduce her anywhere. Must I always have the black shadow of my past trailing after me? . . . God knows how hard I tried to civilize her so as not to blush with shame when I take her anywhere. I dressed her in the most stylish Paris models, but Delancey Street sticks out from every inch of her. Whenever she opens her mouth, I'm done for. You fellows had your chance to rise in the world because a man is free to go up as high as he can reach up to; but I, with all my style and pep, can't get a man my equal because a girl is always judged by her mother.[28]

More often it is the dress itself that exposes them as non-American. As a newcomer, Shenah Pessah is not aware of the rules governing American ladies' fashion and goes for the wrong dress. When she appears in front of John Barnes in her flamboyant new outfit—a very green, crisp organdie dress and a straw hat adorned with the reddest cherries—the American man is startled by her "sudden display of color." To his ambivalent remarks Shenah replies: "I'm through for always with old women's shawls. This is my first American dress-up."[29] Jewish identity is only a thin veneer enveloping her true, American soul, and Shenah is convinced that she can discard it as quickly as she can cast off her immigrant shawl: "There's something in me—I can't help—that so quickly takes on to the American taste. It's as if my outside skin only was Russian; the heart in me is for everything of the new world," she exclaims in another short story.[30]

Yet this is not what John Barnes, who is interested in her because she is "a splendid type for his research" and is both attracted and repelled by her lack of restraint, thinks.[31]

In spite of his intellectual curiosity about ethnic difference, his aim is precisely to destroy it and to teach the Jewish girl the subdued elegance of the American lady. When they enter the library, Shenah is fascinated by the quiet looks of both the place and its attendants and quickly understands that there are hidden codes that she will never master because their purpose is to exclude those who do not belong:

> "How the book-ladies look so quiet like the things."
>
> "Yes," he replied, with a tell-tale glance at her. "I too like to see a woman's face above her clothes."
>
> The approach of the librarian cut off further comment. As Mr. Barnes filled out the application card, Shenah Pessah noted the librarian's simple attire. "What means he a woman's face above her clothes?" she wondered. And the first shadow of a doubt crossed her mind as to whether her dearly bought apparel was pleasing to his eyes. In the few brief words that passed between Mr. Barnes and the librarian, Shenah Pessah sensed that these two were of the same world and that she was different. Her first contact with him in a well-lighted room made her aware that "there were other things to the person besides the dress-up."[32]

Shenah feels as overexposed in her first American outfit as by her "greenhorn rags" and looks forward to the protection afforded by the dark streets of the ghetto. When they stroll together through the Lower East Side, her appearance is no longer strident and out of place, even to Barnes's eyes: "It was all so wonderful to Barnes that in the dirt and noise of the overcrowded ghetto, this erstwhile drudge could be transfigured into such a vibrant creature of joy. Even her clothes that had seemed so bold and garish awhile ago, were now inexplicably in keeping with the carnival spirit that he felt steal over him."[33]

Shenah's romance is destined to fail, like all interethnic romances in Yezierska's works, because of the cowardice of Anglo-American men, who long for passionate and enthusiastic ethnic women to light up their lives but are ultimately too cold and weak to cope with their lack of restraint. Yet the ethnic woman's desire for beautiful clothes will be gratified, and even her flashy style or, more generally, the aesthetics of the ghetto will become fashionable. Sonya Vrunsky, the protagonist of *Salome of the Tenements,* passionately declares her determination to share the privileges of American women including fashion: "Sometimes I'm so infuriated by the ugliness that I have to wear that I want to walk the streets naked—let my hair fly in the air—out of sheer protest."[34] In order to seduce and marry the Anglo-American millionaire John Manning, she convinces a famous couturier to design a dress for her, described as absolutely simple and apparently subscribing to mainstream notions of propriety and restraint. But the sartorial ideology behind Sonya's dress is less assimilationist than it might appear. Not only is Sonya's perfect dress—a plain, "nun-like grey with a touch of sheer batiste"—the creation of a Jewish dressmaker, Jaky Solomon, who passes as a French couturier under the name of Jacques Hollins to sell his models to Fifth Avenue millionaires, its minimalist aesthetic is explicitly defined as not an aping of the Anglo-American taste for understatement even as it expresses a thoroughly modern self, individualistic, self-centered, seemingly alien to the communal ethos of the shtetl:

> Impetuously, [Sonya] grasped [Jacques's] arm: "You made me look like Fifth Avenue–born. Only—I don't want to have the tied-up manners of a lady."
>
> The surging life of her step, the supple swing of her lithe body, fascinated Hollins as she moved around, admiring herself candidly in the revolving mirrors.
>
> "You don't have to be a second-hand pattern of a person—when you can be your own free, individual self," he said.
>
> "I feel I can conquer kingdoms in this dress. Could any man alive refuse me any wish if I came to him in this beautifulness?"
>
> "You'll certainly make my art shine to the heights of your wishes," gloated Hollins. Her frank sense of power—her open egoism delighted the artist because it was the same quality that had made him, Hollins, the unconquerable.[35]

Sonya's simple dress seems to reject the loud, flamboyant aesthetics of the ghetto, yet its wearer as well as its creator are far from succumbing to gentility and its prudish rules of decorum. Their understanding of fashion is performative. They regard clothes and style as strategies to get rid of static identities and achieve their place in the world. Their advocacy of simplicity on aesthetic, not moral, terms sounds markedly modernist. In fact, they scorn politeness and the American manners forced upon the immigrants in settlement houses, as much as they despise clothes that cage women like prison walls and kill their desire for the sake of propriety. Though Sonya has a taste for plainness, she is fascinated by Rosie, "a Carmen-type factory girl" she meets at Manning's settlement, who has been turned out of the dance hall for wearing too much makeup and for her coquettish behavior: "Her rouged cheeks and highly tinted, full lips were flaming like roses. Her robust young body was vibrant in a tight-fitting princess dress that was the last word in Grand Street fashion."[36] What they have in common is a vibrant erotic vitality—a will to rise in the world—that American ladies lack and that Sonya and Hollins will try to preserve in their work to make beauty available to the Lower East Side.

Working-class ethnic young women had already started to change American gender ideology and its notions about proper womanly behavior in the early twentieth century. Sonya is a positive embodiment of the vamp who would dominate the big screen in the following decades, with all her energy and no ambivalence about her lack of morals. As a young Anglo-American woman remarks at the party that John and Sonya have thrown to celebrate the encounter between Fifth Avenue and the Lower East Side, "It is hardly fair to compare Sonya's opportunity to learn the wiles of the art [of seduction] with ours. Unluckily, we've been so carefully shielded!"[37] Another guest, in a bitter remark about Jewish women's predatory nature, comments that imitation in fashion has reversed its direction, and now ladies copy the styles of the lower classes:

Russian Jewesses are always fascinating to men. The reason, my dear, is because they have neither breeding, culture nor tradition. . . . With all to gain and nothing to lose . . . They are mere creatures of sex. . . . And much as we may dislike to admit it, men uptown and downtown are the same. . . . Why do our débutantes go to theaters and cafés? To imitate, my dear . . . Let us recognize, my dear, that our smartest clothes are but imitations of the creations of the demi-monde.[38]

What the Anglo-American girl wants to imitate is the pleasure of excess and hypervisibility, its countercultural appeal. As Jane Addams perceptively remarked in 1909, working women's street culture, the flamboyant aesthetics of the slum, was not evidence of the immigrants' unwillingness to assimilate American manners but, quite the contrary, a creative response to their encounters with the United States.

> We see thousands of girls walking up and down the streets on a pleasant evening with no chance to catch a sight of pleasure even through a lighted window, save as these lurid places provide it. Apparently the modern city sees in these girls only two possibilities, both of them commercial: first, a chance to utilize by day their new and tender labor power in its factories and shops, and then another chance in the evening to extract from them their petty wages by pandering to their love of pleasure.
>
> As these overworked girls stream along the street, the rest of us see only the self-conscious walk, the giggling speech, the preposterous clothing. *And yet through the huge hat, with its wilderness of bedraggled feathers, the girl announces to the world that she is here.* She demands attention to the fact of her existence, she states that she is ready to live, to take her place in the world. The most precious moment in human development is the young creature's assertion that he is unlike any other human being, and has an individual contribution to make to the world. The variation from the established type is *at the root of all change, the only possible basis for progress, all that keeps life from growing unprofitably stale and repetitious.*[39]

Wearing outrageous clothes was the strategy through which young immigrant and ethnic women, turned by the city into mere laboring bodies, affirmed their right to exist as desiring, modern subjects. In so doing they became an epitome of American modernity.

1. "A Chapter on Shawls," *Harper's New Monthly* 2, no. 7 (December 1850): 39.

2. See Graham J. White and Shane White, *Stylin': African American Expressive Culture from Its Beginnings to the Zoot Suit* (Ithaca, N.Y.: Cornell University Press, 1998).

3. See the website "Uncle Tom's Cabin and American Culture: A Multi-media Archive," http://www.iath.virginia.edu/utc/, an invaluable resource directed by Stephen Railton, containing many of the illustrated editions of the novel published between 1852 and 1930, along with playbills, posters, postcards, and other *Uncle Tom's Cabin* memorabilia.

4. Harriet Beecher Stowe, *Uncle Tom's Cabin,* in *Three Novels,* ed. Kathryn Kish Sklar (New York: Library of America, 1982), 213.

5. Louisa May Alcott, *Little Women* (New York: Penguin, 1989), 288–89.

6. Ibid., 289.

7. Henry James, *The Tragic Muse,* ed. Philip Horne (London: Penguin, 1995), 28. My emphasis.

8. Ibid., 29.

9. Edith Wharton, *Madame de Treymes,* in *Novellas and Other Writings* (New York: Library of America, 1990), 24.

10. Anne Hollander, *Sex and Suits: The Evolution of Modern Dress* (New York: Knopf, 1994), 9.

11. Ibid.

12. Charlotte Adams, "Italian Life in New York," *Harper's New Monthly* 62, no. 371 (April 1881): 678.

13. Anzia Yezierska, "America and I" (first published in *Children of Loneliness*), in *How I Found America: Collected Stories,* intro. Vivian Gornick (New York: Persea Books, 1991), 146.

14. Georg Simmel, "The Philosophy of Fashion" [1905], in *Simmel on Culture: Selected Writings,* ed. David Frisby and Mike Featherstone (London: Sage, 1997), 188–89.

15. For more on this, see various essays in Cristina Giorcelli and Paula Rabinowitz, eds. *Exchanging Clothes: Habits of Being 2* (Minneapolis: University of Minnesota Press, 2012).

16. On Jewish women immigrants and American fashion, see Barbara Schreier, *Becoming American Women: Clothing and the Jewish Immigrant Experience, 1880–1920* (Chicago: Chicago Historical Society, 1995).

17. Abraham Cahan, *The Rise of David Levinsky*, ed. Jules Chametzky (New York: Penguin, 1993), 444.

18. Ibid., 201–2.

19. Ibid., 530.

20. Ibid., 260.

21. Ibid., 443–44.

22. Maximilian Schele De Vere, "American Dress," *Putnam's* 15, no. 28 (April 1870): 387–88.

23. Helen F. Clark, "The Chinese of New York," *Century* 53, no. 1 (November 1896): 113. My emphasis.

24. Cahan, *Rise of David Levinsky*, 101.

25. Mary Antin, *The Promised Land*, ed. Werner Sollors (New York: Penguin, 1997), 156.

26. Ibid., 149.

27. Anzia Yezierska, "Wings" (first published in *Hungry Hearts*), in *How I Found America*, 9.

28. Anzia Yezierska, "The Fat of the Land" (first published in *Hungry Hearts*), in *How I Found America*, 90.

29. Yezierska, "Wings," 12.

30. Anzia Yezierska, "Hunger" (first published in *Hungry Hearts*), in *How I Found America*, 26.

31. Yezierska, "Wings," 5.

32. Ibid., 13.

33. Ibid., 14.

34. Anzia Yezierska, *Salome of the Tenements*, ed. Gay Wilentz (Urbana: University of Illinois Press, 1995), 23. On the subject of clothes in Yezierska's works and in particular in this novel, see Katherine Stubbs, "Reading Material: Contextualizing Clothing in the Work of Anzia Yezierska," *Melus* 23, no. 2 (Summer 1998); Christopher N. Okonkwo, "Of Repression, Assertion, and the Speakerly Dress: Anzia Yezierska's *Salome of the Tenements*," *Melus* 25, no. 1 (Spring 2000); Paula Rabinowitz, "Meeting on the Corner: Mediterranean Men and Urban American Women," in *America and the Mediterranean, Proceedings of the 2001 AISNA International Conference*, ed. Massimo Bacigalupo (Turin: Otto, 2003).

35. Yezierska, *Salome of the Tenements*, 26.

36. Ibid., 136.

37. Ibid., 121.

38. Ibid., 128.

39. Jane Addams, *The Spirit of Youth and the City Streets* (New York: Macmillan, 1909); Boon-docksNet Edition, 2001, http://www.boondocksnet.com/editions/youth/. My emphasis. On young women's changing cultures at the beginning of the twentieth century, see Elizabeth Ewen, *Immigrant Women in the Land of Dollars: Life and Culture on the Lower East Side, 1890–1925* (New York: Monthly Review, 1985); Kathy Peiss, *Cheap Amusements: Working Women and Leisure in Turn-of-the-Century New York* (Philadelphia: Temple University Press, 1986); and Susan A. Glenn, *Daughters of the Shtetl: Life and Labor in the Immigrant Generation* (Ithaca, N.Y.: Cornell University Press, 1990).

11

A LOVELY LITTLE COFFEE-COLORED DRESS
EDUCATION, FEMALE IDENTITY, AND DRESS
IN LATE NINETEENTH-CENTURY ITALY

Carmela Covato

> *Marianna! I have a terribly bad sin to whisper to you, in your ear! . . . If only*
> *they'd make me a lovely little coffee-colored dress . . . without a crinoline, there now!*
> *No, that's too much! . . . But a dress that wasn't black, so that I might run about*
> *and climb over walls, one that wouldn't remind me all the time, like this ghastly*
> *habit, that down there in Catania, when the cholera is over, a convent awaits me.*
>
> GIOVANNI VERGA, *Storia di una capinera*

It is a lovely little coffee-colored dress that Giovanni Verga symbolically entrusts with the task of expressing the longing for freedom felt by Maria, the protagonist of his novel *Sparrow: The Story of a Songbird,*[1] written in 1869 and published for the first time in 1871 in Milan in Giovanni Battista Lampugnani's fashion, style, and culture periodical, *Il giornale delle famiglie La Ricamatrice.*[2]

Maria is a convent-educated girl who (because her family has decided it) shall become a nun. Due to a cholera epidemic then threatening Catania, she is allowed to stay home with her family in the country. There she falls suddenly and passionately in love with young Nino, a feeling that overwhelms her, setting her off balance in the space of a few days. But Maria does not dare resist her destiny, which appears to her at times a choice, at times a life sentence. Renunciation, strife, and the convent will lead first to madness, then to death.

In painfully dramatic fashion, Verga solves the dilemma between resignation and assertion, destiny and emancipation (a strongly marked feature of identity among some middle-class women during the second half of the nineteenth century). His is one of many testimonies to a widespread pessimism regarding the social and individual inertia of the period and to the profound chagrin men felt about the effects of female freedom due to a number of radical changes in women's position and behavior. Fin de siècle literature in Europe and America offers frequent examples of an inevitably tragic conclusion to the struggle between autonomy and constriction.

If Gustave Flaubert's *Madame Bovary* or Leo Tolstoy's *Anna Karenina*, the two most famous female heroines of the nineteenth-century novel, like Luigi Capuana's lesser-known *Giacinta*, opt for suicide as their only possible escape, in several other cases, the other choice capable of redeeming them after their rebellion against the given social order is illness, usually consumption, which both symbolically and physiologically seals their inevitable death sentence, as happens with Theodor Fontane's *Effi Briest*.[3] The positivist, natural or verist, literature of the time presents an excruciating exposé of female reality. It is pervaded, nonetheless, by a tendency to label women as innately natural, endowed with strong, conflicting feelings, though almost devoid of any personal history and, therefore, of any real chance of changing. Clothing often appears as the outward mark of a painful existential parable, as a sign or a figurative projection of behavioral restraints.[4]

Dress seems to act, at times, as a kind of disguise, as a tangible expression of compliance with a socially imposed code, the passive representation of an identity molded by the projection of other people's expectations, of a "coercive conformity" based on the dominant social norms of a given historical reality.[5] According to Daniel Roche, fiction, as it narrates the strife between being and appearing, is a topos aligned with moral philosophy. Already in a number of eighteenth-century texts

> the emphasis placed on this strife serves to underline, above all, the difference between people's true identity and the identity invented to comply with the exigencies of a triumphant *sociabilité,* a life of relationships devoted to the cult of forms, where the manifestation of true natural feeling is a problem, because people exist only in the eyes of others.[6]

Refusal of the norm places the individual within areas of conscious transgression or involuntary exclusion due as well to certain modes of dressing. The tragic outcome of Maria's desire for freedom in *Sparrow: The Story of a Songbird,* as expressed in the girl's vain yearning for "a lovely little coffee-colored dress" as an alternative to her black nun's habit, is the socially acceptable codified literary resolution of the strife between destiny and freedom, a kind of antidote to the problem of female subjectivity. An example is the seventeenth-century English noblewoman Lady Eleanor Davies, a prophetess deemed insane, whose story is told by Roy S. Porter.

> In actual terms [Porter holds] Lady Eleanor broke the rules because there was nothing "feminine" in either her behavior or her assertions. Women were allowed to be spiritual and devout, but prophesy was the task of men. When she became Daniel—identifying herself with the Prophet Daniel—Lady Eleanor chose to wear trousers. Her behavior was considered inappropriate to her sex. After her death, the epitaph formulated by her family, making virtue of necessity, praised her for having had, as was said of Queen Elizabeth I, the soul of a man in the body of a woman.[7]

Italian educational functions played by clothing during the final decades of the nineteenth century highlight the ethical-normative clash between conservatism and change reflected in the paradigms of femininity dominant at the time, when, in many European countries, new possibilities, however contradictory and conflicting, were created by the entry of women into the fields of education, politics, and social work. The emergence of new definitions of female self-determination and subjectivity, ushered in by a society altered by industrialization, had a profound impact on the rigid interpretation of gender roles, codified within the ideology of the rising bourgeoisie, which assigned men an unquestioned primacy in public affairs while it entrusted women with exclusively domestic tasks as wives, mothers, household angels, and missionary custodians of the middle-class nuclear family.[8]

This very clash led to the extensive cultural clamp-down on sexual matters so hotly debated during the whole of the nineteenth century. Influenced by the harshening of various forms of misogyny, it took the form of a composite political and cultural front (ranging from the official stance of the Catholic Church to the theoretical ravings of a number of positivist scientists), united in their intent to demonstrate, by every possible means, the intellectual and physical inferiority of women while proclaiming their exclusively maternal vocation.[9] As Bruno F. P. Wanroij notes in *Storia del pudore* (History of modesty): "It is clear that, due to their 'scientific' character, theories of parallelisms between somatic form and psychosocial behavior provided extremely convincing arguments against the female emancipation movement. Insofar as they were earmarked for motherhood, women could not claim the right to work outside of the home, to enter the professions, or to vote."[10]

This cultural climate widened the enormous gap between the ideological emphasis placed on motherhood as a missionary cult—demanding appropriately simple and modest clothing—and the custom encouraging women of the middle or upper-middle classes to flaunt their social prestige with displays of elegant apparel and accessories such as costly fabrics, jewels, and plunging necklines. In the fashion magazines, this contradiction is particularly vivid, demonstrated by a series of ambiguous proposals as the simultaneous and conflicting

invitations to save money and to exhibit ephemeral or superfluous goods, praise of modesty and of shamelessly erotic attire . . . censorship of make-up and approval of

unnatural or harmful bodily practices and rituals, sermons on healthy clothing and un-
failing presentation of deleterious garments such as corsets, criticized because of their
deforming, harmful effects, and evening dresses with plunging necklines accused of
causing sickness, including some serious ailments, caused by chills caught during the
winter season of balls.[11]

The rigid protocols of female apparel did not answer aesthetic requirements alone,
but served to mark the differences between various social groups (class, age, cultural
level, geographical area, as well as marital status). "Dress—depending on its form and
color—marks sociopsychological membership: in the case of women, it indicates age and
respectability above all."[12] Thus the vestal of the nuclear middle-class family suffers
from the quandary between the demands for modesty, as dictated by her mission as a
mother, and the displays of ostentatious elegance through which she is allowed to exhibit
the wealth or power of the man (the head of the family) to whom she belongs.

In the case of women who decided to study or work (and who because of this were
often condemned to singleness), sobriety or austerity became an inevitable social imper-
ative, self-imposed instinctively by intellectually committed women and codified as written norms in the case of training schools where women studied to become primary-
school teachers. Austerity became a necessary defense against the danger of being
considered morally objectionable. There appears to be a relationship between the significantly greater desire to enter the world of education (which some women manifested
during the second half of the nineteenth century) and matters of dress. Other differences in attire are found, for example, between those who chose to enter the forbidden
world of scientific research and those who opted for the socially more acceptable solution
of embracing the primary-school teaching profession.

If complete ignorance among the female population was no longer tolerated because
of new social demands made on women—following the spread of primary education to
the general public that required a new kind of female professionalism, designed, above

all, to enhance the maternal, educational, and teaching capacities of women—access to higher intellectual studies, the traditional preserve of men, was still considered subversive of the moral and social order. Like the emancipated woman, the female scientist ceased to be a woman; she became a monster, a kind of terrible third sex.

Because their desire to gain knowledge and practice the professions implied considerable intellectual commitment and a refusal of traditional models of female behavior, these ambitious women needed to forge new identities devoid of previously consolidated rhetorical codes. But if it is easy to gain access to literary, philosophical, religious, medical, anthropological representations (or the world of fashion by analyzing magazines dedicated to it), it is more difficult to reveal the inner world of women who found themselves, more or less consciously, faced with the difficult task of redefining their subjectivity, their private and public behavior, and therefore their dress, as facets of broader existential choices. Science and higher education in general were deemed contrary to the nature of women. One can find traces of these women's dilemmas, including their sartorial choices, in their biographies and autobiographies, which serve as significant sources on the matter.

Austerity is, generally speaking, the feature that best characterizes the garments of the intellectual woman. An unwritten moral code denied women who gained access to education or the professions the power of seduction. In her biography of her mother, Marie Curie (1867–1934), Eve Curie describes her mother's experience as a university student, around 1891:

> Often in the echoing galleries young men would encounter this shy and stubborn-faced girl with soft, light hair, who dressed with an austere and poverty-stricken distinction, and would turn to each other in surprise, asking: "Who is it?" But the answer, if there was one, was vague. "It's a foreigner with an impossible name. She is always in the first row at the physics courses. Doesn't talk much." The boys' eyes would follow her graceful outline as it disappeared down the corridor, and then they would conclude: "Fine hair!"

The ash-blonde hair and the little Slavic head were, for a long time to come, the only identification the students at the Sorbonne had for their comrade. But young men were what interested this girl least at the moment.[13]

Before Marie's decisive encounter with Pierre Curie, the biography pictures a future of solitude as the necessary complement to her life of scientific study.

Sibilla Aleramo (1876–1960), in her autobiography, *Una donna,* informs us that her precocious interest in literature and learning, mediated by a strong identification with her father, caused her mother considerable worry. "She admired me in silence, regarding me with something of the same pride which she felt for her husband's daring and energy, but she disapproved of the kind of education to which I was devoting myself with so much ardour. She was afraid for me, imagining, doubtless, that I would grow up devoid of sentiment, that my brain alone was being developed; yet she lacked the courage to openly put herself in opposition to my father's system."[14]

Having decided to help her father in his work because of serious financial problems, the young woman "remember[s] a photo of me taken a year later. I was already regularly employed at the factory and had adopted a hybrid costume consisting of a straight-cut jacket with a multitude of pockets for my watch, my pencil, and my note-books, and a short skirt. My hair, cut short, fell over my forehead in curls, lending a boyish look to my physiognomy. My pretty tresses, with their streaks of gold, had been sacrificed at my father's suggestions."[15]

There is considerable evidence of the uneasy or, at least, conflicting feelings toward traditional female clothing on the part of women who chose unconventional paths. For example, in her autobiography, Lou Andreas-Salomé (1861–1937) describes the dislike she felt as a child toward high-heeled shoes. While her mother, who wore a beautiful curled wig "and forced her rather long and thin body into stays as was the fashion at the time, won the hearts of most of the young officers," she "liked only shoes without heels, which [she] willingly took home from [her] dancing lessons to glide around the parquet in the drawing-room as if skating on a large sheet of ice."[16] Even more daring was Anna

Kuliscioff, who attended the Zurich Polytechnic Institute during the 1870s, where girls from many different European countries came to study at a time when women were not allowed to enroll at university anywhere in Europe except Switzerland. "They lived together in the small towns, attending school, frequenting cafés and political circles; they walked about the quiet streets of Berne, Lugano, Geneva or Zurich in groups, under the curious though not always benevolent eye of the local population; besides, they demonstrated their anti-conformist attitude in their behaviour and dress; they smoked in the streets, they were often in the company of male classmates."[17] Furthermore, another foreign student, Angelica Balabanoff, declared that female students "expressed their contempt of exterior show by dressing in the drabbest of manners, in some cases in the most indecent way possible, anxious as they were to distinguish themselves from the parasite women of the dominant classes."[18]

From early childhood, Barbara McClintock (1902–92), perhaps the greatest geneticist of the twentieth century, showed a keen interest in activities (sport and learning) regarded as unfit for her sex; she, too, was considered different, atypical, a problem. "Throughout adolescence it became increasingly clear that she was committed to 'the kinds of things that girls were not supposed to do.'"[19] For these kinds of things one needed to dress properly, remarks her biographer Evelyn Fox-Keller.

"At that time," she recalls, "one didn't go to a store to buy one's clothes. We had a dressmaker for the girls and had their clothes made for them." Very early she insisted, and persuaded her parents . . . "that I should have bloomers made of the same material as my dresses so that I could do everything that I wanted. I could play baseball, I could play football, I could climb trees, I could just have the same kind of completely free time, that my brother and the people on the block had." She remembers having no girlfriends at this time, only boyfriends.[20]

Even more extreme was the case of Concepción Arenal (1820–93), Spanish writer and jurist, connected with Catholic reform movements, and a supporter of moderate feminism, who, in order to study for her degree, entered Madrid University dressed as a man, only to reveal her true identity at a later stage.[21]

The idea of altering exterior identity to pursue intellectual interests (whether barely tolerated or considered a danger to the prevailing moral and social order) is addressed differently by women who entered primary-school teaching as a profession.[22] For the women attending the *scuole normali* (Italian state teacher-training secondary schools), especially those who were boarders because they came from other cities or from the country, austerity was codified as the norm. This regimented austerity, and not the conscious choice of the intellectually *engagées,* also dictated, as is the case in all college-type institutions, uniformity. For the young boarders, the norms of behavior, set down in their prospectus, are worthy of a nunnery.

One reads, for example, in the prospectus of the boarding school associated with Milan's Regia scuola normale femminile (Royal Teacher Training School for Females), a document kept at the Central State Archives in Rome:

Art. 30.

The pupils shall take great care of the cleanliness and orderliness of their own clothes; uniformity is prescribed, and must be accompanied by the utmost simplicity and modesty of apparel.

And, furthermore

Art. 31.

The compulsory wardrobe is the following:

N° 6 blouses;

″ 4 skirts;

″ 4 pairs of knickers;

″ 2 pairs of stockings;

″ 2 corsets;

″ 4 bodices for day wear;

″ 2 bodices for night wear;

″ 2 dusters and a cloth for ironing or a (flat-iron) holder.

N° 4 bedsheets;

″ 4 pillowcases;

″ 2 bathrobes;

″ 12 handkerchiefs;

″ 4 bedroom towels;

″ 1 tablecloth 1.50 x 0.75 m.;

″ 1 tablecloth no shorter than 2 m. or 1 m. wide;

″ 4 table napkins;

N° 2 bags for laundry to be washed;

″ 2 simple, modest, house dresses, besides the black one belonging to the uniform, used for outings along with a short black overcoat;

N° 2 black over-all aprons with bodices, standard cut;

″ 3 white pinafores with halter;

″ 1 pair of black or dark removable sleeves;

″ 2 pairs of booties for indoor use and one pair for outings;

″ 1 pair of bedroom slip-ons or slippers;

″ 1 black mantilla;

″ 1 small black umbrella;

″ 1 box for combs and hairbrush or accessories;

″ 1 work box containing what is required;

″ 1 bone spoon or glass for the bedroom;

″ 1 wicker basket 0.60 m. long and 0.25 m. high.

NB—The clothing need not be new.

Art. 32.

All the clothes must be numbered for identification.

This list from 1899 is characteristic of those prescribing clothing for boarders in similar female boarding schools. The severity, the sobriety, the frequent reference to black, and the rigid uniformity clearly denote a type of dress explicitly related to a behavioral model based on restraint and discipline, two traits absolutely indispensable to the "virtuous educator" in the making. The convent-like atmosphere of boarding-school life continues in most of the norms contained in the school's rules, for example, in the rules of conduct and the nature of punishment or regulations governing visits by relatives. Relations with the outside world were kept within well-defined bounds. Article 42 reads: "On Tuesdays or Thursdays after school and on Sundays having carried out their religious duties, pupils may, weather permitting, take walks accompanied by the headmistress or her aides. The walks shall never take place at times or in places where the presence of large numbers of persons is foreseen."[23]

Thus the training of future primary-school teachers took place within very strict boundaries, keeping out all echoes of the nascent tensions connected with emancipation, including all desire for knowledge beyond the confines sanctioned by the dominant stereotypes. The cultural content within the curriculum of the *scuole normali* was of a general nature because gender and class discrimination viewed the key function of primary schools as moralizing rather than educating or culturally uplifting the lower classes. The pupils attending the *scuole normali* came primarily from the lower and lower-middle classes. For this reason, the boarding-school uniform, besides stressing sobriety and austerity, also indicated a step up on the social scale. Elvira Mancuso's novel *Vecchia storia . . . inverosimile* (An old . . . unlikely story), first published in Caltanissetta in 1906, describes an episode where a mother from the country, anxious to see her daughter, the young boarder Annuzza, now dressed as a lady, pays a visit to the school in the company of the girl's boyfriend, also from the country:

The boarders began coming out and the two country folk had just enough time to find a place next to the front door.

"What lovely clothes they're wearing! Annuzza must look great dressed like that, Pasquà?"

"Look; there she is," exclaimed the youth pointing her out, trembling with joy and pride.

"Annù!, Annù!" The gesticulating woman began shouting.

"Look this way, it's your mama! . . . Humph! . . . how stuck up," she muttered, offended, as Annuzza passed right in front of them, her eyes lowered, pretending not to have either seen or heard them.

Her mother ran after her followed by Pasquale, and continued shouting, "Annù, that hat looks really great on you!"[24]

This modest but significant change in social status points forward to the painful emergence of a conflictual generation and social gap, of which clothing becomes a symbol. Even for the teacher-trainee who becomes a school mistress, clothes are destined to continue performing an important symbolic function.

FIGURE 11.1 "Italian school girl reading" (1928, photographer unknown). Archivio dell'Ente Cantadini dell'Agro romano. Museo Storico della Didattica Mauro Laeng dell' Università degli Studi Roma Tre.

FIGURE 11.2 Italian school class picture with teacher (ca. 1920, photographer unknown). Archivio dell'Ente Cantadini dell'Agro romano. Museo Storico della Didattica Mauro Laeng dell' Università degli Studi Roma Tre.

During the final decades of the nineteenth century, the schoolmistress, even if her profession was seen as an appropriate one for women because of its missionary intent, was a figure that, from another perspective, could be considered destabilizing and transgressive. That a woman who practiced a profession, however lowly, might achieve economic independence and thus travel and live alone contradicted common social norms, giving rise to discrimination animated by unresolved prejudice. This became a theme eloquently reported in the literature of the time.[25] Among other things, there was much discussion about the problem of schoolmistresses from the cities importing into the places where they taught in the provinces clothes, habits, and activities considered unsuited to rural values and habits. Paradoxically, the schoolmarm's clothes became vehicles used to furtively implant transgressive urban behaviors among her students.

In the debate regarding the lack of schoolteachers, male and female, especially in rural areas (while in the cities at the end of the first decade following the 1870 unification of Italy the problem was less urgent), the prevailing opinion was that it was important to train teachers from the countryside by setting up special *scuole normali* there, to avoid clashes between excessively different cultural modes. And so the young countrywomen "once they become schoolmistresses remain humble, modest and dress in local costume, the pride of their families and a blessing to the town."[26] Equally alarming was the practice of provincial girls who migrated to cities to train as schoolmistresses. "The girls from outside the city," writes education minister Michele Coppino in a report accompanying the bill on compulsory education passed on July 15, 1877, "among their companions, lose their native simplicity and acquire the ideas and habits of the others; they begin to loathe the places from which they come and return there with ideas and behaviors unsuited to village girls, making themselves less acceptable than strangers would be."[27]

In a pamphlet housed in the Central States Archives in Rome of the Italian Ministry of Education, primary-school and teacher-training department (Archivio centrale dello Stato, Ministero della Pubblica Istruzione, Div. scuole primarie e normali) (1860–96), entitled *Considerazioni intorno al riordinamento delle scuole normali regie* (Considerations regarding the reform of the royal teacher training schools), the pedagogue Domenico Failla argued that

> in the training schools in the larger and smaller cities vigilance is required to keep the girls away from magazines and models of various modes of dress and hairstyle, so that these educators may be spared the vortex into which the women here are drawn so easily, altering their dress and hairstyles, monthly, weekly, hourly, the wealthy spending what they have and which they could put to better use, the less wealthy and the poor

failing to satisfy other needs or worse, the former and the latter growing accustomed, like weathercocks on towers or campaniles, to flitting restlessly from one desire to another, failing to acquire or losing those virtues which ennoble human nature, that is, perseverance and firmness.[28]

The emphasis placed on the maternal mission of the schoolmistress, which was harped on in the pedagogical literature, in ministerial instructions accompanying primary-school and teacher-training syllabi, and even in parliamentary debates, was far removed from the reality of teachers' lives filled with loneliness and poverty. All assert that clothing is one of the most important markers of compliance with ideals of modesty and decorum. In his 1886 novel *Cuore*, Edmondo De Amicis, for example, describes two totally different schoolmistresses, the melancholy "little nun" and the cheerful "teacher with the red feather," using clothing and appearance to highlight their opposition: the "little nun . . . is always dressed in dark colors, with a black pinafore, and has a small white face; her hair is always straight, her eyes are light-colored, and her voice is so subtle that she always seems to be murmuring prayers. . . . But there's another one . . . the young one with the rosy face, who has two dimples in her cheeks and who wears a big red feather in her little hat and a cross of yellow glass around her neck."[29]

Much later, when the echoes of emancipation died down (awareness of which had spread among schoolmistresses too at the beginning of the twentieth century) and the Fascist regime was in full sway, an even more radical depiction of the maternal, sacrificial, and saving graces of the female primary-school teacher (within the context of a more traditional view of male and female roles, one permeated by sex phobias) returned with a vengeance. A circular from the Education Ministry (February 12, 1929) strongly recommended to schoolmistresses "sobriety of behavior, the use of dark-colored clothing, moral austerity and ladylike conduct, even as far as exterior aspect is concerned, so that the female pupils may see reflected in them a superior ideal of maternity to which it is a source of joy and pride to sacrifice all feminine vanity." In 1935, the minister, Cesare M. De Vecchi, underscored the importance of decorum and austerity of dress and conduct, by forbidding schoolmistresses to wear makeup.[30] For women, access to higher education and the sciences, as well as to the primary teaching profession, contributed significantly to the construction of a historically novel identity, one marked by the struggle between emerging pathways of subjectivity and the regimentation of behavior imposed on them by social custom. The curious history of the rapport between the will to learn and the imposition of dress codes, whether freely chosen or passively accepted, contains numerous traces and significant echoes of this process.

NOTES

1. Unless indicated, all translations are mine. Giovanni Verga, *Storia di una capinera* (Milan: Newton, 1993). This book was translated as *Sparrow: The Story of a Songbird* by Christine Donougher (Sawtry: Dedalus Books, 1994). Regarding the crinoline, Yvonne Knibiehler, in "Corpi o cuori," in *Storia delle donne: L'Ottocento,* ed. Georges Duby and Michelle Perrot (Bari: Laterza, 1991), 310, observes: "Clothes, still tight-fitting and tubular under the First Empire, widen later to reach the apogee of the crinoline (between 1854 and 1868): a skirt could be as much as three meters in diameter and require 30 meters of cloth. . . . This fashion increased the production of ephemera to prevent any form of democratization." On the relationship between feminine identity and cultural models, see Carmela Covato, ed., *Metamorfosi dell'identità: Per una storia delle pedagogie narrate* (Milan: Guerini, 2006).

2. Literally, "The families' magazine, the embroiderer." On fashion magazines, in particular those by the publisher Lampugnani, see Silvia Franchini, "Moda e catechismo civile nei giornali delle signore italiane," in *Fare gli italiani,* ed. Simonetta Soldani and Gabriele Turi, vol. 1 (Bologna: Mulino, 1993), 341–84. For an in-depth examination of the issue, see A. M. Curcio, *La moda: Identità negate* (Milan: Franco Angeli, 2002).

3. The parallelism between suicide and consumption as "the biological destiny which assumes the task of that society" is emphasized by Giorgio Pressburger in his introduction to Theodor Fontane's *Effi Briest,* Italian trans. Enrico Ganni (Milan: Feltrinelli, 1993), viii. The crisis of female identity, hovering on the brink between imprisonment and emancipation, in Europe between the

nineteenth and twentieth centuries, is highlighted by Francesca Borruso in *Donne immaginarie e destini educativi: Intrecci pedagogici nel teatro di Ibsen, Čechov e Strindberg* (Milan: Unicopli, 2008).

4. See Daniel Roche, *Il linguaggio della moda* (Turin: Einaudi, 1989); Pierre Perrot, *Il sopra e il sotto della borghesia: Storia dell' abbigliamento nel XIX secolo* (Milan: Longanesi, 1981); Franchini, "Moda e catechismo civile." Philippe Ariès, on French children's clothing in *Centuries of Childhood: A Social History of Family Life*, trans. Robert Baldick (New York: Vintage Books, 1962), 58, notes: "boys were the first specialized children. They began going to school in large numbers as far back as the late sixteenth century and the early seventeenth century. The education of girls started in a small way only in the time of Fénelon and Mme. de Maintenon and developed slowly and tardily. Without a proper educational system, the girls were confused with the women at an early age . . . nobody thought of giving visible form, by means of dress, to a distinction which was beginning to exist in reality for the boys but which still remained futile for the girls."

5. On the relationship of "dynamic conformity" to "coercive conformity," see Antonio Gramsci, *Quaderni del carcere*, ed. Valentino Gerratana, vol. 2 (Turin: Einaudi, 1975), 862–63. See also Gramsci, *The Prison Notebooks*, trans. Joseph Buttigieg (New York: Columbia University Press, 1996).

6. Roche, *Il linguaggio della moda*, 396.

7. Roy S. Porter, "Lady Eleanor Davies, la pazza," in *Barocco al femminile*, ed. Giulia Calvi (Bari: Laterza, 1992), 40.

8. See Bram Dijkstra, *Idols of Perversity: Fantasies of Feminine Evil in Fin-de-siècle Culture* (New York: Oxford University Press, 1986), and A. Giallongoed, ed., *Donne di palazzo nelle corti europee: Tracce e forme di potere nell'età moderna* (Milan: Unicopli, 2005).

9. On this issue, see Eugenio Garin, "La questione femminile nelle varie correnti ideologiche degli ultimi cento anni," in *L'emancipazione femminile in Italia: Un secolo di discussioni (1861–1961)* (Florence: La Nuova Italia, 1964), 19–44.

10. Bruno P. F. Wanroij, *Storia del pudore: La questione sessuale in Italia 1860–1940* (Venice: Marsilio, 1990), 201.

11. Franchini, "Moda e catechismo civile," 374.

12. Michela De Giorgio, *Le italiane dall' Unità ad oggi: Modelli culturali e comportamenti sociali* (Bari: Laterza, 1992), 66. For a reconstruction of the role of female identity in relation to the emergence of the traits of "Italianness," see Marina D'Amelia, *La mamma* (Bologna: il Mulino, 2005).

13. Eve Curie, *Madame Curie: A Biography*, trans. Vincent Sheean (New York: Da Capo Press, 1937), 95.

14. Sibilla Aleramo, *A Woman at Bay*, trans. Maria Hornor Lansdale (New York: G. P. Putnam's Sons, 1908), 9–10.

15. Ibid., 24.

16. Lou Andreas-Salomé, *Il mito di una donna*, ed. Uta Olivieri (Florence: Guaraldi, 1975), 46.

17. Marina Addis Saba, *Anna Kuliscioff: Vita privata e passione politica* (Milan: Mondadori, 1993), 4, 7.

18. Angelica Balabanoff, as quoted in Addis Saba, *Anna Kuliscioff*, 3.

19. Evelyn Fox-Keller, *A Feeling for the Organism: Life and Work of Barbara McClintock* (New York: W. H. Freeman, 1983), 25.

20. Ibid., 24.

21. See Maria Campo Alange, *Concepción Arenal (1820–1893): Estudio biográfico documental* (Madrid: Ediciones de la Revista de Occidente, 1973). Special thanks to Giuliana Di Febo for bringing this work to my attention.

22. The Casati Law of 1859 set up the *scuole normali* with a view to training primary-school masters and mistresses. Courses lasted three years, and the trainees were separated by sex.

23. The prospectus was approved by the Board of Governors during a meeting held on January 28, 1897: Rome, Archivio Centrale dello Stato, Ministero della Pubblica Istruzione, Direzione generale per l'istruzione primaria e normale, 1897–1910, busta 302, fascicolo "Regolamenti dei Convitti femminili annessi alle scuole normali," 10. The question is discussed in S. Franchini and P. Puzzuoli, eds., *Gli istituti femminili di educazione e di istruzione (1861–1910)* (Rome: Ministero per i Beni e le Attività Culturali, 2005).

24. Elvira Mancuso, *Vecchia storia . . . inverosimile* (Palermo: Sellerio, 1990), 37–38.

25. See Giorgio Bini, "Romanzi e realtà di maestre e maestri," in *Storia d'Italia: Intellettuali e potere*, vol. 4 (Turin: Einaudi, 1981), 1197–1224.

26. *Minutes of the Fifth Italian Pedagogical Congress Held in Genoa, September 1868, at the Expense of the City of Genoa* (Genoa, 1868), 124–25.

27. Quoted in Giorgio Bini, "La maestra nella letteratura: uno specchio della realtà," in *L'educazione delle donne: Scuola e modelli di vita femminile nell' Italia dell' Ottocento*, ed. Simonetta Soldani

(Milan: Franco Angeli,1989), 344. See also A. Santoni Rugiu, *Maestre e maestri: La difficile storia degli insegnanti elementari* (Rome: Carocci, 2006).

28. Domenico Failla, *Considerazioni intorno al riordinamento delle scuole normali regie* (Naples: De Pascale, 1875), 15.

29. Edmondo De Amicis, *Cuore* (Milan: Treves, 1929), 54; see also *Cuore (Heart): An Italian Schoolboy's Journal. A Book for Boys,* trans. Isabel F. Hapgood (New York: Thomas Y. Crowell, 1915).

30. Quoted in Ester De Fort, "I maestri elementari italiani dai primi del Novecento alla caduta del fascismo," *Nuova Rivista Storica* 68 (1984): 528.

12

GENDER AND POWER

DRESSING ''CHARLIE''

Cristina Giorcelli

Kate Chopin wrote "Charlie" in 1900, the year after the publication of her second and final novel, *The Awakening*. The story may have fallen victim to the mostly bad reviews that greeted the publication of her (at the time misunderstood) masterpiece: rejected by two magazines, it lay among her papers until 1969.[1] "Charlie" deals with the strong tie binding a widowed father, who is "preposterously young looking—slender, with a clean shaved face and deep set blue eyes . . . and dark brown hair" (644), to his favorite, the seventeen-year-old Charlie, the second of his seven daughters. In this story, Chopin, with her usual daring and the deftest of touches, tackles a theme—a psychologically and emotionally incestuous relationship[2]—that lurked within much nineteenth-century fiction and was often addressed by women writers of so-called domestic fiction.[3] Following the dictates of a certain male ethic,[4] such a fiction implied the construction of a female identity shaped by and according to the father's will within the ever-complex gender relations at play in the patriarchal family. Physically, this heroine was usually a bloodless beauty, while psychologically she was sweet, devoted, innocent, submissive, dutiful, and generous to the point of self-sacrifice (like Antigone and Electra).

In this type of father–daughter relationship, a dialectic of attraction and repulsion often develops.[5] Within Freudian readings, if the daughter does not identify with any female role model, she may wish her father to bestow a kind of masculinity on her; thus the attraction: "She turns to her father in the hope that he will make her into an honorary boy. In her imagination, her father has the power to confer the emblem of maleness (penis or phallus) upon her. It is for this reason that she wishes to seduce or to be seduced by him. By establishing a special and privileged relationship with her father, she seeks to be elevated into the superior company of men."[6] There is, however, also repulsion resulting from the incest taboo,[7] because "if the father desires his daughter as daughter he will be outside his Oedipal desire for his mother, which is to say also beyond 'the phallic phase.' "[8] Therefore, although this dialectic of attraction and repulsion can be colored (albeit implicitly) with eroticism,[9] it can also be seen—when consciously recognized and overcome—as the foundation of heterosexual desire.[10]

In "Charlie," Chopin makes this father–daughter relationship particularly complex by creating a tomboy of a daughter (thirty years after Jo March in Louisa May Alcott's *Little Women* [1868]).[11] Charlie does not fully correspond to the model daughter, either in her looks or in the way she behaves and dresses: she is devoted, innocent, and generous almost—as we shall see—to the point of self-sacrifice, but she is not feminine in the bloodlessly beautiful, sweet, and elegant sense. In her father's heart, this tomboy takes the place of the son he never had. He sees her quite explicitly as his "ideal son" (644) and (perhaps for this very reason), being his most beloved daughter ("She never seemed to do anything that anyone except her father approved of"), he makes her feel the most protected of the seven sisters (641). Likewise, Charlie's devotion to her father ("She really felt that nothing made much difference so long as her father was happy") heightens her role as go-between within a social group that is totally female (634). As in *Little Women,* an aunt—the father's sister—makes an occasional appearance as well as a governess who, according to convention, is strict with everyone and particularly fierce with Charlie: "Miss Malvern . . . prided herself on her firmness—as if firmness were heaven's first law" (649).[12]

In the second half of the nineteenth century, when the middle-class female model cast the woman as angel of the household, the figure of the tomboy was a popular one in women's fiction. While this popularity showed a fervent desire on the part of female writers (and readers) for a more dynamic, more adventurous, and more independent life, the tomboy was acceptable because she appeared in an age in which "walking, running, climbing, battling, and tumbling [were] as normal female as they [were] male activities."[13] Furthermore, once the New Woman appeared on the scene—to some extent diametrically opposed to the stereotype of woman as angel of the household—tomboys became popular because a new awareness was developing in both male and female readers:[14] "When the initial description mention[ed] a girl's untidiness and careless dress, readers knew at once that she would be jolly, wholesome, and active."[15] Fifty years before, the tomboys' task was simply not to annoy the general reader; now tomboys were actively appreciated. Moreover, as the New Woman became an undeniable presence, the bildungsroman registered a growing importance as a literary genre.[16] In these novels, young women would find their true identities after a radical search to discover their real aspirations and after a tough internal and external struggle to achieve a satisfying form of social integration.

Formerly, the period of adolescence had generally been treated as a time of transition preparing for the only desirable future prospect for a young woman: courtship, marriage, and motherhood. Chopin is both thematically and stylistically among the avant-garde of this new age, and to make her point, she depicts the conformist and conservative Louisiana society of the time.[17] Her tackling of this theme in "Charlie" may, however, also exemplify that "hysterical" ambivalence found by Juliet Mitchell in many women writers of the nineteenth century: a woman choosing a woman as the lead character focuses her attention on the "female world," but at the same time, as a writer of fiction, she must maintain a detached objectivity.[18]

The woman novelist must be an hysteric. Hysteria is the woman's simultaneous acceptance and refusal of the organization of sexuality under patriarchal capitalism. . . . I do not believe there is such a thing as female writing, a "woman's voice." There is the hysteric's voice which is *the woman's masculine language* (one has to speak "masculinely" in a phallocentric world) talking about feminine experience. It's both simultaneously the woman novelist's refusal of the woman's world—she is, after all, a novelist—and her construction from within a masculine world of that woman's world. . . . It touches . . . on the importance of bisexuality.[19]

At seventeen, however, Charlie is a bit too old to be a tomboy. Usually tomboys were presented at an age when shifts in gender were still acceptable/accepted[20] (the period between puberty and adolescence).[21] Chopin, who was the mother of a daughter (and five sons), must have chosen Charlie's age with a purpose—as we shall see.[22]

The opening of the story sets out Charlies's typical attributes: "Six of Mr. Laborde's charming daughters had been assembled for the past half hour in the study room. The seventh, Charlotte, or Charlie as she was commonly called, had not yet made her appearance" (638). A conventional attribute ("charming") groups the six sisters into an indistinct whole. Indeed, Mr. Laborde, who rules over this female universe unopposed (even by his wife, who is dead and whose name we are never told), considers the girls "always like a bouquet of flowers, in a bunch, as it were" (665). Only the seventh daughter is not part of the group: she is the second eldest, but she is mentioned last as she is different from her sisters. Charlie stands out and is not "charming" like the others. Her distinctive characteristic is not that she tries to escape her father's dominance, but that she is emotionally attached to him. The story begins with a number, and numbers symbolically signify. It is therefore no coincidence either that Charlie is seventeen, a number that symbolizes change and rebirth, or that she is the second of seven sisters: seven standing for a dynamic wholeness while two, appropriately, symbolizes ambivalence.[23]

With Chopin's typical directness, the difference that Charlie represents is foregrounded from the opening of the story: not only is her nickname epicene, but even her name is a semantic hybrid.[24] Charlotte derives from Charles, which etymologically goes back to old German and means "man" or "male."[25] Therefore Charlotte—with its feminine suffix—indicates the "woman" within the "man," the "female" within the "male," thus incorporating both sexes in one, in a kind of androgynous paradigm.[26] The writer, as is clear, subtly leads the reader along the road of ambiguity from the very start. As both her name and her nickname indicate *(respondent nomina rebus suis)*, Charlie's gender is not (yet) socially and culturally defined. It is implicit that in presenting the heroine by her nickname alone—a familiar appellation, used among intimates—the story will tend to examine her inner being with honesty and sympathy.

Charlie's clothes and appearance reflect her character. From the moment that she (quite literally) bursts onto the scene, she shows how she differs from the models proposed by her social class (the solid bourgeoisie) and her world (conservative, late nineteenth-century Louisiana):

> Her hair was cut short and was so damp with perspiration that it clung to her head and looked almost black. Her face was red and overheated at the moment. She wore a costume of her own devising, something between bloomers and a divided skirt which she called her "trouserlets." Canvas leggings, dusty boots and a single spur completed her costume. (639)

Dark, with short hair, spirited, sweating and dusty, Charlie is proposed as the complete antithesis of the other sisters, particularly—as will become apparent—the perfectly mannered eldest sister, Julia. Significantly, this reserved, composed, diligent, slender, pale-skinned, blue-eyed nineteen-year-old with long, light brown hair also has a "very womanly" (649) deportment.[27] Charlie dresses differently: she wears "bloomers," trousers gathered at the waist and tight around the ankles and originally donned either with a loose knee-length vest or with a skirt that reached to below the knee.[28] Sponsored in 1848 by the American feminist Amelia Bloomer, bloomers were intended as a more "hygienic" item of clothing that would give women greater freedom of movement and liberate them both from their atavistic subjection to men (justified by supposed female weakness and physical inferiority) as well as from the constrictions of their expected social role.[29] This role was sanctioned by clothing: if a middle-class woman's aim was to become the angel of the household (and be totally dedicated to propagating and protect-

ing the species), her clothing should have helped her seduce men. Women's clothes in that period were usually too long—to the extent that they dragged across the floor—and were weighed down by various petticoats, while rigid, tight corsets imprisoned the torso. The whole outfit was completed by rather high-heeled shoes. Bloomers were attacked so violently in the press (and ridiculed by aesthetes) that they only survived a few years.[30] In the 1880s, however, a feminist writer had them still in mind: "Something of the nature of the American costume—the gymnasium dress, the beach suit, *the Bloomer*, call it what you will—must take the place of our present style of dress, before the higher life—moral, intellectual, political, social, or domestic—can ever begin for women."[31]

Indeed, forty years after Bloomer's campaign, coinciding with the appearance of the New Woman on the social scene, trousers once again became part of bourgeois women's attire thanks to the vehicle that, not by chance, the heroine of "Charlie" mounts just after her first appearance: the bicycle (643).[32] In the 1890s, "the knickerbocker bicycling costume . . . came into fashion."[33] In fact, "the look of legs in motion did not become interesting or problematic until the widespread use of the bicycle at the end of the nineteenth century. Only then did divided skirts and knickerbockers seem necessary in order to articulate the legs."[34] Whereas in the large Northeastern cities, emancipated women —especially if they played a sport—were increasingly abandoning traditional clothing,[35] in Louisiana, some still proudly asserted that

> The New Orleans woman notably differs from her sister in any other leading city of the Union. . . . She is domestic, winsome, *looks askance upon bloomers*, falters before ballot privileges, and prefers to address the public, if at all, by pen rather than by platform; rather cherishes the Old than embraces the New Woman. . . . Nowhere is there a sweeter womanliness and nowhere daintier tastes.[36]

In the South, women's trousers—called bloomers, even though those worn in that period were more like a kind of long culotte or Zouave knickerbockers—could still be considered a scandalous piece of clothing. Having lived in Louisiana, Chopin was well aware of this attitude, and therefore, she deliberately intended to position her heroine outside the strict canons of traditional femininity to which her elder sister Julia conforms. As if to incorporate male attire, trousers, to a woman's world, Charlie—who has a creative ability with language—rechristens them "trouserlets" (639), feminizing the masculinity of pants with a diminutive.[37] Half "bloomers" and half "divided skirt," these trousers are no less of a hybrid than the identity of their wearer.

Charlie's adoption of a semimale attire—completed by a phallic symbol like the "single spur"—supports Marjorie Garber's theory that not only can women cross-dress (contrary to what Freud believed), but that cross-dressing shows the wearer's intolerance of both gender categorization and social distinctions.[38] Indeed, while demonstrating that a fixed gender for each biological sex is unsustainable (along with the roles and behaviors laid down by cultural stereotypes), the transvestite defines an edge where oppositions break apart and realign.[39] Charlie, in fact, does not only overcomes the barriers of gender: she also challenges those of race, wealth, and social station.[40] She is the only one of Mr. Laborde's daughters who has good (albeit paternalistic) relations with the black servants and the Acadian families with whom she mingles. She eats and plays with their children in their homes in idyllic fashion, almost outside history—oblivious to the ferocity of slavery, the horrors of the Civil War, and the injustices of Jim Crow Reconstruction. Charlie often even adopts their language, "falling into the 'Cadian speech as she sometimes did" (652). Charlie is thus a go-between not just between genders, but also between social classes and ethnic groups. Signally, before packing her off to a private school in New Orleans, her father sends her for a couple of weeks to stay with her aunt, because "Two weeks at Aunt Clementine's would enable her [Charlie] to be fitted out as became her age, sex, and condition in life" (654).

With all this, it is clear that Charlie is presented as a sort of female Tom Sawyer or Huck Finn, who, like her, were motherless, could not bear bourgeois social norms, and lived in the rural South.[41] When Charlie goes against the governess's (and her father's) orders and spends time with her young and innocent Acadian and black playmates, she indulges in dramatic boasts in the comic frontier-style tradition found in Twain's heroes. She claims that she has killed "bears," "tigers," "panthers," and "alligators" in the woods around the estate and that the diamond ring she inherited from her mother and wears on her middle finger is a powerful amulet that, when necessary, allows her to become invisible (646–47).

In perfect consistency with the clothes she wears, Charlie thus behaves like a young man: she does not like to play the piano, draw, or take dancing lessons, the cursus honorum for a young lady of her social class. Nor does she like the sports practiced at her school (tennis and basketball [659]). She prefers cycling, horse riding, fishing, or handling a gun (rather too casually). She also feels an urge to write. In her family and at school, she is the only girl who composes poetry: "one day it fell upon them [her school friends] with the startling bewilderment of lightning from a clear sky that Charlie was a poet" (658).[42] By knowing how to use a pen—a phallic-generative symbol par excellence—she presents herself as heir to masculine power, thus aspiring to authorial status (even if the story is not told from her point of view, but from the narrator's).[43] At some imprecise time before the narrative begins we are even told that her writing skill had reached an extraordinary effect: it happened when her father had "vaguely entertained the expedient of a second marriage." On that occasion Charlie wrote such a "touching petition," signed by all her sisters, against the prospect that he did not go ahead with it (643). In order to keep the family united in her mother's absence, Charlie had implicitly taken her place, stopping Mr. Laborde from marrying again by making use of her excellent skill—her *mastery*—of the written (literary) language: that is, the paternal, patriarchal language, the only one her father understands and that can affect his feelings. In obtaining this success, however, as anthropologists and psychologists tell us, Charlie pays an unspoken, but terrible price: if need be, she will dedicate herself to sharing her father's life, become his consort, and never betray him by choosing another man (unless it is her father who chooses him or approves her choice). In short, she gives herself up as a kind of pledge, a tacit pact: "Daughters are expected to marry, but there is still a tradition which decrees that there be one daughter who takes care of her father, who remains single to assume her mother's role as it becomes necessary, or who marries only when her father dies."[44]

The quiet life of the Laborde family is turned upside down when Firman Walton, a "good looking, intelligent looking" young man, arrives on business from his native New Orleans (650). Slightly wounded in the arm by a chance bullet recklessly fired by Charlie, he stays at their house to be looked after for a few days.[45] Here he begins to fall in love with Julia—attracted, conventionally enough, to her beauty—admitting to Charlie, "Your eldest sister is beautiful, isn't she! It seems to me she's the most beautiful girl I almost ever saw" (651). Charlie, on her part, immediately develops a one-sided and unacknowledged crush on him. Thus, on the very evening that Walton arrives, when Mr. Laborde announces to his daughter that she has to go to school to acquire some discipline, "Charlie was exceedingly astonished to discover that the arrangement planned by her father was not so distasteful as it would have seemed a while ago" (654). As her infatuation is still in its formative, initial stage, Charlie, who never felt anything like it before, is unaware of it, and the author will not put it into words. It is, however, already clear to the reader from their first meeting—when Walton mistakes Charlie "for a boy" and calls her a "scamp" (648)—that he, a true son of Louisiana, is not captivated by a young woman so lacking in traditional femininity. Walton's interest in Julia is also conveyed by the attention paid to her clothes, which are conventionally seductive.[46] On the first day of Walton's stay at the plantation, Julia wears a pale blue muslin dress that "brightened her color and brought out the blue of her eyes" (651); a little later, her gowns are described as "quite too young-ladified; they touched the ground, often with a graceful sweep" (653). She displays the voluptuous s-shaped figure then in fashion. Charlie, instead, appears at table in a dress that Julia has lent her, but the adjustments needed to fit her seem a bit ungainly: "the effect, if not completely happy, could not have been called a distinct failure" (653).

When Charlie arrives in New Orleans with her sister, the governess, and Walton and plans her new wardrobe for school, however, she gives the impression that "the feminine instinct had been aroused in her" and that the decision to be masculine had only been a phase to please her father while waiting—like Sleeping Beauty—for a Prince Charming to wake her into femininity (656). Charlie throws herself into acquiring clothes that have so much lace, embroidery, ribbons, and frills that they appear almost grotesque, arousing the criticism of both Julia and her aunt: "She wanted lace and embroideries upon her garments; and she longed to bedeck herself with ribbons and *passementeries* which the shops displayed in such tempting array" (656).[47] In addition, while Julia arranges her long, light brown hair "wound round and round till it formed a coil as large as a dessert plate" (649)—the culinary metaphor perfectly suits a character who embodies such a domestic calling—Charlie curls her short dark hair with irons until she makes her head look like a "prize chrysanthemum" (657). If at first Charlie was a cross-dressing hybrid female, she is now an overdressed female, almost a cross-dressing hybrid male.

Her clothes humiliate her gender and women's fashion (which, at the time, was particularly flamboyant). Faced with such caricature-like results, for the first time the authorial voice defines Charlie as a "young thing" (656). No longer vivacious, independent, and assertive—no longer herself—Charlie does, or rather overdoes, whatever is necessary to make herself conventionally attractive. But, in so doing, she has become a "thing," and a poor thing at that, arousing feelings of benevolent compassion. At the school, Charlie gives voice to the inspiration "bubbling up inside of her" by writing a poem that she hides alongside the pictures of her parents in the gold locket she wears around her neck (657).[48] On this occasion too, the authorial voice calls her "Poor little thing!" and adds, "Let her alone. It would be cruel to tell the whole story" (658). Indeed, the reader never discovers the contents of the poem and is never privy to her powerful emotions (a destiny of silence, neglect, and invisibility traditionally suffered by women), which are gleaned only from her behavior.

In the first three sections of the story, the ties that bind father to daughter are imbued with essential tenderness. He treats "his beloved daughter" as if she were a little girl (653): "Mr. Laborde took a fresh linen handkerchief from his pocket and passed it over her face as if she had been a little child" (644). Indeed, this father, as if to compensate for his deceased wife's absence, is remarkably nonauthoritarian, mild-mannered, and maternal. He has no wish to be separated from his daughters, he does not like making definitive decisions, he is quiet ("she regretted that her father was not a more talkative man. His silences gave her no opportunity to defend herself" [644]),[49] and he has the suitably meditative characteristic of being "perplexed."[50] When he tells Charlie of his (difficult) decision to send her to school, almost begging her forgiveness, "He took her in his arms, and kissed her fervently" (654). "Fervently" might seem a little exaggerated if it were not for the fact that he has already been portrayed as possessing feminine and maternal characteristics.[51]

In New Orleans, Charlie dresses differently, deciding "to transform herself from a hoyden to a fascinating young lady" (658). Her father, who had already been to visit with two of his daughters (and must have seen for himself how she had changed), goes back to spend a whole day "alone" with her. He does not even tell his sister that he has arrived in town: "her father came alone one morning quite early" (661). First, the authorial voice reveals his feelings, his absolute joy and almost uncontrollable excitement: "He did not tell her in so many words how *hungry* he was for her, but he showed it in a hundred ways. He was like a *school boy* on a holiday; it was like a *conspiracy;* there was a flavor of *secrecy* about it too" (661; emphases mine). Immediately afterward we are shown his chivalrous behavior and perfect gallantry toward his daughter: "He carried her jacket and assisted her over the crossings like an experienced cavalier," and he showers her with presents (661). He gives her various items of clothing (a hat, a hat pin, a fan, some handkerchiefs) and books, thus satisfying her vanity without neglecting her education. This phase, which might be seen as a kind of courtship, is followed by a quasi-seduction scene. At breakfast, the two of them are described as "exceedingly young persons" (661), thus reminding us that at the beginning of the story he had been presented as "preposterously young looking." By showing youthful feelings and behaving like a "school boy," he makes the generation gap between them disappear. They sit beside a lake, "looking across the glistening water, watching the slow sails and feeling *like a couple of bees in clover*" (662; emphasis mine). Even the description of the surrounding nature is laden with sensuousness: "the air was soft and moist and the warm sun of early March brought out the scent of the earth and of distant gardens and the weedy smell from the still pools" (661). And while "He held [her] hand fondly in both of his" to check—on her insistence—if it was as white as Julia's (in order to appear feminine she had persistently used a whitening night cream), Charlie "threw an arm around his neck and hugged him." Sensuality does not necessarily entail sexuality, but witnessing this scene in astonishment are "a lame oysterman and a little Brazilian monkey" (662). If the oyster symbolizes femininity, the oysterman, being lame, signifies an unbalanced femininity, marked by moral or spiritual weakness. What is more, the monkey—a symbolically complex animal—also stands for lust and the actions of the unconscious.[52]

Only a few months have passed since Charlie left the plantation, and yet the unconscious—but no less real—process of seduction, on the part of the father, is sustained by a behavior that would be more suitable when dealing with a young woman or a fiancée than with a "little child" of seventeen. It is at this point that another telling reference to the ring that Charlie wears—which is the symbol of her mother's commitment to marriage, the bond of her love and of possession by Mr. Laborde (662)—appears. In a scene that is so emotionally charged, which grows in intensity and occurs at such a delicate moment in her life, when she is trying out her seductive powers and potential, Charlie seems to encourage the process of seduction enacted by her father. Mr. Laborde's behavior may, however, be covertly determined also by another emotion that may indicate his deepest impulses. During their day out together, father and daughter—who for the occasion is perfectly dressed complete with gloves and a parasol—encounter just one person:

> They saw no one they knew except Young Walton. . . . The young fellow turned crimson with unexpected pleasure. . . . He showed a disposition to be excused from the office and to join them, a suggestion which Mr. Laborde *did not favor,* which rather *alarmed* him and *hurried his departure.* Moreover he [her father] could see that Charlie did not like the young man, and he could not blame her for that, *all things considered!* She gave her whole attention to her gloves and the clasp of her parasol while there. (661; emphases mine)

This lack of awareness is remarkable for such a sensitive and attentive father, unless (as his thought leaves us to intuit) he himself has unconscious, but strong feelings of jealousy toward the young man. In fact, the latter is called either "young man," "young fellow," "young gentleman," or above all "young Walton" no fewer than fourteen times in the course of the narrative. In this passage, not only are three of these four appellatives used, but "Young Walton" capitalizes "Young" as if it (rather than Firman) were his first name.[53] This continual insistence on his youth can only be explained by the father's desire to contrast Walton's inexperience with his knowledge of life, unquestionable authority, and absolute supremacy over his daughter-heroine, while concurrently belittling the age difference between him and his daughter thanks to his "youthful" appearance and feelings.[54] It is as if Charlie's father unconsciously recognizes a potential rival in "Young Walton."

Later, when Charlie shows her father her hand that she hopes has become paler and asks him "Notice anything?" (662), she indirectly reveals her plan to become feminine. Given her age, she should be available for marriage; but her father, either obtusely or craftily, fails to understand and, referring instead to the ring that she is wearing—and therefore to the vicarious commitment he once made and that the ring symbolizes—he returns the question, "No stones missing, are there?" (662). Fearful, therefore, of being abandoned by his daughter (or ousted from his position of affective superiority), he either evades or minimizes her attempts to show him that she is no longer a child but a young woman ready to be engaged. Charlie, however, wishes to be seen as such, but without losing the acceptance and support of her father: at night she protects her hands with "a pair of her father's old gloves" (659).

And this may be the reason why Chopin depicted Charlie as a seventeen-year-old young woman. Charlie not only is presented at an age characterized by change and rebirth, but she has already emerged from puberty. As the story intends to fully explore the complex relationship between father and daughter, Charlie must be older and more mature biologically than the typical tomboy to make ambiguities apparent. The father does everything to make their day out together memorable and magical.[55] For his daughter, in fact, the vision of him, "robust and beautiful, clasping her with loving arms," is truly indelible: "For weeks the memory of that day lasted" (663).

In the last section of the story, having lost his right arm in an accident at the sugar mill on the plantation, Mr. Laborde asks his daughter to come home.[56] When Walton arrives for a visit, Charlie—who has continued to use skin creams and tried out new hairstyles—dresses up in feminine fashion: "Charlie wore her pink organdie and her grandmother's pearls . . . and puffed her hair" (665). By now the metamorphosis from tomboy to conventional, middle-class, marriageable lady seems complete. A little later, however, Charlie learns that Julia—who has spent much time in New Orleans with their aunt—has become secretly engaged to Walton. Transported by anguish and anger, Char-

FIGURE 12.2 "We are getting there fast." Illustration for cover of *Puck*, December 25, 1895. Courtesy of Library of Congress, LC-USZC2-1229.

lie accuses her absent and unsuspecting sister of hypocrisy and puts her defensive strategies into action. Refusing the passive role her feminine dresses signify, she goes back to her tomboy outfit, and after an afternoon and evening spent wildly riding her horse as she did in the past, she frees herself of the "girlish infatuation which had blinded her." Using a telling metaphor, she confesses to her father, "I've been climbing a high mountain, dad" and concludes, referring to the typical symbol of womanhood, "I saw the new moon" (667).

The return to male clothing (and, consequently, to the tender, secure love of her father) might seem a regressive choice. By dressing as a tomboy again and barricading herself in claustrophobic family relationships, she might appear to be retreating into the past and isolating herself from the outside world, but the fact that Charlie reemerges from the experience as a "woman" shows that this is not the case. To demonstrate that the old phase of her life has passed, Charlie removes her mother's ring from her finger and, exercising the power of one who can give, sends it to Julia as a wedding gift.[57] Charlie therefore divests herself of the traditional emblem of matrimony, because, as far as her relationship with her father is concerned, she knows that she does not need such a romantic, external symbol. It is not the ring but her own self that constitutes the pledge she unwittingly makes. Thus the ring goes to Julia, who, following in the footsteps of her mother, obtains the reward for her conventional femininity (will it lead her to a marriage of subordination, if not, like her mother, to death?).

Within a year, Charlie matures into a woman through pain, frustration, and disillusionment, but she also achieves a great victory. At just eighteen, she manages the plantation in her father's place. Now an invalid, Mr. Laborde can no longer work as he did before nor go on considering his daughter "a little child." He must reluctantly recognize that she has grown up; he must admit that she has become a "little woman" (668). From now on, therefore, Charlie will act as his "right hand" (668) on a permanent basis and also as his nurse, confidante, and, to all effects, consort ("Charlie forgot that she was young" [664]). She even refuses, or at least postpones to some vague date in the future, Gus Bradley's proposal of marriage.

Gus is the neighbor of mature appearance who has been clumsily courting her for a long time and who was the only one not scandalized by her masculine appearance. Indeed, when she put on a dress, he "was so flustered at seeing Charlie in frills and furbelows that he could scarcely articulate" (655). It seems that it is the destiny of tomboys to attract the interest of men who are old-fashioned in appearance, men who are rather staid, shy, and a bit uncouth. Gus had earlier presented her with a dog and a riding whip—very different gifts from her father's—and then, when he sees her after she returns home to the plantation, Les Palmiers, he has nothing more scintillating to say than "Poor old Charlie" (664). Gus is a true father figure; affectionate and reserved, he is different from her real father, who is charming and seductive: "Mr. Gus . . . was a big fellow and awkward only from shyness and when in company. . . . His hair was light and fine and his face smooth and looked as if it belonged to a far earlier period of society and had no connection with the fevered and modern present day" (654). Perhaps it is to avoid the risk of falling back into her role as daughter that Charlie evades (or defers) marriage to him. She does not want to substitute the father–daughter (male–female) pairing, with one that, as Claude Lévi-Strauss states, is between men (father–husband—or even between two fathers who trade her as merchandise). Significantly, her father is not jealous of his daughter's admirer this time: "From his window Mr. Laborde watched the two [Charlie and Gus] mount their horses under the live oak tree" (668). He has a good opinion of Gus because he knows—as does his fourth daughter, Irene (655)—that Charlie is not in love with him. Neither youthful nor very attractive, Gus cannot compete with her father and thus cannot be a serious rival. Moreover, although Gus offers to help Charlie administer Les Palmiers as a second assistant to her father ("I'm always ready to lend a hand" [668]; "couldn't he have two right arms!" [669]), she strongly opposes the suggestion, declaring "I'm jealous of Mr. Gus" (667), who is now her father's consultant. She intends to manage the estate on her own: "I know as much about the plantation as you do, dad; you know I do" (668). The syntactic structure of this last sentence—in which the subjects switch and the verbs alternate sequentially—indicates the interchangeability of the two characters.

After the disappointing experience of falling in love, Charlie entrusts herself to her father, the man who has never disappointed her, and in so doing, sublimates eros.[58] Not by chance, Charlie's initiation to traditional femininity (fashionable clothes, pale skin, well-groomed hair as well as music and dancing lessons) begins after she shoots Walton in the right arm and ends just after her father loses his right arm. These arms, one wounded and the other amputated, signal a symbolic castration the men in her life suffer, and this rebounds back on her.[59] However, she not only finds consolation and refuge in filial love but becomes a conventional female figure: vicariously, both a protective mother (she looks after her younger sisters) and an attentive wife (she looks after her father). And she succeeds in also being loved in an exclusive fashion both by her father and by Gus (in a certain sense a putative or vice-father).[60]

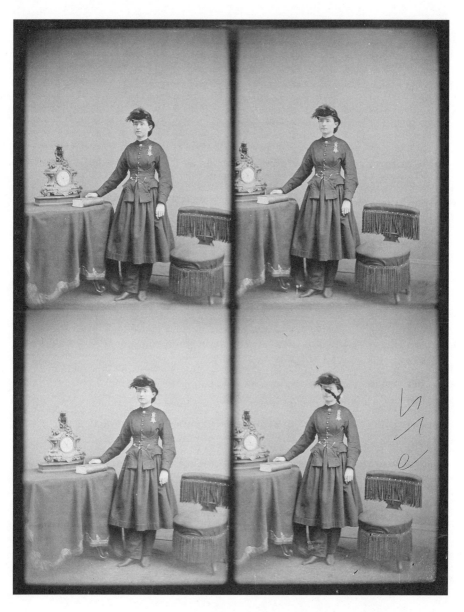

FIGURE 12.3 "Doctor Mary Walker." *Carte de visite*
by Mathew Brady (ca. 1866). Still Picture Records
Section, Special Media Archives Services Divisions,
United States National Archives, III-B-2112.

There are shades of metaphorical endogamy when the daughter returns to live at home (either as an unmarried woman or even after she has married). Indeed, when the father is weak (passive, feminine, and, as in this case, with physical and seductive powers depleted), the tomboy daughter must assume the authority to find a way "to approximate the culturally correct solution—she must be married, or at least at rest and settled— while still properly reverencing the father or father figure who couldn't pull it off himself." In such cases, the daughter, who still remains at the service "of the pieties of home, church, state, and the exogamous circulation of daughters," even comes to substitute her father's prerogative in managing women on the marriage market: forebodingly, thanks to Charlie Walton and Julia had the chance to get to know each other.[61] In any case, "it is her bond with her father that preserves the freedom and authority she enjoys as his favored surrogate."[62] As the daughter who knows how to handle both a pen and a pistol, Charlie is portrayed from the start of the story as the one who saved the plantation "when her father was away" (641).

By now Charlie does not imitate others: neither the language (and behavior) of the Acadians nor the clothes (and language of femininity as social construct) of Julia. She faces the world with a strong, adult sensibility, and her ego is no longer caught between latent femininity and an apparent masculinity. She has faith in herself and possesses a newfound authority. If she stops writing poetry, her talent as a writer will be put to the less romantic, but more profitable, needs of the plantation ("I know as much as he [Gus], more perhaps when it comes to writing letters" [667–68]). Unlike Jo March, who marries Professor Bhaer and becomes a wife and perfect mother, Charlie seems to have a third option to the two that are destined for the March sisters (marriage or death).[63] Dressed as a tomboy, Charlie combines the figure of the angel of the house with that of a manager of a large estate who, as a New Woman, must demonstrate that she has initiative. Dressed in male clothes—with all their sexual and political power—Charlie has doubled her potential, charging it with male and female qualities. It is more than a sort of bisexuality that Charlie claims; she assumes the power and the existence of what Marjorie Garber calls a "third" "space of possibility."[64] Charlie has discovered how to take from another gender what enriches her own identity.

At the turn of the century, between old and new eras, Charlie accepts a sort of self-sacrifice that is not without its own gratifications. First, she imposes her will: even faced with her father's opposition and her aunt's proposals, she stays on the plantation and runs it. Second, and shockingly for a patriarchal society with covert, insidious, misogynist tendencies, she gives a powerful blow to the gender divide, even if her femininity is still harnessed to the usual stereotype of servicing the needs and interests of others.[65] This may be a "hysterical" ambivalence or quite simply the ambivalence of the times. This story shows that a narrative of education can have a woman as its central character with a structure that is circular (the heroine returns to her home and dresses as she once did) and open: "Sartorial borrowings from the other sex . . . display a modern kind of knowledge that sexuality is fluid, unaccountable and even uncomfortable, not fixed, simple and easy. Besides sex, fashion insists on risk."[66]

NOTES

1. Chopin sent "Charlie" to *Youth's Companion* and *Century,* without success: Emily Toth, *Kate Chopin* (New York: William Morrow, 1990), 337. See also Emily Toth, *Unveiling Kate Chopin* (Jackson: University Press of Mississippi, 1999), 209–30. It was finally published as part of the complete edition of her works. *The Complete Works of Kate Chopin,* ed. Per Seyersted (Baton Rouge: Louisiana State University Press, 1969) (all citations are from this edition; page numbers appear in the text); Per Seyersted, *Kate Chopin: A Critical Biography* (Baton Rouge: Louisiana State University Press, 1969), 183–84. Since then, and despite the reassessment of her output, the story does not appear to have received the attention it deserves. Indeed, it is mentioned in passing in a few studies: Anne Goodwin Jones, *Tomorrow Is Another Day: The Woman Writer in the South, 1859–1936* (Baton Rouge: Louisiana State University Press, 1981), 143–44; Peggy Skaggs, *Kate Chopin* (Boston: Twayne, 1985), 63–64; Barbara C. Ewell, *Kate Chopin* (New York: Ungar, 1986), 178–79; Wendy Martin, ed., *New Essays on The Awakening* (Cambridge: Cambridge University Press, 1988), 10–11 of the Introduction; Martha J. Cutter, "Losing the Battle but Winning the War: Resistance to Patriarchal Discourse in Kate Chopin's Short Fiction," *Legacy* 11, no. 1 (1994): 17–36, 32–34; Nancy A.

Walker, "Her Own Story: The Woman of Letters in Kate Chopin's Short Fiction," in *Critical Essays on Kate Chopin,* ed. Alice Hall Petry (New York: G. K. Hall, 1996), 219–20. The incest theme is denied by Anne M. Blythe, "Kate Chopin's 'Charlie,'" in *Kate Chopin Reconsidered,* ed. Lynda S. Boren and Sara deSaussure Davis (Baton Rouge: Louisiana State University Press, 1992), 207–15. Only recently, one scholar has dealt with it: Bonni James Shaker, *Coloring Locals: Racial Formation in Kate Chopin's "Youth's Companion" Stories* (Iowa City: University of Iowa Press, 2003), 99–109.

2. For a discussion of the incest theme, see Otto Rank, *The Incest Theme in Literature and Legend,* trans. Gregory C. Richter (Baltimore: Johns Hopkins University Press, 1992).

3. Incestuous overtones are often found in marriages such as that of Jo March to the mature, paternal Professor Friedrich Bhaer in *Little Women.* See Alfred Habegger, "Precocious Incest: First Novels by Louisa May Alcott and Henry James," *Massachusetts Review* 26, nos. 2–3 (Summer–Autumn 1985): 233–62.

4. "Women's domesticity enhanced men's power by undermining any possibility of genuine female equality and by placing wives in a position akin to that of possessions of men." Barbara Leslie Epstein, *The Politics of Domesticity* (Middletown, Conn.: Wesleyan University Press, 1981), 80.

5. One of the pamphlets published in the first half of the nineteenth century and intended to educate young women offers evidence of the total obedience that a daughter was expected to show her father: "We are struck with the Roman instance of filial piety, in which the life-blood was shed by tender woman to save a father. . . . Let the daughter confide then in her father, and seek so to demean herself that his eye might dwell fondly on the very secrets of her heart. Let her refer to his opinions, consult his wishes and conform to his tastes and habits." A. B. Muzzey, *The Young Maiden* (Boston: William Crosby, 1842), 87–88. "Daughters were urged to obey their fathers as unquestioningly as wives their husbands. . . . In both cases . . . women should show their gratitude for male support and protection with childlike docility and admiring love" (Epstein, *Politics of Domesticity,* 78).

6. Judith Lewis Herman with Lisa Hirschman, *Father–Daughter Incest* (Cambridge, Mass.: Harvard University Press, 1981), 57. In Nancy Chodorow's words, "The penis, or phallus, is a symbol of power or omnipotence whether you have one as a sexual organ (as a male) or as a sexual object (as a mother 'possesses' a father's). A girl desires it for the powers which it symbolizes and the freedom it promises." Nancy Chodorow, *The Reproduction of Mothering: Psychoanalysis and the Sociology of Gender* (Berkeley: University of California Press, 1978), 123.

7. "If social organization had a beginning, this could only have consisted in the incest prohibition. . . . It is there, and only there, that we find a passage from nature to culture, from animal to human life." Claude Lévi-Strauss, "The Family," in *Man, Culture, and Society*, ed. Harry Shapiro (New York: Oxford University Press, 1971), 350. Jane Gallop sees an impenetrable vicious circle in the father–daughter relationship: "The daughter desires a heterosexual encounter with the father. . . . But the only way to seduce the father, to avoid scaring him away, is to please him, and to please him one must submit to his law which proscribes any sexual relation." Jane Gallop, *The Daughter's Seduction: Feminism and Psychoanalysis* (Ithaca, N.Y.: Cornell University Press, 1982), 71. But, as Juliet Mitchell notes, the incest taboo is more a consequence of social need than of biological disgust: "Contrary to popular belief, it is not that there is anything biologically 'wrong' with incest that is important; it is rather that the command to exchange exogamously forbids the cul-de-sac of endogamy. The subjective depth of the taboo indicates social necessity, not biological revulsion." Juliet Mitchell, *Psychoanalysis and Feminism* (New York: Pantheon Books, 1974), 373. Also, according to Jacques Lacan, "The primordial Law is . . . that which in regulating marriage ties superimposes the kingdom of culture on that of nature abandoned to the law of copulation. The interdiction of incest is only its subjective pivot, revealed by the modern tendency to reduce to the mother and the sister the objects forbidden to the subject's choice, although full licence outside of these is not yet entirely open." Jacques Lacan, *Speech and Language in Psychoanalysis*, trans. Anthony Wilden (Baltimore: Johns Hopkins University Press, 1981), 40.

8. Gallop, *Daughter's Seduction*, 76.

9. Initially, Sigmund Freud (in "The Aetiology of Hysteria," 1896) held that neuroses were caused by sexual trauma suffered by daughters and caused by their fathers. In 1897 he dismissed these revelations that his patients had made to him during analysis as "fantasies" and later formulated the theory of the Oedipus complex. Only much later did he reluctantly accept the idea of the father as potential seducer. In the 1930s, however (in "Femininity," 1933), Freud again claimed that it was always the mother, or another female figure who could be identified with the mother such as a nurse or governess, who did the seducing, even though he admitted that the mother might seduce unintentionally. This was a grim burden laid on people in a socially inferior position, as Gallop argues in *Daughter's Seduction*, 132–50.

10. Lynda Zwinger, *Daughters, Fathers, and the Novel: The Sentimental Romance of Heterosexuality* (Madison: University of Wisconsin Press, 1991), 11, 119.

11. Harbour Winn, "Echoes of Literary Sisterhood: Louisa May Alcott and Kate Chopin," *Studies in American Fiction* 20, no. 2 (Autumn 1992): 205–8. Apart from the numerous similarities between *Little Women* and "Charlie" identified in this essay, it should also be noted that both writers' work was often aimed at an adolescent readership and that both of them were greatly influenced by Ralph Waldo Emerson (the only writer who is explicitly read by Edna Pontellier in *The Awakening*). Alcott openly declared that she had been a tomboy when young, reflecting, "I'd rather be a free spinster and paddle my own canoe" and "liberty is a better husband than love to many of us." Ednah D. Cheney, *Louisa May Alcott: Her Life, Letters, and Journals* (Boston: Little, Brown, 1923), 30, 122, 197. With pre-Freudian candor, she admitted, "I am more than half-persuaded that I am a man's soul, put by some freak of nature into a woman's body . . . because I have fallen in love in my life with so many pretty girls, and never once the least little bit with any man." Louise Chandler Moulton, "Louisa May Alcott," in *Our Famous Women*, ed. Elizabeth Stuart Phelps (Hartford: A. D. Washington, 1884), 49.

12. Miss Malvern's attitude to Charlie is undoubtedly caused by the latter's rebellious behavior. On a metatextual level, however, suspicion may arise that Miss Malvern might be attracted to this "preposterously young looking" widower and therefore be jealous of the special relationship between Charlie and her father. This type of relationship, between master of the house and governess (often only implicitly suggested), occurs frequently in nineteenth-century fiction (Henry James's 1898 *The Turn of the Screw*, for example). Furthermore, as a figure that purveys the language of the father through her teaching, the governess can be seen as a kind of phallic mother, all-seeing and all-powerful.

13. Ellen Moers, *Literary Women* (Garden City: Doubleday, 1963), 130. There was a significant discrepancy in the nineteenth century between the parameters of the "ideal woman"—mild, passive, and dependent—and those of the "ideal mother," who was supposed to be strong, self-confident, efficient, and capable, if necessary, of supporting her husband and children; Carroll Smith-Rosenberg, "The Hysterical Woman: Sex Roles and Role Conflict in Nineteenth-Century America," in *Disorderly Conduct: Visions of Gender in Victorian America* (New York: Knopf, 1985), 197–216. Toward the end of the first half of the nineteenth century, some courageously argued that the young lady needed to live in the open air: "Let physical vigor, attended by mental excellence and moral soundness, become a part of her noble adorning. No more may childhood and youth be the only seasons, in which public opinion shall tolerate those generous exercises in the free air, by which

buoyancy and vigor may be prolonged even to old age" (Muzzey, *Young Maiden,* 115) and also "the body was made *for use.* Every part of it is formed for activity. . . . The body . . . needs exercise, to keep it in a healthy state. . . . It requires *motion* to give it power. There is nothing, therefore, so bad for it as *laziness.*" Harvey Newcomb, *How to Be a Lady: A Book for Girls* (Boston: Gould, Kendall, and Lincoln, 1849), 105. See also Frances B. Cogan, *All-American Girl: The Ideal of Real Womanhood in Mid-Nineteenth-Century America* (Athens: University of Georgia Press, 1989).

14. To someone who asked who the New Woman was, a married woman replied, "A creature who smokes and wears *bloomers* and rides a bicycle and hates men and votes" (*Woman's Journal,* October 1, 1898, 318; emphasis mine). The independent, creative, and courageous woman was almost always from the middle classes: "she is well-read, learning the facts of life from French novels and medical textbooks, and deriving her feminist principles from Herbert Spencer and John Stuart Mill." While they tended to recognize and study female sexuality quite openly, "most New Woman novelists . . . did not equate women's liberation with sexual liberation . . . they did not endorse 'free love' or promiscuity." Indeed, "Sex in the New Woman novel mainly takes the form of the heroine's frank sexual discussions, which serve to symbolize her new-found sense of self and freedom." Jane Eldridge Miller, *Rebel Women: Feminism, Modernism and the Edwardian Novel* (London: Virago, 1994), 14–15.

15. Sally Mitchell. *The New Girl: Girls' Culture in England 1880–1915* (New York: Columbia University Press, 1995), 131.

16. According to Eldridge Miller, women's bildungsroman were not possible in the nineteenth century because "Women in the nineteenth century did not really attain maturity . . . rather than becoming economically independent and self-determining, maturity for women meant marriage, and thus merely moving from one state of dependence to another" (*Rebel Women,* 115).

17. Eldridge Miller notes that the new themes required a new model of writing (ibid., 122–24). The circular and open form chosen by Chopin for both *The Awakening* and "Charlie" perfectly suits the modernist aesthetic.

18. See also Sandra M. Gilbert and Susan Gubar, *The Madwoman in the Attic: The Woman Writer and the Nineteenth-Century Literary Imagination* (New Haven, Conn.: Yale University Press, 1979), and Mary Jacobus, *Reading Woman: Essays in Feminist Criticism* (New York: Columbia University Press, 1986).

19. Juliet Mitchell, *Women: The Longest Revolution* (London: Virago, 1984), 289–90. As Zwinger

states, "Like her daughter character, the woman novelist . . . has been reread—by her culture, its stories, and her 'own' desire—to want what she doesn't want" (*Daughters, Fathers, and the Novel*, 120).

20. According to Freud, the sexuality of a young girl has a relatively masculine quality until puberty and, as he considers the clitoris a male organ, he sees the young girl as a male *manqué*. Before Freud, doctors and educators maintained that during childhood there were no significant sexual (or emotional, psychological, and physical) differences between males and females. Dr. J. H. Kellogg, *Ladies' Guide in Health and Disease* (Des Moines, 1883), quoted in Sharon O'Brien, "Tomboyism and Adolescent Conflict: Three Nineteenth-Century Case Studies," in *Woman's Being, Woman's Place: Female Identity and Vocation in American History*, ed. Mary Kelley (Boston: Hall, 1979), 354.

21. One of the many pamphlets written by women and published in the 1880s reads: "The young girl should be *fitted* with some one of the numerous excellent bodices or corsets now in vogue, by the time she is thirteen or fourteen." Marion Harland, *Eve's Daughters; or, Common Sense for Maid, Wife, and Mother* (New York: John R. Anderson, 1885), 350. Therefore, it would seem that this was taken to be the age of puberty. Differing on the basis of data from English studies, Alison Lurie states that in the nineteenth century the average age of the menarche was around seventeen in the 1830s, sixteen in the 1860s, and fifteen in the 1890s: Alison Lurie, "She Had It All," *New York Review of Books*, March 2, 1995. Jo, who is fifteen years old in *Little Women*, is therefore more plausible as an adolescent tomboy than the seventeen-year-old Charlie. However, one notes at the end of the century a tendency in girls to prolong "boy privileges . . . into the teens, through them, perhaps even into the mid-twenties" (Mitchell, *New Girl*, 104).

22. The *Oxford English Dictionary* states that the word "tomboy" was introduced in 1592 and describes (in the following order) "a rude, boisterous or forward boy," "a bold or immodest woman," and "a girl who behaves like a spirited or boisterous boy; a wild romping girl; a hoyden." For a psychological and clinical study of the tomboy, see John Money and Anke A. Ehrhardt, *Man and Woman, Boy and Girl* (Baltimore: Johns Hopkins University Press, 1972), 10–11. According to Carolyn G. Heilbrun, "Achieving women are statistically likely to be from all-girl families. . . . Not uncommonly, if the unconventional woman is not the only or oldest child, she will be the one among a father's daughters selected by him as his 'son.'" "Louisa May Alcott: The Influence of *Little Women*," in *Women, the Arts and the 1920's in Paris and New York*, ed. Kenneth W. Wheeler and Virginia Lee Lussier (New Brunswick: Transaction Books, 1982), 22.

23. Jean Chevalier and Alain Gheerbrant, *A Dictionary of Symbols,* trans. John Buchanan-Brown (Oxford: Blackwell, 1994), 866–67 (seventeen), 859–66 (seven), 1050–52 (two).

24. Chopin seems to have been uncertain about her protagonist's name. Less interestingly than in her final choice, in some drafts she called her "Jacques" and "Jack" (Toth, *Unveiling Kate Chopin,* 167). The names of some of Charlie's other sisters are also significant. Irene—etymologically speaking the "bringer of peace"—is the one who worries the most about Charlie and who tries to speak in her favor; Amanda—etymologically "she who must be loved"—appears as the most selfish (653); Fidelia—the "faithful one"—is always with the governess and obeys her orders; Julia—from Jupiter—is strict and serious.

25. Patrick Hanks and Flavia Hodges, *Dictionary of First Names* (Oxford: Oxford University Press, 1990), 60–61.

26. Carolyn G. Heilbrun, *Toward a Recognition of Androgyny* (New York: Knopf, 1973), x: "Androgyny seeks to liberate the individual from the confines of the appropriate."

27. Almost all female tomboy characters have nicknames and dark hair and skin, thus emphasizing their difference from feminine heroines who are usually known by their full name and have blond hair and light skin; Elizabeth Segel, "The *Gypsy Breynton* Series: Setting the Pattern for American Tomboy Heroines," *Children's Literature Association Quarterly* 14, no. 2 (Summer 1989): 67–71. Furthermore, Charlie, who is also on friendly terms with blacks, is portrayed as in some ways similar to them. Hence her hair and skin are darker than those of her sisters.

It is perhaps worth noting that Julia does not have blond, but *almost* blond (it is light brown) hair. It is as if Chopin, knowing the ethnic mix in Louisiana—and subsequent intermarriages (see her tale "Desiree's Baby")—felt that she should maintain an element of cautious realism in the depiction of her characters.

28. From a pamphlet translated from the French that enjoyed much success when it appeared: "a young girl should learn that dress is a language; it has a hidden sense, and announces the idea that each person means to give of herself." Madame Necker De Saussure, *The Study of the Life of Woman* (Philadelphia: Lea and Blanchard, 1844), 167.

29. Bloomers were seen as purveyors of social unrest, given that they represented "only one of the many manifestations of that wild spirit of socialism and agrarian radicalism which is at present so rife in our land." William M. Nevin, "The Bloomer Dress," *Ladies' Wreath* 3 (1852): 253. The debate on clothing was extremely lively both in the United States and in England where in

1899 the Rational Dress League of England held a meeting to celebrate the fiftieth anniversary of the invention of bloomers. Participants from London traveled to the meeting in Reading by bicycle.

30. Oscar Wilde pronounced them "sensible" but ugly; Oscar Wilde, "More Radical Ideas upon Dress Reform" [1884], in *The Complete Writings of Oscar Wilde, Miscellanies,* vol. 6 (New York: Nottingham Society, 1905), 62.

31. Elizabeth Stuart Phelps, *What to Wear?* (Boston: Houghton, Mifflin, 1880), 34 (emphasis mine).

32. The first women's bicycles were made about 1890 and became immediately popular. In England, for example, "By mid-decade, cycling was a national passion. . . . The archetypal New Woman image is a healthy young person in dark skirt and white shirt standing beside the bicycle that gave her freedom to travel independently in town or country" (Mitchell, *New Girl,* 110).

33. Anne Hollander, "Women and Fashion," in Wheeler and Lussier, *Women, the Arts, and the 1920's in Paris and New York,* 112.

34. Anne Hollander, *Seeing through Clothes* (New York: Viking, 1978), 340.

35. "In the second half of the nineteenth century, feminine dress made strong visual demands, and the elements of conspicuous consumption had a vigorously gaudy flavor and an imposing social importance. Modest simplicity in dress and furnishing was unfashionable and socially degrading." Anne Hollander, "Reflections on *Little Women,*" *Children's Literature* 9 (1981): 30.

36. "The New Orleans New Woman," *Woman's Journal,* June 24, 1899, 196 (emphasis mine).

37. Male attire can have the effect of making a woman even more desirable, as in the case of George Sand who "showed herself to be interested not in female concerns like child-bearing and domesticity . . . but in a female erotic life that depends on an active imagination, on adventurous and multiform fantasy." Anne Hollander, *Sex and Suits: The Evolution of Modern Dress* (New York: Knopf, 1994), 41.

38. In the context of this story, the term cross-dressing is used in a broad sense as Charlie's dressing in male attire does not imply perversion (or paraphilia), which occurs only when "the aim of the act" is "sexual excitement and sexual performance." Louise J. Kaplan, "Women Masquerading as Women," in *Perversions and Near Perversions in Clinical Practice: New Psychoanalytic Perspectives,* ed. Gerald I. Fogel and Wayne A. Myers (New Haven, Conn.: Yale University Press, 1991), 132. See also chapter 1.

39. Marjorie Garber, *Vested Interests: Cross-dressing and Cultural Anxiety* (New York: Routledge, 1992).

40. In "Charlie," the heroine gives some outgrown clothes to the young Acadian Aurendele (653). This was common practice on plantations where "House servants . . . had a proprietary interest in their mistresses' clothes. They took pride in having their mistress always look her best and outshine the other ladies. After her clothes had served that purpose, they were usually handed down to her maids and the other women of the quarters." Elizabeth Fox-Genovese, *Within the Plantation Household: Black and White Women of the Old South* (Chapel Hill: University of North Carolina Press, 1988), 216–18. Regarding the generosity of the tomboy, Segel notes that "Because of their unconventional ways and warm hearts, tomboys were prone to befriending lower-class people; they were, in fact, democrats" (*"Gypsy Breyton* Series," 69).

41. There are similarities between Twain and Alcott; see Linda Black, "Louisa May Alcott's *Huckleberry Finn," Mark Twain Journal* 21 (1982–83): 15–17; John W. Crowley, *"Little Women* and the Boy-Book," *New England Quarterly* 58, no. 3 (September 1985): 384–99.

42. In *Little Women,* Jo—who usually writes in prose—also sends a poem to her mother when the latter is in Washington taking care of her husband. As Ann Douglas states, in the nineteenth century, women who wrote were considered de facto aggressive and competitive—in a word, masculine; *The Feminization of American Culture* (New York: Knopf, 1977), 95–96. On women writers' doubts about their creativity and sense of guilt (as well as shame) for writing and therefore committing what was generally regarded as an illegitimate act, see Mary Kelley, *Private Woman, Public Stage: Literary Domesticity in Nineteenth-Century America* (New York: Oxford University Press, 1984), 180–214.

43. Gilbert and Gubar, *Madwoman in the Attic,* 6; Susan Gubar, "'The Blank Page' and the Issues of Female Creativity," *Critical Inquiry* 8, no. 2 (Winter 1981): 243–63. Hollander observes that, in *Little Women,* writing for Jo "is the agent of her retreat from sex—she uses it to make herself more like a man" ("Reflections on *Little Women,"* 33). In "Charlie," writing is a means of communicating with others (with the governess, for example) or a very private means of expressing one's emotions.

44. Judith Aracana, "Fathers: The Men in Our Lives," *Chrysalis* 8, no. 2 (Summer 1979): 72. According to Herman, "Daughters of seductive fathers thus learned that they had two choices in life. They could remain their Daddy's good little girls, bound in a flirtatious relationship whose

sexual aspect was ever present and never acknowledged, or they could attempt to become independent women . . . and in the process risk their fathers' anger and rejection" (*Father–Daughter
Incest,* 118).

45. Apart from Charlie's masculine habits and, therefore, besides being a symbol of male power
and aggression, this casual handling of a gun by a seventeen-year-old girl can be explained by the
fact that, on an isolated plantation, the masters—of any age—particularly after the experiences of
the Civil War and the Reconstruction, had to be ready to face any emergency. In an (unexplained)
earlier occasion, Charlie is said to have "once saved the levee during a time of perilous over-
flow. . . . It was a story in which an unloaded revolver played a part" (641).

46. From the 1880s, women's clothes were "increasingly elaborate, colorful and decorative, even
theatrical and excessively feminine, tending to stress the hourglass figure, great extent of skirt especially at the back, and great diffuseness of embellishment" (Hollander, "Women and Fashion,"
112).

47. According to Gilles Lipovetsky, fashion is intrinsically excessive: "Governed by the logic of
theatricality, the fashion system was inseparable from excess, disproportion, outrageousness. It
was destined to be carried away, inexorably, in an escalation of extremes, exaggerations of volume
and amplifications of form that braved ridicule." Gilles Lipovetsky, *The Empire of Fashion: Dressing
Modern Democracy* (Princeton, N.J.: Princeton University Press, 2002), 27.

48. "Charlie had a way, when strongly moved, of expressing herself in verse" (641).

49. "The seductive fathers were able to control their families less by intimidation and force,
and more by withdrawal and unavailability" (Herman, *Father–Daughter Incest,* 111). In this case, the
father is not distant and inaccessible. Closed up in his "perplexity," however, he may become mysterious and capable of subtle emotional blackmail.

50. "She realized that she was a difficult and perhaps annoying problem for him, and did not
relish the idea of adding to his perplexity," and later "Then she knew that he was perplexed again"
(643, 644). "Perplexity" seems to be a distinctive family trait, given that even Mr. Laborde's sister,
Aunt Clementine, shares it: "Aunt Clementine would do no more than shrug her shoulders and
look placidly and blamelessly perplexed" (657).

51. As Zwinger writes, when it is a woman novelist who depicts a daughter figure, there is "a
certain twist given the father figure: he generally exhibits paternal inadequacy to some important
aspect of his narrative and cultural authority, thus making room, indeed necessitating, some

amount of daughterly authority" (Zwinger, *Daughters, Fathers, and the Novel*, 124–25). Moreover, this inadequacy often takes the form of mildness or weakness.

52. Chevalier and Gheerbrant, *A Dictionary of Symbols*, 732 (oyster), 586–88 (lameness), 664–67 (monkey).

53. "Charlie," 648, 650, 651 (three times), 655 (twice), 656, 657 (twice), 661 (three times), 665. The name derives from the Latin *Firminus*, which, etymologically speaking, means "resistant" or "stable."

54. Because, in a patriarchal society, no man has power over an unmarried daughter like her father, "no particular man's rights are offended, should the father choose to disregard this rule [the incest taboo] . . . of all possible forms of incest, that between father and daughter is the most easily overlooked" (Herman, *Father–Daughter Incest*, 60).

55. Zwinger, *Daughters, Fathers, and the Novel*, 99: "In the face of the paradoxical requirement that to be desirable she must be both dutiful and unpossessed, our stories of heterosexual desire have produced a version of the desirable daughter who can't say yes but doesn't say no."

56. Traditionally, a father's incestuous love leads to death; here, the purely emotional incest leads to a mutilation and may preannounce the demise of future prospects.

57. On the power of the gift giver, see Marcel Mauss, *The Gift: The Form and Reason for Exchange in Archaic Societies*, trans. W. D. Halls (London: Routledge, 1990).

58. Chopin seems to be fully aware that in the 1890s the "marriage problem" was at the heart of the feminist debate. A little later, in fact, novels would be published with such revealing titles as *Modern Marriage and How to Bear It* (1909) and *Marriage as a Trade* (1909) (Eldridge Miller, *Rebel Women*, 41).

59. "In the wounding of young Walton, Charlie metaphorically wounds herself in her sudden experience of love" (Ewell, *Kate Chopin*, 178).

60. "The place of the daughter, particularly in a motherless household, can be managed to everyone's advantage by placing her in a maternal position" (Zwinger, *Daughters, Fathers, and the Novel*, 33); "the daughter who [after her marriage] refuses to leave the father's house confuses the orderly syntax of genealogy . . . occupying . . . two inappropriate familial positions: her father's in heterosexual exchange, her mother's in heterosexual desire" (ibid., 137).

61. Ibid., 127.

62. Ewell, *Kate Chopin*, 179. According to Cutter, "while mimicking the role of a dutiful daugh-

ter, Charlie is actually finding . . . a niche of independence and voice in the patriarchal world she inhabits" ("Losing the Battle but Winning the War," 33).

63. In *Little Women,* Jo the tomboy dies when Beth, the angel of the household, dies; thus Jo takes her younger sister's place in the bosom of the March family. This is at least true of the first two novels in the trilogy, *Little Women* and *Little Men* (1871); however, in *Jo's Boys,* the heroine seems to have some doubts about her choice of husband. See Angela M. Estes and Kathleen Margaret Lant, "Dismembering the Text: The Horror of Louisa May Alcott's *Little Women,*" *Children's Literature* 17 (1989): 101: "Young Jo—fiery, angry, assertive—represents all that adult Jo can never be . . . for an independent, self-determined Jo, no future is possible."

64. Garber, *Vested Interests,* 11.

65. Before the Civil War, "At all levels, southern culture reflected and reinforced a view of the world in which women were subordinate to men. The view proved the more powerful because it conformed so closely to intuitive notions about 'natural' differences between men and women" (Fox-Genovese, *Within the Plantation Household,* 195).

66. Hollander, *Sex and Suits,* 40.

13

IMAGINATIVE HABITS

FANTASIES OF UNDRESSING IN THE AMBASSADORS

Agnès Derail-Imbert

Henry James's favorite novel, *The Ambassadors,* situated in turn-of-the-century fashion-able Paris, is among his most concerned with dress, even if descriptions of clothes, ac-cessories, and furniture almost never fulfill a realistic or documentary function. Return-ing once more to the transatlantic theme, addressing the confrontation of cultures, the clash of civilizations, James sends his hero, middle-aged Lewis Lambert Strether, from the heart of neopuritanical, materialistic, and provincial Woollett in New England di-rectly to the world capital of fashion, taste, *art de vivre,* where he is instantaneously over-whelmed with a surge of aesthetic emotions incompatible with Woollett's rigid moral standards. Hired as ambassador by Mrs. Newsome to return her wayward son Chad from corrupt Europe to the family business, and from an illicit liaison to a sanctioned marriage, Strether is sent on an errand for the benefit of a community that defines itself intensely by its national and local social codes and values. Bespectacled Strether, in his capacity as ambassador, is then expected to scrutinize the mores, customs, and costumes of the social microcosm he encounters, in posh and historic Faubourg St. Germain. Strether's mission—tearing young American Chad away from the seductive dresses of the wicked adulterous French Countess de Vionnet—demands that he learn to keep his thread in a sophisticated maze where flounces and ribbons, evening dresses, hats, and pink parasols weave an intriguing plot, unreadable for someone used to the coarse canvas of the Woollett social register. Crucial to the success of the mission is the exploration of "imaginative habits" in many senses of the phrase: habits as customs, as the way one acts collectively in a given community—protocols, decorum, fashion, food—and more specifically habits as costume or dress, through which one imagines one's sense of self and offers this decked-out self to the scrutiny of others.[1] Reading clothes, or for that matter, seeing through them, is a litmus test for one who is sent on a delegation from one social set to another, for one who initially takes clothes as tokens to be interpreted in order to enter the social game. Dress plays an undeniable role in the epistemological crisis around which the plot hinges. Strether's cognitive adventure, a speculative journey involving intense critical activity, is presented as a process of uncovering, unveiling, stripping appearances to discover stable essences or types. It calls almost naturally for the figure of clothes, of clothing and disclosing, as the metaphorical substitute for the process of the inquiring mind in the course of its investigative errand.

Yet dress does not merely provide a fancy vehicle to convey the reflexive patterns of the novel's central consciousness and its American obsession with laying bare a single truth finally exposed in its most naked state. On the contrary, the book, which is also a portrait of the artist as a not so young man, very minutely unthreads this fantasy of undressing by exposing the character to a much more puzzling perception of clothes. No matter whether the European dressed self is devised to be meaningful or deceitful, uncovered or muffled, invulnerable or alluring, in all cases it gestures toward the variation of unsettled identities; it is the locus of potentially conflicting encounters between convention and subversion, between the collective and the private, between social standards and intimate desires. The instability of the dressed self is more and more tightly interwoven with Strether's "process of vision" (2), with the expansion of his constricted perceptive organ to the scope of unimagined sensuous vistas, as his consciousness divests itself of Woollett's straightjackets and is gradually altered into a "soft and elastic" garment, a second skin fit to accommodate an infinite variety of aesthetic experiences (20).[2]

Strether's liminal exposure to Europe elicits a perception of himself as inadequately dressed. His survey of himself in the "dressing glass" at the hotel induces a sense of lacking, as he says, "the elements of Appearance" (20). The chance meeting with Maria Gostrey, whom he catalogs as a "woman of fashion" (38), as fully equipped for Europe as he considers himself ill-equipped, further sharpens his sense of looking oddly inadequate. Yet as soon as the woman of fashion guides him through the shops of Chester and London, his "lacks" and "wants" quickly become intertwined with half-guilty desires for discriminations forbidden to a pilgrim from New England. Strether's purchase of a pair of gloves, his interest in tailors, his "affinity with the dealers in stamped letter-paper and in smart neckties," are already signs of his declension from American moral standards, signs of his being in "peril of apparent wantonness" (38). London and its shopwindows fueling the lust of smart clothes is a modern version of Babylon; the Catholic Church advertised by the fashionable woman seen as "a Jesuit in petticoats."

The confrontation with Europe entails a reassessment of the conception of dress in the Woollett circles. It is only in retrospect and by contrast that Strether gradually realizes how clothes are linked to national identity and customs. The way they operate is to secure national features and publicize them, very much on the model of advertising, which is the business Chad is summoned to come back to. This is how stern puritanical Waymarsh, for instance, is perceived as he is compared to Sitting Bull, "wrapt of his blanket": the metaphorical dress here (the blanket) stands for the autochthonous quality constantly on display as the flag signaling an immutable link between the wearer and his nationality, even if, or mostly when, the citizen is in exile. In contrast, Strether has the feeling that his own nationhood is not as immediately legible through his personal appearance. Here again he experiences the shakiness of his national affiliation as an impression of insufficient clothing: "Strether's sadness sprang from his thinking how little he himself was wrapt of his blanket, how little . . . he resembled a really majestic aboriginal" (126). For the American set, dress is closely attached to the ambassadorial function.

The logic of delegation consists in displaying abroad, in foreign or alien milieux, the social and economic power of a community.[3] This is particularly striking in the opposition of the two young girls: if both are depicted as embroiled in adults' strategic games on the marriage market, they are used differently according to national standards, and their outfits point to that difference. In the competition between the two *jeunes filles* for Chad's hand, young Jeanne de Vionnet seems indeed ill-equipped: almost translucent, evanescent in her white dress and soft plumed hat, she appears to Strether as a sacrificial victim. As soon as plump and over-dressed American Mamie Pocock parades her voluminous skirts on the station platform in Paris, Jeanne is doomed to retreat into the background. Mamie's aggressive shift already announces the inevitable defeat of the little French girl: "from the moment Miss Pocock had shaken her skirts on the platform, touched up the immense bows of her hat and settled properly over her shoulder the strap of her morocco-and-gilt travelling-satchel, from that moment little Jeanne was opposed" (212). Whereas Jeanne has been brought up and is dressed to conform to the private desires of her mother, Mamie, with her conspicuous hat and complex hairdo, is exhibited as deputy for the community whose interests she defends. The outfit she wears already casts her as the ideal bride capable of returning the straying son to the family business: "granted that a community might be best represented by a lady of twenty-two, Mamie perfectly played the part, played it as if she were used to it, and looked and spoke and dressed the character. . . . What Mamie was like was the happy bride, the bride after the church and just before going away" (212).

This is why the purchase of clothes, far from being a frivolous feminine activity, plays a decisive part in the mission of conquest, or reconquest, of what the community or the family considers as its collective, permanent property. Clothes eternally must be bought, not only because fashions change, but because they are chosen to represent and maintain the durability of the family, that is, of the family business. It is not by chance that respectable Sarah Pocock is seen at her Parisian hotel dealing with a seamstress and a *lingère* and that she wears an undoubtedly outmoded but very flashy crimson dress at Chad's party. The notion of ambassadorship, which is at the core of the novel, is given its distinctive New England emphasis when seen through clothes: if the first ambassador, Strether, felt undressed on the very first day of his arrival, Sarah's sartorial concerns in Paris only testify to the political correctness of her delegation. Despite the vast range of her outfits, meant also to foreground the family's wealth, her dress fashions her an exact replica of the absent mother, making it visually clear that she will not deviate from her mother's purposes. Sarah presents herself as a representative who can double for her mother, who can deliver the message to the letter. Just as she speaks by the book, her tremendously neat hairdo replicates her mother's, to a lock.

Now, the fact that the business of clothes is left to women does not reflect the conventional divide between gender roles. Women's business is to shop for, buy, and show clothes because all business is inevitably women's business. Strether's awkward impression of feeling undressed is the symptom of his change of allegiance, of his coming out of the sphere dominated by respectably dressed ladies, in which men are mere decorative accessories, only just tolerated to "play into the general glamour" (215). Such is the case with Jim Pocock, meekly trailing behind his wife's skirts, compensating for his insignificance by wearing white hats and smoking very big cigars matched by very little stories. "Small and fat and constantly facetious, straw-coloured and destitute of marks, he would have been practically indistinguishable hadn't his constant preference for light-grey clothes, for white hats, for very big cigars and very little stories, done what it could for his identity" (215).

In this society governed by women, men are decked out by women. A wonderfully comic passage gives a ludicrous description of the transformation, or dressing up, of austere Waymarsh, formerly cast as Sitting Bull and now masquerading as "a Southern planter of the great days" in white panama hat and waistcoat (270). A perverse case of sectional transvestism secretly fomented by Sarah's elegant hand recasts the stern pilgrim from New England into a seductive cavalier, for her own fantasies of erotic glamor.

Strether had at any rate never resembled a Southern planter of the great days—which was the image picturesquely suggested by the happy relation between the fuliginous face and the wide panama of his visitor. This type, it further amused him to guess, had been, on Waymarsh's part, the object of Sarah's care; he was convinced that her taste had not been a stranger to the conception and purchase of the hat, any more than her fine fingers had been guiltless of the bestowal of the rose. (270)

As for Strether himself, if not rigged out as a Southern planter, he is not immune to New England ladies' sartorial traps and trappings. He is also instrumentalized in the collective exhibitionism orchestrated by women: when he first introduces himself to Maria Gostrey, he realizes that whatever rags or scraps of identity he might claim depend on the green review, *the* Review, a minor journal financed by Mrs. Newsome, in which he happens to play a menial role as editor:

> "The Review?—you have a Review?"
>
> "Certainly. Woollett has a Review—which Mrs Newsome, for the most part, magnificently pays for and which I, not at all magnificently, edit. My name's on the cover." Strether pursued, "and I'm really rather disappointed and hurt that you seem never to have heard of it."
>
> She neglected for a moment this grievance. "And what kind of a Review is it?"
>
> His serenity was now completely restored. "Well, it's green."
>
> "Do you mean in political colour as they say here—in thought?"
>
> "No; I mean the cover's green—of the most lovely shade." (50)

In substituting cover for contents and color for thought, Strether's funny cue exposes the book for what it is: sheer varnish or again a fine garment giving luster to the otherwise so trite industrial production that the manufactured object remains unnamed. The unnameable vulgar thing is what the cover actually covers. Strether's name in gold letters on the cover, ornamental as it is, inscribes him as debtor in Mrs. Newsome's account book. His straying away from her absolute authority becomes the progressive disentangling from the constrictions of the green cover.

Opposed to the collective exhibitionism of the Woollett fashions, the European *art de vivre* strikes Strether as a removal from the social stage, or rather as the cutting out of private niches, or nooks, within the very stuff of social life, as pockets of privacy sewn in the lining of the social texture. The consequences of this "habit of privacy" can first be observed through the revision operated on Chad's physical appearance by Parisian experience (145). On his first, much postponed, meeting with Strether, Chad's spectacular eruption in the theater box has already displaced the spectacle from the stage to the seclusion of the box. His formal evening dress does not prevent him from showing something of his new private self, even of staging it, before Strether's admiring gaze. As he manipulates his crush hat, teasingly uncovering new white hairs in his juvenile black mane, he produces them less as the sign of aging than as the alluring symptoms of sexual maturity. The revised Chad has been fashioned anew by women's taste and desire. The collapsible structure of the crush hat (and that of the phrase, for that matter) discreetly identifies a woman's crush as the cause for transformation just as it intimates Strether's vicarious crush on the newly tailored Chad. A woman's hand of course has retouched Chad's rough shapeless fabric into a smooth comfortable man of the world: "Strether had conceived Chad as patched" (69).

It is in his intercourse with women, however, that Strether more vividly experiences the European way of dressing as an art of undressing. Clair Hughes argues that the novel registers acutely, if not realistically, the fashion changes at the turn of the century. In the evening dress, in particular, "the most dramatic development was the exposure of the bosom," so that, as a satirist said, it was practically impossible to tell what women wore around a dinner table as women dressed for breakfast and undressed for dinner![4] Maria's low-cut dress, the one she wears for her first tête-à-tête dinner with Strether, would be typical of European fashions around 1900. By then, dresses for the evening aspired to the condition of underwear, for underwear itself had become more luxurious and more important. Dresses should be "fluffy and frilly, undulating in movement with ripples of soft foam appearing at the feet."[5] This is not the way things are stated in the novel, because Strether is no fashion critic: he would rather be, in his own passive way, a fashion victim. Enveloped in the warm perfumed image of Maria Gostrey, plunging his eyes into the low-cut decolleté of her dress, he is perhaps not aware that her outfit, by contrast, makes Mrs. Newsome's respectable black dress démodé, but he is bound to record the different intensity of their respective erotic charges. Similarly, the red velvet band Miss Gostrey wears around her neck makes its American version, the black ruche, a neo-Elizabethan ruff, singularly unattractive, with its ominous overtones of virginity, absolute power, and strangulation.

Whereas in New England, voluminous dresses are contrived as combat suits for conquering ambassadors, as weapons of mass seduction, in Europe, soft, evanescent fabrics such as silk, satin, or transparent materials of lace or crepe gesture toward the private body, or rather construe it as something private, as the site for intimate adventures. Again, Strether does not formulate it in terms of fashion changes, but James seems to have been aware that fashion designers such as Jeanne Paquin or Paul Poiret had launched the trend of the loosely draped silhouette, of limp materials and soft hues, of transparent overdresses that were quite damaging to the opaque black or the lurid colors of cumbersome American dresses. Maria's décolleté is only the first step in Strether's initiation journey toward "the habit of privacy," the staging of the denuded body behind the half transparent curtains of clothes. Countess de Vionnet, when he first sees her, challenges his preconceived image of her as older than she is, possibly wearing the yellow gown bad women sported in late-century melodramas: "She was dressed in black, but in black that struck him as light and transparent; . . . her hat not extravagant; he had only perhaps a sense of the clink, beneath her fine black sleeves, of more gold bracelets and bangles than he had ever seen a lady wear" (128). The Countess's black yet almost transparent dress is typical of those clothes one can virtually see through or, even more suggestively, hear through, just as one can hear the clink of bracelets hidden from direct sight by the translucent material of the sleeves.[6] Her clothes conjure up the image of the natural body and its earthly lures whereas the perfection of Sarah's frock suggests she could go to heaven in it. Yet this achievement of transparency, which discloses the body as the locus where the personal, the intimate, harmoniously blends with the social or the historic, is an illusion produced by clothes, accessories, and the staging of the self. What Strether's fantasy tends to embroider as the disclosure of natural intimacy is in fact an artful composition, a form of theatrical make-believe in which clothes are used as props or costumes aiming at an effect of sublime or antique nudity. The vision of Madame de Vionnet's elaborate, exquisite dress at Chad's party triggers images of half-nude goddesses and sea nymphs "waist high in the summer surge." In his fancy, the naked upper body is not the result of this 1900 fashionable dress but is referred to the more stable and proper context of antiquity and mythology. Mythical as it is in Strether's reverie, the dress is obscurely perceived as the costume of an actress, adaptable to the self's "various and manifold" identities. This multiplicity, suggested by the complexity of the garment, the diversity of its textures and hues, and the sophisticated patterns of its gems, induces a contradictory impression of covering and uncovering. While Strether sees her as both "muffled and uncovered," he is not able to realize that her being "uncovered" is precisely achieved by her being "muffled" (160). The more muffled she is, the more uncovered she seems. Privacy in this sense is indeed a habit, a role, a part, a costume. Intimacy is not the disclosed single truth of the self but is as variegated as Madame de Vionnet's shifts. The private, however singular, is as plural as the numerous parts played by the Countess when she was a schoolgirl acting in the "curtained costumed school repertory" (138). So her attachment to Chad can be both virtuous and adulterous.

> She had been in particular, at school, dazzingly, though quite booklessly, clever; as polyglot as a little Jewess (which she wasn't, oh no!) and chattering French, English, German, Italian, anything one would, in a way that made a clean sweep, if not of prizes and parchments, at least of every curtained costumed school repertory, and in especial of all mysteries of race and vagueness of reference, all swagger about "home," among their variegated mates.[7]

The deployment of dress in the novel tends to show that the private—the corporeal, the intimate, or the sexual—is a function of appearances, a product of representation, much more than a disclosure of a fixed reality behind the veils of phenomena. Strether's New England conception of the self prompts him to obliterate the representational dimension of his Parisian experience. The sophisticated art of her appearances is systematically effaced or screened to put into relief her natural, simple, pure character. Thus Strether's sublimating fancy operates two ways: while he reduces the art of dress to a natural state, to a mythical restoration of nature, he embroiders his tale to cover up in vagueness the hard facts that dress or absence of dress may reveal, just as "a little girl might have dressed her doll" (315). Among those hard facts dressed in vagueness stand quite prominently his own repressed desire, his flustered senses. In the climactic scene in Notre Dame, where Strether chances upon Madame de Vionnet, the dressing or embroidering fancy is given free rein in order to pursue hardcore fantasies of a striptease. Stimulated by the red and gold covers of the seventy volumes of Victor Hugo he has just bought, Strether's voyeuristic observation of the praying Countess interprets the adulteress in relation to the holy setting where she happens to be seen. Reflecting on the Catholic practice of indulgences, he himself indulges in an exciting reverie where *Marie de Vionnet* becomes a sexy version of the *Virgin Mary*. Just as the letters MV are turned inside out like a glove to form VM, the fallen woman is dressed up (or better laid bare) as the holy virgin. The fictional embroidery of Strether's fancy, aimed at knitting a spiritualized image of sainthood in accordance with the cathedral and the mysterious woman haunting the place, paradoxically covers up an erotic fantasy of naked bodies. Strether's lofty tale of the sublime is closer to the fiction of some "romance" by a "great romancer"— less a novel by Victor Hugo than a cheap tale of sexual thrills. Just as Madame de Vionnet's dress is multilayered, the dull wine-color suggestive of religious ritual but already heralding the more pagan pleasures of the *déjeuner,* Strether's sublime discourse allows him to picture himself, verbally at least, as "a firm object," one that occasionally "rocks," one that she might desire to "feel in her hand":

and if he happened to affect her as a firm object she could hold on by, he wouldn't jerk himself out of her reach. . . . It was as to this he had made up his mind; he had made it up, that is, to give her a sign. The sign would be that—though it was her own affair— she was free to clutch. Since she took him for a firm object—much as he might to his own sense appear at times to rock—he would do his best to *be* one. (177)

The naked body or organ ("firm object") is produced in Strether's romance by a figure of speech that veils at the same time its nakedness. This is how Strether's mental writing, his fantastic romance, is at the same time the tapestry exhibiting all the motifs of his desire and the decent veil of a tale patching up the naked truth thus revealed. And this ultimately poses very neatly the question of representation that lies at the core of this novel dealing with delegation and ambassadorship, as intimately related to clothing—clothing as the product of representation.

FASHIONING NUDITY

Dress in *The Ambassadors,* and more generally in James, is textually interwoven both with writing and painting but also, to make things more complex, with both at the same time.[8] James's criticism of contemporary artworks bears witness to the close scrutiny he devoted to the representation of clothes, in John Singer Sargent's paintings, in particular, which he valued highly.[9] But more intrinsically, independently from the pictorial representation of dress, James's fiction about painting has also to do, if not with dress, at least with cloth, fabric, canvas. In the tale entitled "The Liar," which is the portrait of a painter trying to paint the portrait of a liar, the painting that provides a reference for the artist while achieving his portrait is *The Tailor* by Giambattista Moroni, as if painting could be represented by the cutting of cloth or clothes. In the wake of Nathaniel Hawthorne's "Prophetic Pictures," a number of James's tales deal with the destruction of the painting through the violent laceration of the canvas.

It is quite remarkable that the first reference to the visual arts in *The Ambassadors* (apart from the oblique and unique mention of Hans Holbein's *Ambassadors* in the title, thus on the cover) should be directly connected with clothes: Titian's *Young Man with the Glove.* Just as the picture by Moroni, Titian's painting forcefully draws attention to clothing and its representation. The spectator is required to look at the gloves, at the gloved left hand holding the limp glove of the bare right one. In addition, the pointed ringed finger of the young man whose hand suggestively holds back the heavy folds of a rich black cloak, the precious gem on his chest half concealed in the opening between the white linen of the shirt and the deep black velvet of the cloak, the finely painted white lace of the shirt visible at the neck and the wrists, all these carefully contrived details powerfully focus attention on the painter's artistic performance, that is, on the painted subject, rather than on the model himself. Yet this is precisely what Strether forbears to do:

> The meeting with little Bilham took place, by easy arrangement, in the great gallery of the Louvre; and when, standing with his fellow visitor before one of the splendid Titians—the overwhelming portrait of the young man with the strangely-shaped glove and the blue-grey eyes—he turned to see the third member of their party advance from the end of the waxed and gilded vista, he had a sense of having at last taken hold. (83)

Typically Strether averts his eyes from the painted young man and his strangely shaped glove to a real young man, himself a painter, walking toward him in the Louvre gallery. Turning away from the canvas, from the fictional character of the painting and its represented gloves, Strether gets the deceitful sense of taking hold of the real thing. To be sustainable, this illusion of taking hold must do away with what calls attention to representation, be it the canvas itself, or the clothes on the canvas, or clothes at large. As Strether construes it, the real thing lies behind clothes, or apart from representation. In other words, the real thing requires the repudiation of clothes as a denial of representation.

The same process is at work in the epiphanic scene on the river when Strether, taking a day off in the countryside, meets by chance the illicit couple and understands at long last the sexual nature of their "virtuous attachment" (112). Before the arrival of the couple, Strether associates the countryside with a painting by Émile Lambinet, a painting he had seen years back in Boston and intended to buy. As he walks through the bucolic scenery, he gets the feeling of walking directly "in the picture" (308). Symptomatically, the painting as it is evoked in Strether's memory does not represent costumed charac-

ters. In fact the painting's title, which the novel does not mention, is precisely *Paysage avec figures*.[10] Strether only records that the human figures are just what he finds missing in this picture. Canceling the figures from the remembered painting, he also dismisses figuration.[11] When the characters do come into the landscape in the guise of a man and a woman in a boat, Strether sees them as pastoral ingredients of the bucolic landscape, bringing the picture, his mental picture, to completion. They are, in his own story, the primitive actors of a pastoral idyll:

> What he saw was exactly the right thing—a boat advancing round the bend and containing a man who held the paddles and a lady at the stern, with a pink parasol. It was suddenly as if these figures or something like them, had been wanted in the picture more or less all day. . . . For two very happy persons he found himself straightway taking them—a young man in his shirt-sleeves, a young woman easy and fair. . . . The air quite thickened, at their approach, with further intimations; the intimation that they were expert, familiar, frequent—that this wouldn't at all events be the first time. They knew how to do it, he vaguely felt—and it made them but the more idyllic. (309)

Just as he has canceled the canvas from the landscape in order to conjure up the illusion of walking directly in the picture, he suppresses from his mental representation the possible meaning of the figures coming toward him in a boat. He treats the lovers as natural participants featured in a bucolic scene. This process of naturalization is of course meant to occlude the violence of sex from the peaceful scenery and the violence of potential betrayal, as the guilty couple might well decide to "'cut' him" (311), like an expendable rag. Chad thus comes to be seen as "the coatless hero" of the idyll (310). The absence of coat at this stage of Strether's construction is interpreted as a kind of sublime nudity: love is natural and pure. The imagined naturism of the lovers is recast as primitive nakedness. Madame de Vionnet's pink parasol is all the more easily woven into Strether's idealized, artless representation since the primal function of the accessory, which is to shade or conceal, is radically evacuated. The parasol is only seen as a pink decorative touch, while all the erotic connotations of the color are suppressed, along with the possibly duplicitous use that might be made of such an object, given the circumstances.

Yet, despite the blurred comfort of the painting (reminiscent of the impressionistic manner in which details and outlines are not distinguishable), the hard facts of sex are more than intimated in the fabric of the text, which constitutes in a way the suppressed canvas of Strether's idyllic painting: the heavy sexual impact of the textual overwhelms the idealizing thrust of the painterly. The absent clothes of the bucolic painting do not, as Strether first believes, signal innocent nudity but, as he realizes in "a sharp fantastic crisis" (a crisis in his fancy too), point to the depth of the lovers' intimacy (310):

> she hadn't started out for the day dressed and hatted and shod, and even, for that matter, pink parasol'd, as she had been in the boat. . . . Her shawl and Chad's overcoat and her other garments, and his, those they had worn the day before, were at the place, best known to themselves—a quiet retreat enough, no doubt—at which they had been spending the twenty-four hours, to which they had fully intended to return that evening. (314)

Thus intimacy is not to be perceived through the obscene removal of clothes, nor by characters streaking across the novel's stage: it looms up in Strether's consciousness as the backdrop of the canvas, as one more cloth, which he sees only obliquely as it were, in the form of missing clothes. This fluid form (significantly imagined by Strether, "without undressing" [313]) only delineates intimacy as infinitely receding in the folds of his imagination, just as Holbein's painting *The Ambassadors* recedes behind the Lambinet, hidden and exposed in the (not necessarily green) cover of the book, or just as the strange anamorphosis of the oblong object in the foreground of *The Ambassadors* requires that the spectator renounce his frontal gaze.

> That was what, in his vain vigil, he oftenest reverted to: intimacy, at such a point, was *like* that—and what in the world else would one have wished it to be like? It was all very well for him to feel the pity of its being so much like lying; he almost blushed, in the dark, for the way he had dressed the possibility in vagueness, as a little girl might have dressed her doll. . . . Verily, verily, his labour had been lost. He found himself supposing innumerable and wonderful things. (315)

Intimacy is neither this nor that, neither here nor there, never to be fully revealed, but only *"like* that," only imagined, restored in the intimate difference of figuration, figured out of the "innumerable and wonderful" forms the perceiving consciousness, "without undressing," consents to fit experience in the folds and creases that ceaselessly retouch and alter it, like a limp garment, a loose overcoat, a crush hat, or again the strange shape of a stripped glove.[12]

NOTES

1. The phrase is excerpted from Henry James's review of Henry Irving's production of Richard III. "The more [Richard III] is painted and dressed, the more it is lighted and solidified, the less it corresponds or coincides, the less it squares with our imaginative habits." Henry James, *The Scenic Art: Notes on Acting and the Drama, 1872–1901*, ed. Allan Wade (London: Rupert Heart-Davis, 1949),

288. Interestingly enough, the semantic environment of the word "habits" suggests a potential pun on habits as customs or manners and habits as dress, both senses being directly connected to the question of representation, and hence the title of this series.

2. All references are to Henry James, *The Ambassadors*, ed. S. P. Rosenbaum (New York: Norton, 1994).

3. This phrase is the title of an article by Julie Rivkin in which the author analyzes the ambassadorial logic at work in the novel as an inevitable "deviation from design." Even if she does not focus on clothes, the response to costumes, looks, habits is part and parcel of a larger scheme of representation, involving both delegation and the mediation of artistic representation. See Julie Rivkin, "The Logic of Delegation," *PMLA* 101, no. 5 (October 1986): 153–75.

4. Clair Hughes, *Henry James and the Art of Dress* (New York: Palgrave, 2001), 122. I am particularly indebted to the chapter on *The Ambassadors*, which provides amply documented information on the historical context of fashion changes at the time when the novel was written.

5. C. Willett Cunnington, *English Women's Clothing in the Nineteenth Century* [1937] (New York: Dover, 1990), 402, quoted in Hughes, *Henry James and the Art of Dress*, 132.

6. Although Hughes mentions the French designers Jeanne Paquin and Paul Poiret, she does not name the female designer Madeleine Vionnet whose very name might have been borrowed by James for the ultrafeminine character of Marie de Vionnet. Born in 1876, Madeleine Vionnet learned the technique of draped fabrics with the most famous English tailors of the period. Inspired by the fluid, liberated forms of Isadora Duncan, she explored the art of the "drapé," rejected the use of corsets, and sought to design a natural, sinuous, undulating silhouette. She invented the revolutionary technique of the *biais* and is now considered by contemporary fashion designers as one of the most talented and inspiring precursors of modernity. For instance, Azzedine Alaïa, noting her ingenuity as a designer in using fabrics and simple line, called her "a virtuoso of the cut." *Beaux Arts*, exhibition catalog, Hors Série no. 134 (Paris: Musée de la Mode et du Textile), December 1996 (my translation).

7. James, *The Ambassadors*, 138. Interestingly, Madame de Vionnet's mastery at foreign languages matches her art of dress, both types of expertise joining in her theatrical skills. The Countess easily shifts from one language to another, while Strether only shyly attempts to speak a few words in French toward the end of the novel.

8. In her study of clothes in Western culture, Anne Hollander argues that the relative scarcity

of James's references to clothes in his fiction points in fact to his deep acknowledgement of the power of clothing, as distinct from other inanimate objects. See Anne Hollander, *Seeing through Clothes* (Berkeley: University of California Press, 1993).

9. See for instance Sargent's portrait of Hylda Wertheimer, painted in 1901. The alluring, fluid, satin, low-cut dress might have belonged to Countess de Vionnet's wardrobe.

10. Émile Lambinet, a French Barbizon school painter, traveled twice to the United States. During one of those journeys, *Paysage avec figures: Vue de Bougival* was sold in Boston in April 1867. Given Strether's chronology, it would then be this particular painting that he saw in Boston and intended to buy.

11. Maud Ellman comments on the passage in the following terms: "In a curious inversion of the order of mimesis, he perceives the real French landscape as a representation of its own representation; that is, of the painting he could never own . . . since the *real* landscape stands for the *represented* landscape that . . . was priced 'beyond a dream of possibility.'" "The Intimate Difference: Power and Representation in *The Ambassadors*," in James, *The Ambassadors*, 510.

12. Besides the conventional metaphors that James uses in his preface, associating the book or the story with the lexicon of clothes, through such words as "material," "stuff," "fabric," "thread," it is interesting that the novel as a genre should be described in the last sentence as the "most elastic, most prodigious of literary forms." The elasticity of the writing suggests that the perceiving consciousness itself is imagined as a loose envelope or fabric, capable of suiting closely a profusion of experiences (James, *The Ambassadors*, 15).

SEEN AND OBSCENE

Paula Rabinowitz

In 1859, Pre-Raphaelite painter Dante Gabriel Rossetti described his new work, *Bocca Baciata,* as "a rapid study of flesh painting" in what was perhaps an extended response to critic John Ruskin's comment to Louise, Marchioness of Waterford, on Rossetti's 1858 painting *Golden Water.* Ruskin had relished that work's "golden glow of Venetian colour," exhibiting a woman "wearing a dress of woven gold, with green-blue lining—showing in a series of waves or indentations at the edge of the robe: her long golden hair falling over all." Such attention to the flow and response of skin, hair, cloth, and color was a central feature of mid-nineteenth-century British painting, which found in the work of Venetian school artists a solution to the "fatal medievalism, the stiffness & quaintness & intensity as opposed to classical grace & tranquility" that for Ruskin had "almost sickened" him because "all the Gothic" had become overly predictable and trite in the paintings of the "Rossetti clique."[1]

Indentations at the edge of the robe, the play of light working between cloth and flesh, were deemed successful by Ruskin, a sign of Rossetti's artistic development, suggesting just how aware of clothing and its relationship to the body and to identity nineteenth-century aesthetes were. Whether imagining ethereal beauties, nouveau riche parvenus, solid middle-class citizens, rebellious young women, or wild dandies, artists and authors relished their attention to dress. By the end of the century, British authors could spoof the fine attention to dress even among middle-class suburban boors as had George and Weedon Grossmith in their 1892 satire, *The Diary of a Nobody,* first serialized in *Punch.* These brothers—one an artist and the other a caricaturist, whose work found its way into operettas by Gilbert and Sullivan—record the daily doings of a man and his wife newly arrived at some Victorian London suburb. An entire entry makes note of the "lavender kid-gloves and two white ties" bought for a ball, the second tie necessary in case one gets wrinkled in the tying. The fictional diarist recounts arguments with his tailor, disputes with friends, and discussions with his wife about his threadbare shirts ("I'm 'fraid they're frayed" he puns badly), creased trousers, and enameled walking sticks in the course of recording the utterly dull daily life among the up and coming.[2] In this satire, despite the lavender gloves of a dandy, we find Victorian middle-class life to be devoid of any secret or perverse dimensions. It will take a much subtler satirist— Henry James, for instance—to display the underside, or undergarments and accessories, supporting propriety.

Since Victoria's Secret has so successfully cashed in on a fascination with the hidden risqué sexuality of the period, one must look to underwear as a gauge of sensuality underneath surfaces. Thus we begin with Anna Masotti's brief memoir of her family business (now no longer family owned) La Perla, purveyors since the mid-1950s of fine undergarments. The play between the seen (from the Old English, visible with the eyes) and the obscene—etymologically that which is inauspicious, left-handed (from Latin *scaevus*) and also associated with filth and mud (L. *caenum*), but folklore links it to the Latin *scaena,* stage or scene—what can be viewed and what is ill-omened, lewd, and indecent is framed and reframed constantly in the literature and art of the nineteenth century. This is the import of Anne McClintock's potent title investigating British class and gender interactions during the era of rampant colonialism, *Imperial Leather,* which suggests the perversions at the heart of Victoriana.[3]

The essays in this volume chart a spectrum of dress and its representations during the long nineteenth century, a period of fashion and fashioning when clothing became industrialized and thus tied to democratization, while at the same time, precisely because of this, took on increased significance as a social marker of class and other differences. The contributors provide a sense of the long trail leading to and from colonialism and the transatlantic encounters with worlds (and adorned bodies) beyond the horizon of limited though often quite extravagant European imaginations. As a prelude to understanding these sartorial exchanges, Carroll Smith-Rosenberg begins long before the 1800s. She charts "Modernity Clothing" through the depictions of America as a naked beast in early maps and atlases (from the sixteenth century when the word obscene enters the English language) through the first appearance of the clothed Columbia draped as a Roman goddess of the early Republic that set the stage for understanding how representations of America were deciphered in part through attention to the dressed, or undressed, body. America, she notes, acquired clothing as it first became incorporated into the European body politic and then asserted its right to independence through appropriating the dress of ancient Rome—it needed to be seen and to stage the scene in which the nation could be recognized. By the end of the eighteenth century, decorum rules, and the wild images of America have been supplanted by visions of a chronological cross-dressing Ben Franklin floating amid a sea of toga-clad putti in the French imagination, while in the new nation, America sees itself as a severely clad Minerva bringing light to the benighted peoples of the world, setting the tone for the new century and new national identity.

Middle-class and wealthy Americans flooded Europe during the long nineteenth century, and it was there that they found a variety of refined habits. The great works of Henry James, as Clair Hughes and Agnès Derail-Imbert show, were attuned to the ways in which the American-European encounter often was expressed through dress and especially through the attention paid to the revelatory aspects of seemingly extraneous details—those accessories surrounding the body that, like all James's details, acquire intense meaning once they are noticed. The perverse, even obscene, relationships Maisie finds herself enmeshed in as the daughter of an ever-expanding set of parents become apparent through various objects—Hughes mentions hats, shoes, and canes but also her mother's jewel-laden breast—connecting her to the series of adults among whom she is exchanged. These accessories are evidence of the crime of which Maisie is both witness (adultery) and victim (incest and neglect). Traces found lying around rooms and casually strewn across bodies, accessories emphasize details partially acknowledged—not the facts but their effects. Like the accessories found on the bodies of her guardians, Maisie is moved across an expanding stage among various actors. In *The Ambassadors,* Mr. Lewis Lambert Strether (named for a Balzac novel) understands the subtle change that has transformed him from a stiff New Englander to a louche expatriate in Paris in part through his recognition that when Madame de Vionnet set out with Chad, the young American Strether is sent to retrieve, she "had not started out for the day dressed and hatted and shod, and even for that matter, pink parasol'd, as she had been in the boat." He sees them from the shore in a boat one lovely day, meaning they have left their traveling clothes—"her shawl and Chad's overcoat"—somewhere nearby ("a quiet retreat enough no doubt"), so her parasol is posed to shield her from the sun, not from public view; it is this undressing of bourgeois habits that Derail-Imbert finds so provocative in James's telling.[4]

That a parasol could be a sign of danger was central to James's conception of Daisy Miller's cavalier attitude about Roman fever in all its various symptoms, including the allure of a cicerone. When Winterbourne finds her and Giovanelli in the Pincio—he leaning against a tree with a "nosegay" in his buttonhole (this the third flower of evil he wears, having been decked out in a "sprig of almond-blossom" at a park and a "bouquet" at a picture gallery), she brazenly walking alone with him—he chastises her for courting danger: of fever, of damaged reputation.[5] Later her open parasol, shielding her and Giovanelli from view in the Borghese gardens, assures Winterbourne that she is more than an "American flirt"; she's "reckless," easily sloughed off, and deserving of the harsh reception she has found among the proper expatriates. That open parasol, offering protection from the glare of what can be seen in sunlight, contrasts with his rigid bearing, "as stiff as an umbrella" tightly wound in anticipation of stormy weather. Daisy complains that he is "so stiff" (as he says, "stiffer than ever") whenever he meets the two young people flaunting themselves across the Roman landscape, courting disaster.[6] This highly sexualized distinction between the open parasol and the tightly rolled umbrella recalls another great nineteenth-century dialogue between fashion and death—as Giacomo Leopardi had staged it in 1824: "Fashion '... look at me.' Death 'I am looking at you' ... Fashion 'I am Fashion, your own sister.'"—and ultimately dooms poor Daisy, who succumbs to malaria as Winterbourne had predicted; but it claims him, too, who clings to his prejudices about proper womanly behavior. Twenty years before, Ruskin had complained about "Rossetti's clique" and its "stiffness" as "sicken[ing]," its "fatal medievalism" lacking "classical grace." Already he had seen how adherence to formality and to formalism stifled aesthetic expression, and anticipated the nexus of sex, death, and cloth.

Like Rossetti, James knew dress conveys hidden sensations. Like Leopardi, he understood fashion as a deadly set piece performed on the stage of both private and public life. In this they were acknowledging the "philosophy of clothes" that mirrored the "philosophy of life" so astutely dissected in Giuseppe Nori's elegant unpacking of how the satirical appropriation of German romanticism by Thomas Carlyle in his novel *Sartor Resartus* helped create Ralph Waldo Emerson's transparent American eyeball: one, it seems, as attentive to the habits of dress as to those of being. After Smith-Rosenberg details how America moved from naked savage to robed statue as colony became Republic, Nori shows how quickly America returned to "nature."

This tension between natural material and fashioned artifact is the central concern of Bruno Monfort who finds in Nathaniel Hawthorne's eerie tale of American expatriate artists in Italy a meditation on the relationship of cold marble to malleable clay that parallels Hawthorne's conceptual inquiry into the ways in which artists make the dead live by casting life as inert and so harks back to Leopardi's dialogue. As Walter Benjamin notes, "Every fashion couples the living body to the inorganic world."[7] The draped statue of Cleopatra, which Hawthorne saw in William Wetmore Story's studio, provided a fitting emblem of the intimate contact between life and death, as the flowing and falling fabric is rendered immobile once carved in stone. The figure of the marble beauty frozen yet evoking a passion within finds its double in the intense, haunted sculptor Miriam, whose dark features contrast with Hilda, her dove-like alter ego, who wanders Rome's streets in gauzy white robes and becomes Kenyon's ultimate companion. Hawthorne unveils how invested nineteenth-century artists were in finding a way to express the changing roles of women as they skirted the selvages of what could be seen and what might be obscene in this murderous romance.

Dagni Bredesen shows that even the Victorian widow, a figure seemingly endowed with the purest of attributes as she enters a realm of perpetual mourning, in effect is reformed through (her husband's) death into a maternal virgin. The widow follows the precedent of the queen herself, becoming an uncanny representation of new womanhood when she dons her widow's weeds, capping them off with her excessive bonnet. In effect, this headdress positioned the widow as a third sex, and her liminality became a delicious topic for nineteenth-century women writers, such as George Eliot and even her heroine Dorothea, who experimented with gender identities and clamored for education and a meaningful life despite the constraints of Victorian-era provincial morality. "*Middlemarch*," says Carolyn Steedman, "is made of fragments from an Unvisited Archive" that Eliot connects directly to the writing of history, tracing its lineage to Herodotus and his recounting of the inauguration of History in a women's "shopping expedition" for new material and patterns to wear.[8]

A woman of letters in Victorian England was clad in contradictions. Lytton Strachey had challenged the portrait of Florence Nightingale as "the Lady with the Lamp," in his 1918 collective biography, *Eminent Victorians,* noting of her "voice" that it "had that in it one must fain call master." Her passion for "*doing* something"—what led her, while nursing, to requisition enough resources that she was "clothing the British Army," as she remarked—"pent up all day in restraint and reserve of a vast responsibility . . . poured itself out in . . . letters with all its natural vehemence, like a swollen torrent through an open sluice . . . a virulence . . . and sarcasm . . . with the deadly and unsparing precision of a machine-gun." Clothing an army and casting "vituperations" at her male superiors, Nightingale remade the image of the nurse from slovenly scrubwoman into orderly professional.[9] In her meditative video *Florence,* Beryl Korot unravels the text/(ure)/(ile) of Florence Nightingale's journals and letters through her own work and identity as video artist and weaver, threading connections between this rebellious nineteenth-century woman's acts of healing and writing and modern and traditional technologies of reproduction that reanimate them as intangible materials for a contemporary artist. The lines of thought connecting video streams to letters and language to cloth form a matrix that takes time itself as its medium.

Appropriating the words of another is a textual form of fashioning in which the adornment of the self is performed and accomplished through assuming the clothing and dress of another. In various ways the theme of cross-dressing takes on significance during the long nineteenth century, as clothing became such an important visual marker of social and other differences. Psychoanalyst Bianca Iaccarino Idelson unpacks the distinctions between transvestism and cross-dressing by going back to Richard van Krafft-Ebing's writings to discern the role of spectatorship in the performance and staging of gender. Her insights into Sigmund Freud's limitations help explain the powerful effects on identity formation played by clothing, especially among young women. In effect, she argues in her dissection of the differences between the Freudian pathologizing of transvestism and the more playful theatricality of cross-dressing that the astute artists and authors of the nineteenth century reveled in the "secret," as she calls it, that requires a knowing audience fully in on the hide-and-seek of both verbal and sartorial double entendre.

Charlie, the seventeen-year-old tomboy protagonist of Kate Chopin's eponymous story, fully understands how her position within her family—as father's favorite, as mother's substitute, as creative and active young woman, as exception—is secured and made visible by her clothing. Cristina Giorcelli's insightful reading of this tale, an exploration of the deep emotional ties between father and daughter, uncoils the ways in which Charlie's changing dress—from her bloomers to her whitened skin, coiffed hair, and lace-trimmed gowns and back again—telegraph her complicated feelings for her father's affections and for the role she assumes as the "master" of the family's estate once he loses his potency. Chopin's deft treatment of a freighted and unspoken subject appears legible only through the exploration Giorcelli offers of how dress and its details reveal the habits and attitudes lurking behind the walls of family life. Charlie's dilemma of femininity becomes most apparent when she is packed off to boarding school away from home: here she assumes new forms of dress, new forms of desire, and new forms of expression as a poet.

Just so, the education of young women in late nineteenth-century Italy served to bring a primarily rural population into modernity and so threatened entrenched patriarchal assumptions about women's capacity to learn and about women's mobility. School uniforms, as Carmela Covato shows, served paradoxically to contain the potential revolutionary force of educated women and also demonstrated a new kind of womanhood—one that was free to undertake new kinds of work—as schoolteachers in the most restricted frame (but who still broke with tradition, including wearing contemporary urban fashions while working in country schools) and as pioneering scientists, like Marie Curie, in the widest. The exodus from home, a mobility that was at once social and geographic, provided nineteenth-century women (especially those like Charlie or Covato's schoolgirls) access to new forms of expression—aesthetic and scientific, but also through attire—even under the highly restrictive limitations set by headmasters.

Anna Scacchi's essay on the shifting use of the shawl by late nineteenth-century American immigrant women explains how cross-dressing not only is a manifestation of gender trouble, but registers through tensions across class and ethnicity as well. In Paris, cashmere shawls, as Charles Baudelaire wrote his mother, were glutting the market in 1865 so he could not pawn one. Made of materials and in designs brought from the imperial conquests by European capital—cashmere, silk, and cotton lengths used for saris and veils—they had been hot women's fashion items among the middle and upper classes as a form of practical exoticism in nineteenth-century Europe.[10] Every proper woman might at some time during the day be wrapped in one. That they were also the everyday wear of Southern and Eastern European peasants streaming into Ellis Island reframed these wraps into something associated with poverty and drudgery especially for the newcomers, who quickly shed their shawls for shirtwaists once they entered work in garment-industry factories. As middle-class women took up tailored outerwear in place of shawls, now associated with immigrants, so too did their immigrant sisters whose labor was altering American clothing through ready-mades.

Flaunting their colorful outfits on the streets of the Lower East Side, these newly arrived "Salomes of the Tenements" became a form of immigrant working-class dandy, who used the spaces of the city to draw public attention to their unique refashioning of bourgeois women's clothing. In this way, they unwittingly mirrored the great practitioners of dandyism, such as Baudelaire, "sometimes called Monseigneur Brummell" who often wore "blood-red cravat and rose gloves . . . his trademark."[11] But dandyism was perhaps most extravagantly displayed by Gabriele D'Annunzio who, in Marta Savini's account, in a late-century Baroque style, remade himself, through clothing and writing, into a decadent aesthete, a national hero, and a Fascist idolater, rising from bourgeois origins—truly obscene in all its senses. In actuality, he is not too far from the schoolgirls fleeing their backgrounds when they donned their uniforms; he knew the body behaved differently depending on how it was cloaked (or unclad). Despite his flamboyance, he appeared to have much in common with the "nobody" who kept a diary of his suburban life, who could by century's end purchase lavender kid gloves at a haberdashery. Spectacular appearances—whether a line of parading young women wearing the same outfit, or dashing ones bent on expressing wild individuality, or even conformist appropriations of them—forged new modes of being.

Being seen and posing for the scene were fundamental to the shifts in dress required of nineteenth-century urban life where anonymity provided ample room for movement and interactions across social divisions. In staging "the coming thing . . . every fashion is a bitter satire on love; all sexual perversities are suggested," noted Walter Benjamin. He goes on: "Beyond the theater, the question of costume reaches deep into the life of art and poetry, where fashion is at once preserved and overcome."[12] This confrontation with the past and its multiplying prophecies for the future is the legacy we have received from the century that fashioned fashion itself.

1. Quoted in Allen Staley, *The New Painting of the 1860s: Between the Pre-Raphaelites and the Aesthetic Movement* (New Haven, Conn.: Yale University Press, 2011), 51, 54, 55.

2. George and Weedon Grossmith, *The Diary of a Nobody* (Harmondsworth: Penguin, 1945), 23, 32, 42.

3. Anne McClintock, *Imperial Leather: Race, Gender, and Sexuality in the Colonial Contest* (New York: Routledge, 1995).

4. Henry James, *The Ambassadors* (New York: New American Library, 1960), 338, 339.

5. Of course the locus classicus connecting flowers to death is Charles Baudelaire's 1857 *Les Fleurs du Mal.* In *The Arcades Project,* Benjamin quotes from Champfleury: "Baudelaire's favorite flowers were neither daisy, carnation, nor rose; he would break into raptures at the sight of those thick-leaved plants that look like vipers about to fall on their prey, or spiny hedgehogs. Tormented forms, bold forms—." Walter Benjamin, *The Arcades Project,* trans. Howard Eiland and Kevin McLaughin (Cambridge, Mass.: The Belknap Press of Harvard University Press, 1999), 258. For an examination of women's appropriation of deadly flowers, see Charlotte Nekola, "The Flowers of Evil and the Lilac Sea: Why Bad Women Wear Flowers," in *Abito e Identità: Ricerche di storia letteraria e culturale,* ed. Cristina Giorcelli, vol. 6 (Rome: Ila Palma, 2006), 147–68.

6. Henry James, *Daisy Miller and Other Stories* (New York: Airmont, 1969), 56, 62, 71, 51, 68, 71, 53.

7. Benjamin, *Arcades Project,* 79.

8. Carolyn Steedman, *Dust: The Archive and Cultural History* (Manchester: Manchester University Press, 2001), 102, 93.

9. Lytton Stachey, *Eminent Victorians* (Harmondsworth: Penguin, 1948), 129, 144, 148–49.

10. "Baudelaire to his mother on December 25, 1865: 'I was told that, with the approach of New Year's Day, there was a glut of cashmeres in the stores, and that they were trying to discourage the public from bringing any more in.'" Quoted in Benjamin, *Arcades Project,* 58. Benjamin notes "A chapter, 'Shawls, Cashmeres,' in Börne's *Industrie-Ausstellung im Louvre*" published in 1862: ibid., 60.

11. Ibid., 259, 248.

12. Ibid., 64–65.

Contributors

DAGNI BREDESEN, professor of English and director of faculty development at Eastern Illinois University, has written on widows and women detectives in Victorian literature and culture. She recently edited two of the earliest yellowbacks to feature professional women detectives: *The Female Detective* and *Revelations of a Lady Detective*. Her essays have been published in *Victorian Review* and *Clues: A Journal of Detection*.

CARMELA COVATO is professor of the history of pedagogy at the University of Rome Three, where she serves as director of the Museo Storico della Didattica (Museum of the History of Education) Mauro Laeng and as director of the doctoral program School of Education and Social Service. She is the author of books and essays on the relationship between public and private life, especially education and gender, the history of childhood, and fatherhood.

AGNÈS DERAIL-IMBERT is associate professor at the École Normale Supérieure/VALE, University of Paris Sorbonne. She is the author of a book on Herman Melville *(Moby-Dick, allures, du corps)* and the coeditor of an anthology of Melville's late poems.

CRISTINA GIORCELLI is the editor of the series *Abito e Identità: Ricerche di storia letteraria e culturale*. She is professor emerita of American literature at the University of Rome Three. She writes on nineteenth-century fiction (primarily Margaret Fuller, Kate Chopin, Henry James, and Edith Wharton), twentieth-century fiction and poetry (especially Gertrude Stein, William Carlos Williams, and Denise Levertov), and the literary iconography of fashion. She is cofounder and coeditor of the quarterly journal *Letterature d'America*.

CLAIR HUGHES was professor of English and American literature at the International Christian University of Tokyo. She is the author of *Henry James and the Art of Dress* and *Dressed in Fiction*, as well as essays on art, dress, and literature. She lives in France and is preparing a book on the cultural life of hats.

BIANCA IACCARINO IDELSON, a psychiatrist and psychoanalyst, was educated in Naples, where she took degrees in philosophy and medicine. Until her retirement in 2011, she directed the Student Psychotherapy Center at the University of Rome Three. She is the founder of De/Creation Art Center at http://www.idelson.eu.

BERYL KOROT is a pioneer of video art and multiple-channel work. She was coeditor and cofounder of *Radical Software*, the first publication to discuss video communication alternatives to broadcast television. Her early works *Text and Commentary* and *Dachau 1974* used weaving structures to create complex nonverbal narratives to express the relationship between the ancient technology of the loom and the digital image; they were exhibited at The Kitchen, Leo Castelli Gallery, Documenta 6, and the Whitney Museum of American Art. A retrospective of her work was exhibited at the Aldrich Museum in 2010, and she has been artist in residence at Dartmouth University and a Guggenheim Fellow.

ANNA MASOTTI grew up in the family business, La Perla, and until recently served as its director of branding and marketing.

BRUNO MONFORT is professor of American studies at the University of Paris, Ouest Nanterre La Défense, where he teaches courses on nineteenth- and early twentieth-century American literature. He has published widely on Washington Irving, Nathaniel Hawthorne, Herman Melville, Henry David Thoreau, and Edgar Allan Poe, focusing on the theory of shorter narrative forms, the politics and ideologies of literature, and the life of images in fictive contexts.

GIUSEPPE NORI is professor of English and American literature and language in the Department of Humanities of the University of Macerata, Italy. He is the author of two books on Melville and of essays on nineteenth-century literature, history, and ideas. He has edited and translated into Italian several volumes, including Thomas Carlyle's *Cartismo*, Herman Melville's *Bartleby*, and Nathaniel Hawthorne's *Wakefield*. He is currently completing a book on early Ralph Waldo Emerson and New England Transcendentalism in a transatlantic philosophical and cultural context.

PAULA RABINOWITZ is professor of English at the University of Minnesota. A materialist–feminist scholar of twentieth-century American literature, film, and material and visual culture, her books include *Labor and Desire: Women's Revolutionary Fiction in Depression America, They Must Be Represented: The Politics of Documentary, Black & White & Noir: America's Pulp Modernism*. She is editor-in-chief of the Oxford Research Encyclopedia of Literature.

MARTA SAVINI taught humanistic literature in the Faculty of Letters and Philosophy at the University of Rome Three. She is the author of several books and essays on Italian literature spanning the fifteenth through the seventeenth centuries.

ANNA SCACCHI is assistant professor of American literature at the University of Padua. She has published extensively on the politics and ideology of American English, nineteenth- and twentieth-century women writers, and children's literature. She translated Charlotte Perkins Gilman's utopian novel *Herland* into Italian and is the editor of *Lo specchio maternol* and *La babele americana* and the coeditor of *Recharting the Black Atlantic*.

CARROLL SMITH-ROSENBERG is Mary Frances Berry Collegiate Professor Emerita at the University of Michigan. She is the author of *This Violent Empire: The Birth of an American National Identity* and *Disorderly Conduct: Visions of Gender in Victorian America*.